WEMBLEY 1972

... And Other Big Feats

GÜNTER NETZER

with Helmut Schümann

Translated and introduced by
Robert Pralle

xxpedient

PUBLISHED BY XXPEDIENT
La Belle Étoile
19290
Chavanac
France

Original text copyright ©2004 by Rowohlt Verlag GmbH
Reinbek bei Hamburg
Alle Rechte vorbehalten
ISBN 3 499 61921 0
Originally published in Germany as
Aus der Tiefe des Raumes – Günter Netzer

This text published in 2022
Translation and Introduction copyright
© Robert Pralle

ISBN: 978-2-9547-111-2-6

Printed in the UK by www.beamreachuk.co.uk

www.xxpedient.com

Für Alana und Elvira,
ohne die alles nicht wäre

Contents

Introduction

They don't come much bigger than England vs West Germany in 1972 in a match that counted.

As well as thunderous noise, there was light drizzle at Wembley on 29 April, as the England XI and their visitors made their way out onto the pitch to contest the first leg of the European Championship quarter-final. They had last met here six years before, when Geoff Hurst's second 'goal' presented ARD's Rudi Michel with the toughest sixty seconds of his distinguished commentating career: should he give voice to a justifiable grievance or repress his true feelings and accept the fait accompli? His characteristic calmness belied the inner struggle. With Kenneth Wolstenholme (: "They think it's all over ...") recently retired, David Coleman is at the microphone for the BBC. Michel is back, providing the perfect, softly spoken accompaniment for anyone who wishes to watch the game on youtube fifty years on. His accurate phrasing of the English players names – Bell and Ball clearly distinguished – suggests a courteous impartiality. But his pleasure at watching the green shirted West German side playing so well and leading against hosts whose dominant

Wembley aura has not entirely evaporated flickers through. As West Germany construct a twenty-one pass move, the simple intonation of their names is, like the spectacle, poetry of a kind. One name in particular stands out: Netzer. Tonight, the full repertoire of his ball playing skills is on show. In contrast to Colin Bell, who gets in an uncharacteristic tangle when he is put in on goal after half an hour, the Borussia Mönchengladbach number ten calmly intercepts the next England ball into Sepp Maier's penalty box. This is defending *à la* Günter Netzer. A cushioned volley with the outside of his boot bisects the white shirts towards Siggi Held who plays a short return pass. With a lengthening stride, his flowing blond mane illuminated by the floodlights, Netzer surges fifty yards down the middle of the pitch, pushing the ball far in front across the sleek Wembley surface. The opposition cannot get close to him. Several are aware of the danger posed by Gerd Müller, who Netzer plays in on the edge of the England box. With two jinking touches, the Bayern Munich striker threads his way through them at pace. His shot nutmegs Hughes on the retreat but Gordon Banks reacts just quick enough to scoop the skidding ball behind.

West Germany's lead is maintained until Francis Lee equalises in the seventy-sixth minute. Wembley is rocking. English hopes though of rescuing something against such fluent and steady opposition are jeopardised when, eight minutes later, Bobby Moore concedes a penalty. The obvious candidate to take it, Müller allows Netzer the honour. The responsibility stimulates rather than intimidates him. Nevertheless, diving to his right, Banks (: 'Safer than the Bank of England') gets a hand to the ball.

There are two schools of thought concerning tonight's meeting of two football civilisations, which comes a few days after Chancellor Brandt's triumphant re-election, endorsing his Ostpolitik, and as the Heath government settles itself following the first miners' strike. A dissenting opinion is offered by the *Frankurter Allgemeine Zeitung*'s (*FAZ*) football correspondent. Ulfert Schröder was no fan of Netzer's. He thinks that 1-1 would be a fair scoreline, indicating how England pushed West Germany hard. The hand of Banks very nearly keeps it there. It is by a fine angle that the ball rebounds off the post into the net.

The dominant view however is that 1-3, the final score once Müller had capitalised on the open spaces left by the home side in pursuit of a second equaliser, accurately reflects West German superiority. Whereas England seemed to be anxious both to offload or to hoist the ball forward, the visitors played what Netzer describes as, 'a light-footed, rhythmic football having little to do with the traditional virtues of the German game, repetitively drilled home down the years'. Their demeanour was pleasing too: 'From the [long] Charlie George hairstyles to the occasional small courtesies in the blazing heat of the match,' there was little that was teutonic about it, noted Ian Wooldridge in the *Daily Mail*. The consensus in the Press was that the hosts were left chasing shadows by (arguably) the best German side of all time producing its best performance in which, another English paper reported, Netzer was ably assisted by Wimmer and Beckenbauer – as he happily quotes on page one hundred and one of this book.

Its original title is *Aus der Tiefe des Raumes*, the phrase coined by the *FAZ* literary critic, Karl Heinz Bohrer to describe Netzer's performance in a piece he wrote eighteen months after the event. 'Out of deep space' has overtones of *2025, A Space Odyssey*. *L'Équipe* hailed this instant classic as, 'Dream football from the year 2000'. So perhaps it is appropriate that nearly a quarter of the way into the new century we can learn a little more about Günter Netzer, as he is pulled *Aus der Tiefe des Raumes*, and out of the shadow of Franz Beckenbauer.

The background to what Netzer refers to as one of his 'Big Three' matches, was the 'historic compromise' which, with the blessing of the coach, Helmut Schön, the two players came to as they prepared for it. While he appreciates that this might be a rather grand way to describe how he and the libero were to randomly interchange positions so as to befuddle the English, there was more to it than that. The compromise was really a merging of the different playing styles of Netzer's Borussia and Beckenbauer's Bayern. Since 1966 the two dominant Bundesliga sides had not been separated by more than two places. Without dwelling on the point that on 29 April 1972 there were six Bayern players and only two from Mönchengladbach (, Berti Vogts being injured), the centrality of a Netzer feeling confident in the company of his fellow Gladbacher, Herbert Wimmer in West Germany's first successful campaign since winning the 1954 World Cup (: 'The Miracle of Bern') meant that the performance did meld the creativity of the back-to-back champions with the solidity of their great rivals, who provided the spine of the team: Maier, Beckenbauer, Hans-Georg Schwarzenbeck and Müller, as well as two names for the future, Paul Breitner and Uli Hoeneß.

Wembley is not a one-off. The West Germans will go on to sweep aside Belgium in the next round and then the Soviet Union in the final. Netzer continues to command, constantly available to interlock their game and unlock that of the opposition, with discriminatingly sprayed long balls which bypass even the best laid game plans. He has produced similar performances for the national side in the past, for example in a 2-2 draw against Brazil at the Maracanã in 1968. But only now, aged twenty-seven, has he become a regular choice. (Wolfgang Overath, of course, waits in the wings.)

The first game in which it was shown that the two clubs' systems could function together harmoniously had come a year before, when *Die Mannschaft* were what Netzer calls '*souveränes*' 3-0 victors in Istanbul. This was also the match in which Schön finally agreed to play Beckenbauer as sweeper. For the previous two years, since he had been converted into that role for Bayern, the player had been trying to persuade his coach, who thought putting him in defence would be a waste of talent, that this was how he operated most effectively.

It was not hard at the time, with Willy Brandt as chancellor and the Republic beginning to shed the protective shell which, out of necessity, Konrad Adenauer – "No Experiments!" – had placed around it, to read political significance into the principal footballing rivalry of the day. 'Borussia and Bayern: radicalism or rationality, reform or pragmatism.' (And Puma (Netzer) or Adidas (Beckenbauer), too.) These were the things which interested Karl Heinz Bohrer for example and which were reflected in the names bestowed upon each team by two other writers: '*der Bayern-Pack*' (Professor Walter Jens) and the Borussia 'Foals' (Wilhelm August Hurtmanns).

Their dissimilar attitudes would be encapsulated for Günter Netzer when the luck of the 1976 European Cup draw brought Real Madrid, where he and Paul Breitner were now playing, up against first Borussia at the quarter- and then Bayern at the semi-finals stages. On his homecoming he received a standing ovation, whereas at the Olympic Stadium Breitner was booed every time he got the ball. Statistics might suggest that the contrast between the clubs was overstated. But what side with Gerd Müller, who scored 365 goals in 427 league appearances, could fail to achieve a healthy goal tally? It was not so much the 'what' as the 'how' which separated the two. Borussia played flowing football, at pace; Bayern's game was channelled down the middle of the pitch. It was tight and attritional, in keeping with the philosophy of their disciplinarian coaches, first Branko Zebec and then Udo Lattek. Beckenbauer recalls that it was because opponents were so concerned about himself that he was able to be the provider for Müller, left in open space. Netzer joked that *Der Kaiser* was only able to play on until he was thirty-seven, in his untouchable libero position, because he left it to Schwarzenbeck in front to do the dirty work for him. While he might have his own protector, Netzer himself operated in a more exposed, central position as he teased and spread the flow of play around the pitch. For ten years, Borussia satisfied his ambition. That of a Beckenbauer, always aiming to achieve more, "was foreign to me. Playing such wonderful football with Mönchengladbach I had already achieved everything I wanted to."

Beckenbauer's and Bayern's ambitions were realised to the full in the European Cup from 1974-76. But when they overcame Leeds United in the second of their three successive final victories, they were described by the *Daily Mail* as the 'parasites of football'. The following year, France's answer to

Borussia, Saint-Étienne, hit the woodwork twice before finally going down 0-1. In the 1970s it was still possible, as Ipswich Town also showed, for a provincial club to dazzle.

The symbolism cultural commentators invested in Borussia was a considerable amount for a small city side with a run-down stadium (30,000 capacity) on the Lower Rhine to bear. Perhaps the unlikelihood contributed to its aura of progressiveness. Not only the 'who' but the 'where' of Mönchengladbach raised questions: when the club competed in the European Cup for the first time and were drawn against Everton in the second round, the English 1969-70 champions' manager, Harry Catterick was unsure where on the map he could locate this town with the unpronounceable name. A year later it was Inter Milan's turn to have to find their bearings, having first assumed Mönchengladbach to be a satellite of Munich. (More about that encounter, another of Günter's 'Big Three', later.)

The RAF had a clearer idea of its location when, reacting to the German invasion of Belgium, it targeted road and railway infrastructure there on the night of 11 May 1940. It was the first town in the Reich to be bombed. A much deadlier raid was reserved for the end of the war. Netzer had not long been in the world when he, his mother and everyone else on the MariaHilf maternity ward had to go and shelter in the basement. When they emerged the following morning, 20 September 1944, it was to find Mönchengladbach reduced to a pile of smoking rubble. The cotton industry which had been its raison d'être would not rise from the ashes. In the working-class district of Geroweiher only one street remained inhabited. Its social hub was Barbara Netzer's corner shop, supplementing her husband Christian's income as a wholesale seed salesman to horticulturalists and farmers. Gasthausstraße was where the young Günter learned to play football.

The city's commercial revival would see a shift to the service sector. Its clothing manufacturing history lay behind the success of its fashion school, second only to Hanover's. At the same time as Borussia climbed the Bundesliga, the old town suddenly became a magnet for those involved in Düsseldorf's social and artistic scene, on the lookout for variety. Its attraction also had something to do with Mönchengladbach's proximity to the Dutch border … dope being a basic ingredient of the counter culture which thrived from 1968 into the following decade: the Brandt years.

Like Netzer, who signed for Borussia from 1. FC Mönchengladbach in 1963, most of his teammates were either from the city or the surrounding region. There was loyalty to the jersey, as well as to the cavalier footballing philosophy cultivated by Hennes Weisweiler after he arrived a year later to coach them. Coaches still tended to be authority figures. Weisweiler stood out because, most of the time, he was prepared to listen to what his young players, particularly Netzer, had to say in a debating society atmosphere that coincided with Brandt's campaign promise of "more democracy". This openness and the matchday fruits it bore were what made the No.10's ten years at Borussia such a satisfying time.

It was certainly not the pay which kept players at the club, one reason for Netzer's non-footballing ventures while he was there. 'Lovers Lane', the intimate discotheque he opened at the time of Borussia's second successive title in Spring 1971, established itself straightaway as the hub of the Mönchengladbach scene. This was a first for a player in the eight-year-old Bundesliga, just as his ear lobe length hair, now down to his shoulders, had been. It was worn in the Ilie Nastase style.

West Germany was casting off the shadow of the war. Not only was it the leading European economy as of 1970; Brandt's Ostpolitik began to loosen the straitjacket which had been placed on the country's divided status after its defeat. As the enthusiasm of the sixties tailed off elsewhere, the Federal Republic aroused interest. Munich, a city Netzer headed to whenever he had the opportunity, was representative of both the attraction and the danger of the country at this moment. Naturally, Jack Nicholson, *The Passenger* of Antonioni's 1975 film, in which locale and ambience counted for much, passed through it en route to Barcelona, another city in the process of being rediscovered, during the final years of Franco's dictatorship. Led Zeppelin, the Rolling Stones and others did not come to the Bavarian capital just because of the recording opportunities presented by Musicland Studios. They came because Munich was a happening place. Günter had already moved on to Spain when Jimmy Page and Keith Richards arrived. Had he still been an habitué of Munich nightlife it is interesting to imagine meetings between them. Besides being wartime only children, he, Page and Richards all share a quietly spoken manner belying great determination. His farewell to Borussia in June 1973 had been made in Roy of the Rovers fashion; the *FAZ* likened him to Achilles. And here were Led Zeppelin recording 'Achilles Last Stand' at Musicland.

Listening to the Stones and Bob Dylan for the first time had been a revelation for Netzer. He rebels though against the idea that he was a rebel. He was more a loner with a cause: that of protecting his integrity. This individualism, which he freely admits could be self-centred, did not help his international career. Because he only ever played twenty-one minutes of world cup football during his time as an international, which spanned the 1966-74 tournaments, a suspicion of underachievement attaches to him. This is his record as a player:

Bundesliga champion: 1969-70; 1970-71

Pokal Cup (FA Cup): 1973

Bundesliga Player of the Year: 1972, 1973

La Liga champion: 1974-75; 1975-76

Copa del Rey (FA Cup): 1974 (in which he did not play in the final); 1975

West Germany: 37 caps. European champion: 1972

Then, as manager – general manager, not coach – of Hamburg SV (HSV): Bundesliga champion: 1978-79, 1981-82, 1982-83

European Cup: 1983.

It is an undeniable record of high achievement, yet somehow it remains … ambiguous. For example, while Johan Cruyff's Barcelona years are considered to match those he spent at Ajax, Netzer fails to receive credit for being central to Real Madrid's revival in the brief time he spent there alongside Paul Breitner. Once he left, their slump resumed. Cruyff of course had a higher profile, captaining a great Dutch side at a world cup. When he arrived in the Catalan capital, at the same time that Netzer moved to Madrid, he was hailed as 'El Salvador'. On 17 February 1974 Barcelona were 5-0 victors at the Bernabéu, before going on to win La Liga for the first time since 1960.

After that? Nothing in his five years as the *Azulgranas* kingpin, until winning the Copa del Rey in 1978.

It could have been Netzer at the Nou Camp, but Rinus Michels balked at building his team around a German. Once again, the war was casting its long shadow. So did the Spanish Civil War. Cruyff's insistence that he would never play for Real Madrid because of the club's identification with the Franco regime was applauded. Having been on the more attractive side of the supposed political argument between Borussia and Bayern, Netzer now joined the club with clout. This was the vantage point from which he could watch a society in transition. Back in West Germany, Brandt's forced resignation brought the highly competent, pragmatic Helmut Schmidt to power. The Press again drew the football parallel to political developments: was the twenty-nine-year-old Netzer's time also past, almost as soon as, internationally, it had begun?

As the Schmidt era commenced, Bayern Munich's own pragmatic penchant was not limited to the pitch. They were the first club, now that the Bundesliga was firmly established, to appreciate the game's publicity potential. Netzer's transfer abroad made him the first player both to head in that direction since its founding and, after many years of Spanish isolation, to opt for La Liga. With the world cup to be hosted by West Germany only a year away, it received a lot of negative press attention. This was the cue for Bayern to make a great play of venturing to bring the prodigal son back home, and generate much positive press coverage in the process. The reality was that Real Madrid were hardly likely to accept Netzer's return lightly; he had only just arrived. One of the contractual terms left him free to play for his country anyway. But perception of the actual facts tended to be blurred, to Netzer's detriment, as it was in the comparison with Cruyff. Even if he was allowed to play, there were those who questioned whether the 'traitor to the fatherland' should be allowed to, having made his decision to head for the sun and abundant pesetas. Once again, Ulfert Schröder led the chorus of criticism. 'Netzer mistakenly believed,' he wrote, 'that he could lead his teammates by the nose and that they were bound to accept him as their chief. Now Netzer makes the further mistake that he can follow a fourteen-day fitness crash course to regain the strength that he has frittered away for a whole year, flying here and there, with his business ventures and his fun seeking and' – the coup de grâce – 'his Spanish football.' In the case of Uli Hoeneß, Netzer may indeed have been mistaken, since he allegedly went on to call the Bayern player a "bandit" for sabotaging his own performance in a friendly played early in the year, in order to get him thrown out of the squad.

Not long after Netzer's experience abroad, Bob Paisley's feelings when Kevin Keegan left Liverpool for HSV were no different to Helmut Schön's for his playmaker – that he had turned himself into a "soldier of fortune". Both players however were determined not to capitulate in the face of their respective difficult first years abroad: on the pitch, gaining acceptance in the dressing room and culturally acclimatising themselves. Keegan's situation would change for the better following Netzer's unexpected arrival in Hamburg in early 1978. 'Günter was one of the most reliable and trustworthy people I have ever known,' he remarked. The following year HSV were champions, though, regrettably, celebrations at the Volksparkstadion on 9 June 1979 came close to tragedy when the fenced ground was invaded, an event that has been taken to signal the end, both on and off the pitch, of a golden footballing decade, which stretched back to Borussia Mönchengladbach's first title.

The Rhinelander's determination to overcome the problems he faced in the 1973-74 season was the making of him as a man. He could no longer, as he might otherwise have been (, his brief, 1972 preeminence in the national team notwithstanding) be considered a smalltown legend. Before, he tended to walk away from confrontation, for example vowing to never play for the national side again because Schön unfairly singled him out for criticism when, in the build up to the Mexico World Cup, West Germany produced a chaotic performance in Seville, and lost 2-0 to the hosts. Once he became a manager himself, Netzer was not afraid to make tough decisions with players if that is what the team interest required. During his three years in the Spanish capital, he also became imbued with the Real Madrid way of doing things. When it came to personnel, this meant shielding players and high maintenance coaches from any paraphernalia that surrounded and might distract them from the football essentials. Man management was key to his success at HSV. Since he never felt entirely certain that his brilliant coach, Ernst Happel's dependability could be assumed to endure, he would take the died in the wool bachelor off to Sylt, or back to his native Austria for a few days, as a token of his appreciation, and to keep the danger of the 'Grantler' burning out at bay. At Madrid he had also learned patience. He demonstrated it now, making forty journeys over a three-month period to sign the goalscoring phenomenon Horst Hrubesch from second division Rot-Weiss Essen and from under the nose of Eintracht Frankfurt. His instinct told him that, whatever *Das Kopfball-Ungeheuer*'s (The Header Beast) technical shortcomings, he must sign the big centre-forward. As for Happel: "I understood this man from the first second. I did not even need to hear him speak."

By the time Netzer retired, aged forty-one, the emotional effort had taken its toll, just as the physical grind had ten years earlier, when he brought his playing career to an end. 'I was no longer fully committed,' he admits. 'My enthusiasm had dwindled, partly because my instinct was no longer as lively and, therefore, reliable as it had previously been.' In 1983 he signed Wolfram Wuttke, 'one of the most outstanding players Germany has ever seen,' from Schalke 04. 'Unfortunately,' Netzer continues, 'Wuttke was not one of the most outstanding human beings Germany has ever seen.' He is one example whom, in his autobiography, *Ich*, Franz Beckenbauer gives of unfulfilled talent. Which is fair comment: he had no medals to show for it. The other is Netzer, whose record has been listed above. There seems to be a difference, all the same …

Beckenbauer took over as national coach. Netzer left the city for the Swiss countryside, in need of rest. (He already knew the country from the final season of his playing career, with Grasshoppers Zürich, where one of his first games was a friendly against Arsenal: the opportunity for Malcolm Macdonald to observe, "I have never seen such big feet in my life – his boots must have been size 14". Another Gunner had known about this for years. Brought in by Alf Ramsey to deal with Netzer in the return leg following the Wembley defeat, Peter Storey kept one of his (size 12 in fact) boots as a memento of an ugly 0-0 played out at the Berlin Olympiastadion. Günter Netzer's own memento? "The whole England team autographed my legs.") Later he would reflect that Hamburg suited his temperament perfectly but at the time he had been too busy, working seventy-hour weeks, to notice much of his surroundings. It was while he was there, he confides, that he learned to talk. The job demanded it. Speaking to the media, he was composed and considered. Two years after retiring, at the same time as pursuing a new business career with the sports marketing firm, CW Lüthi, he was chosen to partner Uli Potofski in Germany's first dedicated television football show, broadcast by the independent channel, RTL. Clearly, the producers were attracted by his renown and aura. But the chatty younger Potofski, a strapping thirty-something with dark curls, soon found that Netzer was not particularly forthcoming as his *Kick-Off* co-presenter. At least not in the context of a three-and-a-half-hour-long extravaganza which was too obviously trying to entertain. After the first broadcast he remarked, "*Er ist ein introvertierter Typ. Das ist problematisch.*" When Netzer teamed up with Gerhard Delling for the public channel, ARD the chemistry and more concise format worked. Now that he had turned fifty, Netzer's charisma was better understood. It was not based on superficial glamour but the confidence to hold the camera's gaze and to speak his mind succinctly, as well as with more than occasional irony. The debonair Delling was businesslike himself. Rather than stirring things up unnecessarily, the duo saw their role as that of offering a candid assessment of the spectacle being provided, which hopefully they could enjoy and compliment. The German game, unfortunately, was no longer what it had been during the golden, Netzer, era. A "new low point," he concurred with Delling, following a European championship qualifier in Reykjavik which ended Iceland 0 – Germany 0 in September 2003. The pair's assessment so enraged the national coach, Rudi Völler (, a big Netzer fan, incidentally) that, when interviewed later that evening, he demanded, "You know how much shit they played in Netzer's days? You couldn't watch that, it was football without running …". Günter may have elsewhere agreed that, "from the outset, I found somebody to do the running for me," and that, "I expended more energy during a game talking than running". He was, as often, being self-deprecating. Widely held though Völler's viewpoint had become, it was an exaggeration. On a good surface, like Wembley's, the pace of the game back then was not so far off what it later became. Those players were athletes too.

After the Völler outburst, Netzer explained, "I accept that we played a lot of shit in the past. I say that often enough. But the regularity of bad games of Völler's team is worrying. We used to have poor games, but they were followed by ten outstanding ones." Of the kind to get Karl Heinz Bohrer excited in his 'Aus der Tiefe des Raumes' piece: ' 'Thrill' is the moment things start to kick off, the unforeseen move, the creation of energy out of fine angles. […] 'Thrill' *ist* Wembley.'

"That's not the case here," continued the onetime street footballer in his response to Völler. "We weren't overly critical," of this German team. "They got off lightly over the course of the last year."

As he sat down to write this book, with the assistance of the author and journalist, Helmut Schümann, the perspective for the national side appeared brighter. Germany's hosting of the 2006 world cup was eagerly anticipated. Still, *Die Mannschaft*'s renaissance from "footballing methods that come close to desperation," as Netzer put it in Reykjavik, awaited Joachim Löw moving up in the hierarchy to take over from Jürgen Klinsmann.

Before Löw, and in contrast to the suspicion of Netzer's own personal underachievement, the national side's competitive results since the 1972 triumph had for a long time flattered it. The Germans were a *Turniermannschaft*. In 1974, Cruyff's side were victims against the hosts of their own overconfidence. At Italia '90 Franz Beckenbauer espoused pragmatism as the true German virtue in winning the least attractive world cup of all, 1-0, with a penalty. The next victory, in Euro '96, was a workmanlike achievement of the kind to be expected from a team now managed by Netzer's former right-hand man, Berti Vogts. Then there were the world cup runners-up years of 1982 and '86 and 2002, as well as similar positions in the European championship. Rarely exciting viewing, even when the side were inspired by Bernd Schuster, still only twenty years of age, to victory in the 1980 edition.

The 1982 World Cup marked a low point. The stigma of Schumacher's brutal taking out of the French defender Patrick Battiston, as well as the cynical collusion with Austria in their group match, still clung to the West German game, Netzer records, when, the following year, he took HSV to Athens to face Juventus, who were European Cup favourites in both senses of the word. If parallels could be drawn between Brandt and Borussia, is it fanciful to suggest that the boorishness which characterised the 1982 campaign was a sign that, at the same time as it might congratulate itself on having become a model under Schmidt – '*Modell* Deutschland' – this post-war creation might already be entering a more uncertain stage?

Schuster, the most exciting player to emerge since Netzer and Beckenbauer's time, had already broken with Schön's successor, Jupp Derwall in a manner which left no doubt that he disdained his authority. He may have had a similar degree of talent to Netzer, but not his charm. While the *Rebell am Ball*, the title of a first biography, appearing in 1971, preferred to spend his free time with friends he had made at business school or the artistic circle his girlfriend was a part of, he would never insult his teammates in the manner Schuster did his, nor would he show disrespect, as opposed to candour, in his dealings with Hennes Weisweiler or Helmut Schön. The liberties he took allowing himself time off were often on the pretext of injuries. From the outset he had, as the Borussia team doctor, Alfred Gerhards recognised, a less than robust constitution. These liberties may have been outrageous, but they served a purpose: Netzer instinctively knew that if he was forced to keep his nose to the football grindstone he would soon grow stale. His way of playing the game, an unusual combination of languor and drive that was particular to himself, demanded that he have a certain degree of freedom, which other players might not require.

The anti-Netzerites considered him to be someone who let extracurricular business and leisure activities (his discotheque, nightclubbing and Ferraris) interfere with his core activity. This was another misperception. Not unlike David Beckham in this regard, he was capable of distinguishing between what was essential in his life – football – and the rest. However appealing the surprise invitation to join Joseph Beuys, as Professor of Applied Arts at the Düsseldorf Academy might be, he knew he must turn it down. A later Netzer biographer,

Helmut Böttiger, suggests that his charisma is derived from this awareness and acceptance of what both his special (footballing) capabilities and his limits are. He never does or says anything '*falsche*'. While occasionally he will don a gold lamé outfit for the amusement of the TV audience, the mature Netzer look is an elegantly worn suit and tie, and shorter, but still not short, hair. Besides being age appropriate, it matches his cool, analytical style.

Cool playing conditions suited him best. Nothing could exceed a floodlit match in a moist spring or autumn atmosphere, like Wembley, or the Bökelberg stadium on 20 October 1971 for a European Cup tie against Inter Milan. "*Das ist das größte Fußballspiel, das ich bisher gesehen habe!*" raved his national side teammate, Horst-Dieter Höttges. "What a fantastic team! Such pace, power and invention!" enthused Sir Matt Busby. A malign fate however decreed that it was cynical Inter who went through, and eventually on to the final. Netzer is confident that without it Borussia would themselves have progressed to the final and a showdown with Cruyff's Ajax, whom they had already beaten in two friendlies. "A pity," he says. The Borussia – Inter match was not even televised, because ARD were unwilling to pay the extra 6,600 marks which Borussia Mönchengladbach were holding out for to cover sales tax. Instead, the story of the match has been handed down, if not exactly as oral legend, then at least the stuff of it.

And here we come to an interesting aspect of Günter Netzer. Just like those in West Germany who distinguished between Bayern's functional manner and Borussia's progressive game, César Luis Menotti, Argentina's world cup winning coach in

1978, contrasted 'Right' (negative, conservative, authoritarian) and 'Left' (positive, creative, democratic) football. Another difference he drew, participating in the European channel 'Arte's' broadcast, 'Tango or Military Music' was between 'winners' and 'losers'. "For one, being a footballer is work; for the other, play."

That describes the story of Borussia vs Inter in 1971 perfectly. But it is not all. Netzer, to recall his record, was not just an aesthetic 'Beautiful Loser'. He was a pragmatist who, in their ongoing debate, insisted, with eventual success, to Hennes Weisweiler that Borussia Mönchengladbach needed to bolster its defence and temper all-out attack, by introducing different phases into their game in order to make it more sustainable, and successful. He was never a 'winner' though in the Beckenbauer mould. The Gladbacher chronicler, Holger Jenrich, considers that, 'Beckenbauer was seen as being vain and arrogant; at best he became a star, while Netzer turned into a myth'. Most importantly, as a player who raised the German game to one of its peaks; later, as a presence in the country's footballing culture, a rather different personality to the younger 'Rebell am Ball'. It is obvious that nostalgia for what he once was does not interest him. Nevertheless, at a deeper level the player and the analyst are the same man; 'den cleveren Netzer', as Beckenbauer calls him, is still an individualist more than a team player.

With an appealing nonchalance he admits that he remains something of a mystery to himself. In answering the FAZ's Proust Questionnaire, he chose Confessions of Felix Krull, Confidence Man by Thomas Mann as his favourite book.

Asked why, Netzer responded, "Because he is an impostor". In his own case, does the myth which accompanies him have little to do with who he really is, asks Helmut Böttiger? Or, does a myth sometimes possess its own truth, that is not entirely comprehended by the man behind it; even one who avoids striking false notes?

'Never trust the teller, trust the tale,' wrote Eastwood, Nottinghamshire's favourite son. That is, with due respect to the 1. FC Köln and England striker, Tony Woodcock, the novelist D.H. Lawrence. Here is Günter Netzer's tale. Extraordinary at times, but fact not fiction.

Robert Pralle
April 2022

1

We Come from Geroweiher

Things did not get off to a good start. I was five days old – or so I was later informed – when the new mothers at the MariaHilf hospital had to all go down into the basement because Mönchengladbach was being bombed. It was 19 September 1944. When they came up again, me in my mother's arms, it was to see the town reduced to a heap of smoking rubble and ash. At the age of five, I was too small to be allowed to play with the street team in Gasthausstraße. However, I had sweets from my mother's corner shop, and I had a ball. One of those rubber balls which get blown about in the wind and that can end up almost anywhere. Still, it was better than either the scrumpled up material or tin cans which the older kids were used to playing with. Then I got a leather ball, roughly stitched together, with a rubber bladder. If you headed it and made contact with the stitching rather than the leather part, a day long headache was assured. I mostly headed the stitching. A leather ball though was quite something. Together with the sweets, it allowed me to bribe my way into playing with the older boys.

"What shall we do with the nipper?" they asked amongst themselves, before saying to me, "You can watch if you like, shrimp." Then, "Hang on, the little fellow's got a ball. Not a bad one either." So, the older boys let me play with them.

Many years later, it would occur to me that throughout my life someone or other has wanted something which, fortunately for me, I have been able to provide. Back then, the big boys in Gasthausstraße needed my ball. Hey! Fantastic!

They put me in goal. Straightaway, shots were being smashed in above me. "Goal!" they exclaimed, as I retrieved my ball. Every now and again, it would end up down the Geroweiher drains, so I got thrown out of the team. My mother provided more sweets and another ball. The ball counted for a lot, while being in goal and conceding the whole time did not. Just being able to play football was what mattered. And a goalkeeper, trying to prevent the ball from crossing the line, is part of the game after all.

By the age of thirteen I was beginning to make my mark, or so I liked to think. I had not played in goal since the day when one of the Geroweiher outfield players failed to turn up. With no alternative, the older kids got me to take his place. I was lucky. And so were they, to have me playing uninhibitedly, in a more important role than goalkeeper. This was actually meant to be as 'last man', still using my hands when necessary. But I didn't simply stay at the back; I roamed forward too. From then on, the sweets were only needed at school, to make up for my occasional shortcomings.

During this time we had not been idle in Geroweiher. We made a small pitch, next to the plot of land where my father cultivated flower seeds. 'Pitch' is probably an exaggeration. It was a plot of clayish soil surrounded by trees and bushes, which we cleared. Our fathers then put up proper goalposts.

The only inhabited street in the neighbourhood was little Gasthausstraße. Its hub was my mother's grocery. As far as I can remember, other street teams never stood a chance when they played against us there. I scored goals by the dozen for Gasthausstraße and for 1. FC Mönchengladbach, a club suggested to me by the others when I was about eight or nine. I would play either on the left or the right wing – but not in goal. Whichever side of the pitch I was on, I scored goals. Six a game was not unusual; over a season, maybe as many as one hundred and fifty. By the age of thirteen I felt I had made my point. So did my coach, who sent me off to a course at the Duisburg-Wedau Sports Academy. The name of the Association coach there was Heinz Murach. He immediately sent me back home again. I was not yet big or strong enough.

Overall, my thirteenth year was a great success. At school I did just enough to get through it. But by the following year, in the lower third, it was becoming fairly obvious, as it would remain until the eagerly anticipated – by all – end of my schooldays that I was not, how shall we say, fully applying myself. Not that football was the only subject which occupied my mind. No, there was room enough in there to park cars as well. I am not sure where this passion came from, but it was no surprise to my father. Anything to do with automobiles, whether written or photographic, I began to absorb eagerly. I bought car magazines from the moment they first appeared. My keen interest was at the superficial level of how a car looked. I did not have a clue as to what a clutch was or what purpose it served. It would not take long for me to look a fool for my ignorance.

The family's two sources of income were Mother's grocery store and Father's seed business. He was the sales representative for his brother-in-law's shop. Work frequently took him out of our state, visiting peasants, his main clientele. It was a tough job because of the competition from wholesalers undercutting the independent salesmen, and also because his personal engagement was required. He often took me with him, driving along the Lower Rhine from one far-flung village to the next. While he was inside negotiating with a peasant, sometimes for up to an hour, I would be in the car in the farmyard. Inside, Schnapps was reputed to be drunk from time to time.

I am no longer sure why but one day – maybe on account of the Schnapps; perhaps just to make his son happy – he turned down a country lane, brought the car to a halt, and said, "Would you like to give it a go?" I didn't want to. I felt nervous. But my father had made up his mind to teach me to drive.

This first lesson was a fiasco. In order for my feet to reach the pedals, I had to slide so far down the seat that I was unable to see over the steering wheel. A cushion would have helped. The make of car slips my mind; probably a DKW or a Ford 12 M. I do remember it had a steering column gear shift and, most vividly of all, that the way I was sitting made stalling easier than driving. Tears flowed. My father, who was not a patient man, gruffly remarked, "Too dumb to drive," and I howled. It was another bad start.

Then came the matter of my hair. When I think about it, this was the worst and most painful defeat that I had to endure during my childhood and youth. It was all Aunt Triene's fault.

4

My father's sister was well-off and, if one can say this when talking about the Lower Rhine's West Bank in the fifties, very fashion conscious. One day, in the course, once more, of my 'lucky' thirteenth year, she decided that I needed a new hairstyle. She was very determined and persuaded my parents. If there was any protest from them, I do not remember it. They probably thought that Aunt Triene had a good idea of how to keep pace fashion-wise in the booming fifties. She thought the young man looked too childish and callow. He was put on a stool, where the hair roller torture began. He then received the blow drier treatment, sitting beneath one of those hot, strange smelling plastic hoods. When it was lifted up, I was no longer myself. I had a perm. It looked awful.

Geroweiher's and 1. FC Mönchengladbach's marksman, son of the thriving grocer Barbara Netzer and the well-regarded seed agent Christian Netzer, the only child from Gasthausstraße in high school, a little obsessed with football, and cars too, was now running around with a perm. On the football field I was the standing joke of both the older and the younger kids. It was the same at school, after they succeeded in recognising me once again. This was definitely not the hairstyle I wanted.

Some might say that the naughty war baby with curly locks was the chrysalis out of which emerged the midfield general identifiable by his fair hair flowing in all directions; the playmaker with a weakness for eye-catching fast cars, Ferraris in particular. But this development was not obvious: little Günter grew up amidst an apparent absence of luxury.

I was born during the war, although what my mother felt fleeing down into the hospital basement, with me in her

5

arms, I do not know. We did not talk about the war much at home. Nor did we discuss the Nazis, in spite – or maybe because – of the fact that one of their monstrous leaders, the minister of propaganda, Joseph Goebbels was one of the city's sons, as the neighbouring town of Rheydt, where he was born, was later incorporated into it. My father had served as a soldier in the Wehrmacht. I think he drove a lorry in the French campaign. It was something else that we avoided as a topic of conversation when we sat down to play cards in the evening. This silent blocking out of the Third Reich was nothing unusual. But how come I have no real memory of the war's aftermath, during which evidence of it, which I must have seen, was everywhere?

Mönchengladbach was chosen for the first Allied bombing raid on Germany, in May 1940. There were casualties. Before the war it had been a prosperous hub of the Rhine's cotton industry. In the mid-nineteenth century the river Niers, which runs through our city, had attracted thousands of spinners, weavers and dyers. They mostly produced cord, which in the early days was called 'Manchester'. As part of our school homework, we were proud to learn that Mönchengladbach was known as the 'Rhineland Manchester' before the war. By its end, almost half of the city had been destroyed. Rheydt was virtually wiped out.

I have no memory of going out and climbing through the rubble, something I was forbidden to do. Does that mean I never dared do anything? Probably not on my own, because I was too shy then to oppose authority. The summit of my rebellion was the Geroweiher kickabouts, another activity which was not permitted. The first furtive cigarette? Never happened. A little sweet thieving? There was no need for it, sitting in Mother's store. And illegal driving, once I had worked out how to use the clutch and accelerator together, was validated by my father when we drove down country lanes and through off-the-beaten-track villages together. I never had a prang in a car.

With my ball, I already had everything I wanted. I could barely walk when I began to bang it against a wall. It then became my passport into street and team football. There was no real need for me to be rebellious. Were beatings still common in those days? My father never hit me; my mother must have occasionally done so. Since the memory of this is so hazy, her punishments could not have been that painful. When I came back from playing football in bad weather, soaked and covered in mud, she would deliver a twin-handed strike, to either side of my head, before chucking the sludgy garments into the washbasin. One thing I do remember: we had no washing machine at the time.

Besides football, I was lucky to have caring, generous parents. Together, they provided me with a sane outlook on a world that had yet to be put back together again. There was nothing about my own little world which I wanted to change. Did I ever leave the patch between Gasthausstraße and Waldhausener Straße, Geroweiher and my father's business? Very rarely, and, even then, not alone. By the time I first tried to use a public telephone I was already sixteen years old. I hemmed and hawed, without really knowing how the thing worked, or what I should say to the operator or, most importantly, what sort of conversation one was meant to have on the telephone. In other words, I was a shy, rather inhibited lad with little knowledge of the world, besides knowing how to score goals. 'Rebel with a ball' was how I later became known. I admit I liked the name. But that is not what I am! I certainly wasn't then!

I was privileged and knew it. How many have parents who send their youngster off to high school, full of hope, then accept his failure without any kind of drama? What gives me greatest pleasure, even today, is being lazy. Laziness on the football pitch can be set right with a couple of passes. For a long time at school, I was able to hide it with a certain cuteness, which meant one or two of my classmates were willing for me to copy their work. But that is not so easy in geography and biology. And so my schooldays came to an end in the lower third year. These two subjects, that required a minimum of hard work, were my downfall. There were no scenes or reproaches at home. My parents simply accepted, without displaying any disappointment, that the dream of their son becoming a graduate was now over. Perhaps I felt a little ashamed; I cannot remember exactly.

I can still recall the sense of relief I felt on leaving school. It lasted until I enrolled at a tutorial college which provided business courses for football players, something I did to humour my parents rather than because I was genuinely interested in pursuing a professional career.

They were both, as I say, incredibly generous, my father maybe too much so. In my supposedly ill-starred thirteenth year, he had offered me a five mark reward for each goal I scored in a 1. FC Mönchengladbach jersey. It meant I received handsome pocket money for the time. That may not have been the intention: perhaps my father's honourable gesture suggested that he did not fully believe in my talent?

Money placed one in a privileged circle. Aunt Triene was quick to realise this. She and her husband, who was also in the seed business, were a feather in the wind of better times. If one wants to be critical, they were almost a caricature of the newly founded Lower Rhine region's materialism during the early days of the economic miracle. I was not about to criticise. Together with my father, I was happy to join my aunt at this or that holiday resort, while my mother stayed behind at the grocery store. Aunt Triene liked anywhere with a casino. Baden-Baden, Bad Neuenahr and Bad Wiessee were amongst her destinations. What stood out most about her and her husband, Gottlob's lifestyle though was that you could be sure to find the latest consumer goods in their house before anyone else had them. A television, for example. This was a great big thing housed in a chest with carved doors, which could only be opened, as though it were a shrine, by Aunt Triene or my uncle. Whenever I visited, Gottlob obliged.

To own a TV set at the beginning of the fifties was very uncommon. With few exceptions, it was only radio retail shops that had them. When there was a big event, such as a league game, the display model was turned on in the shop window. It did not take long for a crowd to form. Nor did it matter that, in contrast to today's high fidelity broadcasts of entire matches, only fragments were shown.

Summer 1954 though was something different. All across the country groups gathered in front of these shops. Walking through Mönchengladbach, there were people everywhere when I made my way to Aunt Triene's, to take my place on the sofa in front of the great chest. The TV was switched on. It was the world cup in Switzerland. Although not yet ten years old, anything about football, I knew it. I was familiar with Fritz and Ottmar Walter, Max Morlock and Helmut Rahn. I obviously knew Toni Turek, who played in goal for Düsseldorf, on the other side of the Rhine. Whenever football was the topic of conversation with my parents or in company, I soaked up everything I heard. But I was never 'Fritz Walter' or 'Helmut Rahn', 'Max Morlock' or 'Hans Schäfer' in our Geroweiher kickabouts. Not even 'Toni Turek', as my goalkeeping career had ended a while before. Before the reader concludes from this that, even as a child, Günter Netzer was so self-confident and inflexible that he had no need to model himself on any of these heroes, I ought to point out that images of them, making impersonation easy and natural, were few and far between.

Summer 1954 changed that. There they were on Aunt Triene's TV screen, in front of the sofa I shared with her, 'Uncle Triene' and my father. I struggled to comprehend as the German team lost their group game against Hungary 3-8. We consoled ourselves with the shared view that the Hungarians were just too good, unbeatable even. Schnapps was possibly part of the remedy. For the deciding group game, in which the Germans beat Turkey 7-2, we were all in front of the TV once more, as we would be for the 2-0 quarter-final victory over Yugoslavia, and again for the semi-final, a 6-1 rout of Austria in Basle. Then came 4 July, the day of the final – and victory against Hungary. Shy young Günter could not miss that. When I think about it, that was the moment from which things began to go well.

2

The Lilywhites

We crossed the Rhine by train, heading in the direction of Duisburg again. I had received a second invitation from the West German Football Association to take part in a training camp there. I had earned the right and, if I may say so myself, was on the way to becoming an important figure at 1. FC Mönchengladbach: the fourteen-year-old centre-forward, a goalscorer 'at your service', whose record spoke for itself. I cannot remember a single game I played for the club without hitting the back of the net. Usually I scored several times. Afterwards I received vigorous backslaps. I was never on the bench. Nor, I believe, was I ever a candidate for substitution.

The tactics at our small club were limited to this: shoot at goal whenever you have the opportunity. There were three pitches. The grass one was reserved for the first team. A clay ground had a rickety wooden stand, that is still there. It was used by the C and D teams. Then there was a cinder pitch where the eldest juniors played. Not much thought went into its location on the edge of a plateau. If you shot wide of the goal the ball would run down a short hill, and a long break in play would usually take place. I wanted the game to be non-stop and to keep chasing after the ball. Only later did I prefer strolling around the pitch. Back then I just ran and shot.

My father stood on the touchline, looking happy and, increasingly, a little proud even. He was not that interested in sport but, when he saw that I was the focal point of the team, he came to watch regularly.

The new invitation to Wedau, to take part in its talent development programme, was not a complete surprise. It pleased me, although I was not ambitious. I had no plan mapped out for my potential career in football to take off. In place of any immediately obtainable goal, I dreamt for instance of playing for the national youth team. Until now, everything that had happened to me in sport had occurred by hazard. It was not out of dogged determination to improve my shooting technique that I would spend an hour outside, kicking the ball against the wall. When the weather was foul and I nevertheless went out to play in Geroweiher it had nothing to do with wanting to become the best. I did it because I felt like playing football. My focus on scoring goals by the dozen was explained by the enjoyment it brought me, rather than the idea that it might lead to this invitation from Duisburg. Playing for 1. FC Mönchengladbach, the oldest club in the city, with its unusually large Juniors squad, was not that big a deal for me, in spite of the praise, beyond all measure, that we received from those we lived amongst.

At Duisburg, Heinz Murach, the Football Federation coach who had sent me home the previous year because I was too slight, was still in charge. His philosophy was very different to mine. A young lad like me should not just casually improvise as he went along. As he put it at breakfast time, "Young man, you need to become a lot tougher," a message repeated during each training session and every evening five-a-side game. Obviously, the academy's regime came as a bit of a shock for a youngster like me, used to basking in the sun. Nowadays they offer five-star hotel comfort; at the time I am talking about the atmosphere was more like a barracks. Who my three roommates were I cannot recall but I do remember that the cooking was hardly performance enhancing.

The group I was part of were the best young footballers from the Lower Rhine and its surrounding areas. Unlike in my own team, there weren't any I was able to outshine – not remotely. Each of them could do whatever I could; their combined talents easily overshadowed my own. The whisper of one name seemed to hover over each session and some, for example myself, would be frozen in an attitude of respect at its mere mention: Wolfgang Overath of 1. FC Köln. Extraordinary tales were told about him, of how he could control any situation on the pitch, and of his ability to ease himself away from the close attentions of three or four opponents without ever losing the ball. I got to know Overath two years later when we were both in the national youth side; not a word of what was said about him during training or in the canteen was exaggerated.

But before that encounter I first had to get to grips with Heinz Murach. For the first time in my short footballing career, I was obliged to take criticism. "You don't do enough defensive work," he observed. In fact, I did hardly any defensive work. Since turning into a goal poacher, the area between our own goal and the halfway line had become suspect territory for me. "Your tackling leaves room for improvement," he told me.

13

To be honest, my tackling was virtually non-existent. How could it be otherwise for a shy, skinny kid anxious to avoid too much rough-and-tumble? "First you need to learn to head the ball," he said, sending me off to the gym where a ball, which I could barely reach, was suspended by a rope from the ceiling. Nevertheless, I had to reach it – because Heinz Murach said so. Run, jump, head … and then start again. A bump formed on my head. Inside it, my thoughts went back to the way I used to dash after the ball as a kid. I wondered what had become of that carefree game. These evening sessions were anything but play.

The course was attended by fifty or sixty boys of my age group. We were divided into ten teams playing against each other on both the indoor pitch and reduced scale pitches outdoors. That should give an idea of the sort of tight space we were competing in. It was demanding and exhausting. Just as in ice hockey, quick substitutions were made, so that players who were out of breath could come up for air. Everyone came off at some point and rejoined the game once they had got their strength back. Everybody? Not exactly everybody. There was one, whom federation coach Murach was on to, whose fancy notion that football might be fun he wanted to correct with his own philosophy that the game was much more about sweat and tears: little Günter from 1. FC Mönchengladbach. In spite of having done everything Murach asked of him. Me, a rebel? Not now, not then!

This dour attitude of Murach's, as it struck me at the time, was one I reencountered twenty-five years later. By now, as Hamburg SV (HSV) manager, I was just an observer. My coach, Branko Zebec, used the same psychological method, of first pulling a young player off his high horse, before building him up again according to his own principles. Not everyone would agree with this approach. But although Heinz Murach gave me a hard time, he also supported me and I am grateful for that. I am in his debt too, not just for having selected me for the Lower Rhine XI, but for having given me a better idea of my limits. This contributed to my later development.

It was in a Lower Rhine shirt that Dettmar Cramer, the national youth team coach, first saw me play. And when he selected me for the West Germany XI, his first words were, "Günter, you need to toughen up and learn how to compete". As I attended more of these courses, I progressed from being a child to a hardened competitor, even if in other ways I remained green. At fifteen I went to Duisburg once a week for special coaching, otherwise known as boot camp training. If the conversation there turned to academic subjects, which was rare, I could still keep pace; I never came across a footballer who was both a talented player and a gifted student. As footballers we were all more or less at the same level. But that leads to another topic, which is always important for fourteen- and fifteen-year-olds – even more so at this kind of training camp than at school. Here, as a very late developer with girls, I struggled to keep up. When I was eighteen I still did not have a girlfriend. I knew scarcely anything about the opposite sex, quite a lot relating to football and a bit about different car models. I had learned to drive. Aged sixteen, I was also able to make a telephone call without any help.

I was always in a good mood after receiving the summons to come to a training camp at Grünberg in Hesse, knowing that the train fare was fully paid for and that, if I had to justify my expenses being a little on the high side to Hermann Joch, who was then general secretary of the DFB (Deutsche Fußball Bundesliga), however fearful the prospect might be, I could just about handle it. I was happy too whenever selected to play for the Lower Rhine or the West German Association sides or when Helmut Schön, as its new coach, picked me for the national youth team. The footballing part of my life was fine. Aged eighteen, my home life still consisted of evenings spent with my parents, playing cards. Ours was a cosy family. I believed that I had everything I needed in that direction, too.

At some point a change began to take place. I am uncertain how much it owed to Heinz Murach and Dettmar Cramer, or, alternatively, to a new self-assertiveness. In training, it is true, I was still not much of a grafter. I was still reluctant to work hard on my fitness. Neither physically nor emotionally was I fully formed. One advantage of my comparative lack of strength was to avoid the call-up.

Without being sure about it, I think my first argument may have come before the European Championship in Portugal, when Helmut Schön left me out of the squad which travelled there. It was probably the best national youth side Germany has fielded. Sepp Maier was in goal, Wolfgang Overath in midfield and Reinhard Libuda, a superb dribbler, on the right wing. I had no particular position. Sometimes I played on the left wing, on other occasions I stood in for Libuda on the right. My later, central midfield, role was not available, since that is where Overath operated, in the manner we had spoken of so admiringly at Duisburg. It is hard to remember if I was upset. I think I accepted it, neither happily, nor especially disappointed, nor rebellious. Perhaps it was the lesson which nudged me out of my lethargy, indicating that with such an approach to life I stood little chance of achieving anything.

In contrast to my high school failure, I completed the business course, which my parents enrolled me in, without any problems. My father and I agreed that if I spent a spell as a clerk at Mannesmann Engineering's head office in Düsseldorf I would receive a solid grounding in business. While he might be proud of his boy, a hot topic of conversation over an evening beer with his friends, who was often mentioned now in the papers, it was hard to imagine that I might have a future as a professional. There were very few players at the time earning genuine salaries. The Bundesliga did not yet exist, nor was football's business potential necessarily evident. The 1954 World Cup victory had made an immediate impact but, in the conservative climate of the fifties, the perception of the game remained uncertain at best and even that it might be mildly disreputable. I was stuck in a netherworld too. I felt as though I was plodding through life, as I adopted various attitudes which seemed appropriate to the age I was, without being able to picture my future.

Mannesmann was a different world. Amazingly, I got through the interview alright and began the training programme at the Mönchengladbach branch office. The desk side of the business bored me, but I quite enjoyed the practical experience on the workbench. If I had a hard training session the previous evening, it was always possible to take a nap in the toilets. But would I be able to complete the apprenticeship, now that I kept getting selected by the DFB for youth team matches?

Dettmar Cramer made frequent visits to the company's central intern department to ask for my temporary release.

These requests were unusual, given football's questionable status. The section's chief did not have a clue about the game and the role played in it by talent development. Every time Cramer called, a contest ensued between me and my football versus the business world. I could not see my future lying with Mannesmann.

If I think about it carefully, it must have been this business apprenticeship which drew me out of my shyness. The second year at Mannesmann coincided with my second year in the national youth side. This was when Cramer, who had recently replaced Helmut Schön, appointed me captain. He had not selected the passenger, who kept himself to himself; he had chosen a player his teammates would accept in this capacity. For his own part, he believed that he had detected in me the right credentials. It was another moment when, fortunately for me, somebody recognised that I possessed something which they needed, whose existence I had personally never suspected.

My captaincy coincided with the European Championship in England. Against Scotland, aged eighteen, I headed the winning goal. Heinz Murach's harsh regime with the gym pendulum ball had paid off.

In the same year, I travelled with 1. FC Mönchengladbach for a minor tournament in Limoges in France, where I was in sensational form. Whatever I tried, came off. It was a time when I was becoming much sought after. Soon after the team's return to Mönchengladbach, an offer arrived in the post to our house: an immediate 50,000 marks in cash to be followed by a further 150,000, to play for Limoges. The sums were coyly remarked upon, before being officially confirmed a few months later, at the same time that the Bundesliga was set up. 50,000 marks in one fell swoop: even by Aunt Triene's standards it was a tidy sum; for my parents it was an obscene amount. But for me it proved that I could make my living playing football and wasn't destined, once I had completed the apprenticeship at Mannesmann, to end up working in an office.

The relationship with my parents, who naturally wanted to have me near them, my lack of experience in life and inability to cope on my own all argued against the move. As did Helmut Schön when I sought his advice. It was not hard for such a discriminating man to see the risks involved in accepting the spectacular, brash offer that had been made. He was adamant: "*Junge*, are you mad? You are at the very beginning of your career. You need to establish yourself here first. In heaven's name, *Junge*, do not leave this country." That brought an end to any serious talk of Limoges at home. Trying to find it in the atlas, we had been unable to.

Next came an offer from Preußen Münster. Today they are lost somewhere in the lower regions of the Bundesliga. At the time they were not just a club with a proud tradition, but a force in Upper Rhine-Westphalian football. Originally founded at the time of the old Oberliga, Preußen Münster was also one of the founding clubs of the Bundesliga, whose table it had begun to climb. Its ambition was to rise higher still, helped by a powerful and very rich property developer; Oevermann, I believe, was his name. The offer made by Herr Oevermann went a long way beyond the average bid, while the distance to Münster was a manageable one for both my parents and me.

When I received a formal contract proposal though it was from Fortuna Düsseldorf (, even if it might have seemed likelier that, being the homegrown national youth captain, Borussia Mönchengladbach would have taken the initiative with me). That is, the contract *should* have been with Fortuna Düsseldorf. They were another ambitious club. Toni Turek, the world champion, had made his name there. I knew their centre-forward, Peter Meyer. Besides generous wages, there was the lure of a world tour to Asia, Latin America and through a large swathe of Europe. That clinched it for me; I said "Yes". The contract signing was due to take place in a Mönchengladbach restaurant. My father and I were there – but Bruno Recht, Fortuna's chairman, was not. I don't know why he failed to appear. He never commented on what did, or did not, happen. I was left without any explanation, just my disappointment. The world and its sights would have to wait a little longer for yours truly.

The interest being shown in me had obviously not escaped the notice of either the owners or training staff of 1. FC Mönchengladbach. The price to be paid for my ambition to develop and play at a higher level was to incur the club's wrath. Nothing has changed in the attitude of smaller clubs towards their more talented players who attract the interest of bigger fish: they kick up a fuss, try blocking the sale and, when they fail, dismiss them as traitors. Attempting to bar the route to young players like this was, and remains, absurd. I will never understand why the little clubs do not instead take pride in what their youth programmes achieve in producing a player with the desire and the ability to go on to higher things. Just the same as nowadays, 1. FC Mönchengladbach's rage was not softened by the 38,000 marks which their local rivals, Borussia Mönchengladbach bid for me.

Only belatedly, just before I might have gone to Preußen Münster, and Fortuna's first contact from Düsseldorf, did the management at Borussia wake up and take some active interest in the talent on its doorstep. I am still not sure why I moved to the club. It would have been hard to have a worse image than they did in the region. If one wanted to praise the team of that period you would say they were tough. A less generous assessment would be that their game was destructive – horribly destructive – lacked culture and was barren of ideas. The goalkeeper was Manfred Orzessek. I don't think it is unfair to say that he personified the Gladbacher style of play then. Orzessek was thickset, he knew what he wanted, and wherever he wanted to smash his way through … through he came. A good guy, nevertheless. Route one, brutalist: that was the path Borussia Mönchengladbach took on its way up through the regional league. If I had had a proper plan in place for furthering my career, never – not ever – would I have allowed myself to make the choice I did. And yet, Borussia was in every respect the best choice I could have made. It allowed me to carry on living at home, avoiding a separation from my parents, while giving me the chance to play in a team and a league that would provide amusement as well as income.

The money was not bad for the time. When we met to discuss terms, my father and I sat on one side of the table. Facing us were the club directors, Dr Beyer, Herr Grashoff and Herr Hoffmann. Although I was receiving a first-class grounding for business life at Mannesmann, I was still not at the stage to handle negotiations; my father, on the other hand, thanks to all his dealings with small farmers, was a sharp negotiator. We had not forgotten the staggering offer made by Limoges. The payment they had proposed was what my father persuaded Borussia to pay for my transfer fee: 50,000 marks.

My first contract, signed on 19 July 1963, provided that the 'player will receive one hundred and sixty marks monthly' and an 'appearance fee of ten marks for each game played either in the first or the reserve team'. I was now being paid for my hobby. In order to remember the detail of my first season, I need to consult the archives, which record that I played in thirty-five of the thirty-eight west region league games. I do not have to look at the records to recall that Borussia saved on reserve appearances. I was happy, too. A couple of months before, in anticipation of my eighteenth birthday, my father had given me a Mercedes Diesel. It made sense – for me, for my family, who could use it too, and costwise, since it was possible to fill up on the other side of the Dutch border, not far from Mönchengladbach, for six or seven pfennigs a litre. It was great fun to start driving. Even if a Diesel was no Ferrari, I drove it as hard as I could.

So, I had a car. I had a contract and a footballer's licence. Football and cars … that was all I dreamt of as a child. I was no longer a child and this was not a dream.

The proof that childhood was over was called Fritz Langner. Langner was the Borussia coach, whose training routines caused my afternoon naps in the Mannesmann gents to multiply. This first year as a professional was also my last as a business apprentice. It was a demanding time. Langner, with his firm principles concerning drills, was the sternest of taskmasters. We were also put in our place by old staff members, as well as the Orzesseks of the team who, to make way for themselves, would shoo us off the massage tables with a dismissive wave of the hand. They were already family men and wanted to get home, whereas we youngsters had time to kill. One had to accept it, since that is the way football teams operate. At the same time, these senior players initiated us into the hedonistic side of the game by taking us to the pub. It was the first time in my life I had drunk a beer. I did not like it, if I am honest.

Best described as old-school, Langner was irrevocable in his attitudes and unapologetic concerning his view that what counts in the game is strength. In addition, the power of the team talk. To begin with we trained twice a week, on Tuesdays and Thursdays. This changed to daily sessions. We were shattered. When we were barely able to move any more, Langner called a team meeting. First there would be an analysis of the reserve side's last game, then a post-mortem of the first team's match. Once we were all on the verge of sleep, we would finally be released for our evening celebrations. "But seriously, Günter, you see that you need to work much harder?" I would straighten up with a start when he put this to me, my eyes barely open: I didn't see anything. The next day there would be another snooze in the works toilet.

Nevertheless, Langner was the man who was determined to change Borussia's style of play. If we produced a technically impressive performance and lost, he was perfectly happy. Victory was not the number one priority. The team got shaken up. Out went the older players and in came fresh talent. I was one example, Herbert Laumen another. There was also a nineteen-year-old wing-back, named Horst-Dieter Höttges, but soon known as 'Ironfoot'. Unfortunately, he moved rapidly on to Werder Bremen.

If I remember rightly, I scored nine goals in my first season as a pro, which was not bad at all; in fact, it was very good, and helped the team to reach the playoffs for promotion to the Bundesliga. We were less than brilliant in them. In spite of this, we had our photos taken for a collectors' series. That was better, as we were each paid fifty marks for the photo rights. Until then I had no idea that such a concept existed.

Fritz Langner was not satisfied with the season which, besides the potential of greater things, finally amounted to a few attractive regional league performances, like the one against Lüner SV or our match with SpVgg Herten, plus a handful of commemorative photographs. Langner wanted to be involved in the Bundesliga; Schalke 04 wanted Langner; and Borussia Mönchengladbach wanted Hennes Weisweiler.

Hennes Weisweiler? He was a bit of a mystery to us. In fact, we knew scarcely anything about him, other than that he held a diploma and lectured at the sports academy in Cologne. But what a diploma was was a mystery to us, too. Sepp Herberger, still national coach nine years after the world cup triumph, had recommended him. There was nothing surprising about this. Herberger had first encountered Weisweiler just after the war, at a coaching course. He soon came to appreciate him, to the extent that he would later groom him to be his eventual successor as national coach. But Weisweiler, born in Lechenich before becoming an adopted *Kölner*, was not that keen. He was more interested in staying in Cologne and, most of all, developing a brand of attacking football that had yet to be seen. During the fifties he was coach at 1. FC Köln. The team starred the world champion Hans Schäffer, otherwise known as 'Hans

Storm'. Weisweiler then moved on to Viktoria Köln, where he nurtured players who subsequently made the move up to the Bundesliga. These included Carl-Heinz Rühl, Jürgen Sundermann and Willibert Kremer. Together they scored eighty-one goals in thirty matches. That was what Weisweiler meant by attacking football.

We knew nothing about all that. We were simply told how Weisweiler had apparently been due to take over as manager of the Dutch club Fortuna Geelen, before pulling out at the last minute, because he wanted to carry on teaching at the sports academy part time. The distance between Geelen and Cologne was too great. Borussia being only his second choice was not the most promising basis on which to come to the club. Here he was, all the same, standing in front of us.

Almost the first point he made was that he disliked our team colours. What he did not say, as I only learned much later, was that the suggestion to change them came from his wife, Frau Lilo. She found our black jerseys so mournful she had tried dissuading him from signing the contract. Now Weisweiler was telling us that our black kit was emblematic of a defeatist attitude and could not fail to have a negative impact on our psyches. Were we slightly amused by this new kind of team talk, which contrasted so starkly with those we were used to being given by the old warhorse Langner? Probably we were, but the man had a diploma so he must know what he was talking about. He decided that from now on we would wear white – lilywhite. Lilo had probably said that it represented innocence and freshness and radiated energy. As everyone now knows, the colour white did Borussia Mönchengladbach no harm at all. Lilo Weisweiler cannot be thanked enough.

I had turned twenty and was no longer so shy. I wore my hair with a neat parting and played at inside-left. Believing he could deploy me elsewhere, Weisweiler had other plans in mind. He bought a genuine winger from my old club, 1. FC Mönchengladbach, the eighteen-year-old Werner Waddey. This was the first time a coloured player had joined Borussia. Then he recruited Bernd Rupp from Wiesbaden. Out of the reserves, Weisweiler fetched up another attacker, Jupp Heynckes. He had played for the first team before. Who on earth had then put him in the reserves? In all respects Jupp Heynckes was our best player. Even though he was thought of as an out-and-out forward, he could do everything. He was technically brilliant and lightning quick. It's not easy to think of another player with his ability to see situations develop, and who could make timely interceptions with such frequency as Jupp did.

How was I going to slot into Weisweiler's plans? In training, did he notice that I am fundamentally a lazy individual who likes the ball to do the work? Most likely. Quite likely, too, he observed that my teammates granted me a certain recognition and that I had become accepted as their spokesman. However extraordinary this change in my character might have been, it had occurred gradually, without any big bang or great leap forward. Now that I was in my second year as a professional, I had successfully completed the Mannesmann apprenticeship, which had perhaps contributed most to this maturing. The heavy threat of years to be spent working in an office had been lifted. Free from the hindrance of a day job, I felt ready to assume my responsibilities as a player.

In passing out as a business trainee, I had received a bit of help. Our examination day story has been told by Klaus

Bertram, an old schoolmate who I then reencountered at business college. There is no reason to doubt his account. Besides liking him a lot, I know he has a flawless memory. According to Klaus, I drove up in a red Porsche. I barely had time – this much I personally recall – to get to a match later on the same day at Venlo. Even if it is not a long haul from Mönchengladbach, it's always good to have a fast car. (Again, according to Klaus,) when I climbed out of the Porsche, I demanded with a broad Mönchengladbacher accent, "Hey! What's happening?" This must have been a flippant remark; I cannot believe that I really did not know what was going on at the college that day. The exam was an important event, following which I could become a qualified clerk – in the long term; in the short term, of course, I would speed off to Venlo to play football. What Bertram has related about that day is probably not of burning interest to anybody. But I love the man and so shall re-tell the story nevertheless. We were four candidates. The examiner put questions to us in turn. When it came to me, he asked something which Klaus, with his outsized brain, remembers. The question, which I myself do not remember, baffled me. Anyway, the answer was 'three'. With a deliberate movement, the assessor raised his right hand to his mouth and formed his thumb, index and middle fingers into a 'three'. The hint escaped my notice. "Herr Netzer," he said, "if you take a look, then you will surely know the answer." Once again, he slowly raised his hand to his mouth and made a 'three' out of his thumb and fingers. I could not see anything. "Herr Netzer," he patiently resumed, "observe once more; if you take another look, you will have the answer." He repeated the movement.

This time I got it. And since giving the answer, 'Three' I have technically been a qualified clerk, as well as free from the petty inconveniences and pressures of a day job. I was ready to take on my footballing responsibilities.

The manager knew what he wanted. During training one day he drew me aside. "Günter, it's really what you are doing anyway, but you play better in midfield. Waddey can be left wing; you can orchestrate play from the centre." Hennes Weisweiler had discovered my true role. On the football pitch at least. And in life? I don't think I have ever craved to be the centre of attention. But, without false modesty, nor can I deny that is what I often am.

To return to football … I liked the position of playmaker. This is the man who sets the tone, who provides the direction of play. He needs self-confidence and even an egotistical streak. I felt ready for the part.

Weisweiler's seeds began to sprout. We were mostly twenty-year-olds in full ferment. A journalist came up with the term 'Foals' to describe us, probably because our carefree and innocent manner of playing put him in mind of these gambolling young animals at pasture. We scored goals – a total of ninety-two during the season – won our regional league and qualified for the playoffs for promotion to the Bundesliga. Above all, our style of play earned the club a new reputation. We were called extrovert; a breath of fresh air; ballsy and daring; thrilling; phenomenal, courageous and risk assuming; sensational; bubbly. If I may say so, we were all of these. One of our games finished 10-1. Even if Horst-Emscher were bottom of the table, that is not a scoreline to be dismissed with a smile.

I scored sixteen times in the regional league and was goalscorer in the final game of the playoff group too. In the previous matches we had been nervous. We now needed a draw to secure promotion. Our visitors at the Bökelberg were Wormatia Worms. Unfortunately, we let them take the lead. Once again, we were not at our best. We were certainly neither ballsy and daring, nor courageous, nor bubbly. We were straightforward bad. Then, receiving the ball on the edge of the penalty box in the sixty-ninth minute – it was one of those moments you never forget – I thudded it at goal. In it went. That goal gained Borussia Mönchengladbach promotion to the Bundesliga, plus a 1,500 mark bonus for the players. Father had something new to talk about at the bar.

The chemistry between Hennes Weisweiler and the players was good. A two-way learning process began to take place. Weisweiler was not yet the great training guru that he would later come to be revered as. We had yet to become heroes, each of whom could single-handedly destroy an opposition. As a unit, though, we were already strong and positive. Working with our new trainer was novel. Heinz Murach gave orders. So did Dettmar Cramer. Even Helmut Schön, for all his astute man management, wished his own views to prevail in the end. Weisweiler engaged in conversation. He did not ask us for our views only to discard them. The opposite, in fact. He had clear ideas about how the game ought to be played. Most of the time we were in agreement. If there were differences, we were able to thrash these out, and so settle them.

Later, at the peak of our rivalry, we were portrayed as the political alternative to Bayern Munich's conservatism. This had almost nothing to do with our beliefs – we were not political anyway; it probably owed more to our reputation and taste for free debate. What Weisweiler and we had unintentionally arrived at was a kind of football democracy.

One thing the manager never forgot was the importance of identifying with the club. We were not looking for moves to bigger sides anyhow. Back then there was a lot less player movement from one club to the next, in search of better opportunities. Our circumstances were simpler too; at the time of the playoffs we were still changing in a draughty wooden hut. If, leading to the later scandal, players' regular salaries were boosted at some other clubs with under the counter payments, at Mönchengladbach there was not enough money even for this. A close identification with the club was our main incentive to perform better.

When it came to looking for new players, Weisweiler was smart enough to scout those who either shared his conception of the game already or who could adjust to it without too much difficulty. The promotion celebrations were barely over when, right on his doorstep, he found an eighteen-year-old defender playing for the local sports club, VfR Büttgen: Hans-Hubert Vogts, later 'Berti'. We were ready for the Bundesliga.

In 1965 I was also ready for a new beginning in my private life – or a particular part of it. It took place at a bus stop. I was driving along with a buddy from business school in my new car – a charcoal grey E-Type I think it was – when he spotted a friend waiting for her bus. We slowed down. I was now known around the town, almost a local celebrity. My mate introduced us. "The name Netzer means nothing to me," she said.

3

Like a Rolling Stone

We lived in completely different worlds. Hannelore Girrulat's was a goldsmith's; mine, football, interspersed with occasional outings in my sports car. Hannelore's knowledge of football was limited to it being the sport which happened to go by this name. She could not understand why everybody made such a fuss about it. As to Borussia Mönchengladbach being in the Bundesliga: "Aha," she said.

Her world consisted of art, fashion, design and music: what was starting to be called 'Pop' then or, occasionally, avant-garde, which was the cue for me to go, "Aha".

At the time I got to know Hannelore Girrulat I was almost twenty-one and still living with my parents in Gasthausstraße. The dining table was decorated with a lace doily. Potted plants stood in line on the windowsills. There was floral wallpaper. When Father or I wished to read the newspaper match report, to check on how I had performed, either of us would sit in an old, rather hard, winged armchair. Pride of place was given to the television, as bulky as Aunt Triene's, but freestanding rather than housed in a chest. On top of it lay another lace doily. My parents' apartment was not furnished fashionably, but, in its homely way, it was still appealing. No experiments, as Chancellor Adenauer was fond of saying. Today, most would describe this kind of domesticity as musty and drab. I liked it though. It was not musty and drab to me; rather, cosy and familiar. Why would I waste time on thoughts of saying goodbye to a world in which I felt perfectly at ease?

Hannelore's apartment looked like this: the walls were roughly plastered and unpainted, as imitated in a thousand pizzerias since. Instead of potted plants, two naked rose stems stood in a bucket. Rather than the television, it was a bed which occupied centre stage, with large porcelain cats, one black and the other white, standing on either side. The walls were decorated with posters. Marilyn Monroe, the Rolling Stones. The music system and speakers were not hidden away. There was probably a flokati carpet, sheltering bacteria and dust in its long, loose and constantly moulting strands. The reason I say 'probably' is because a shaggy rug was part of the avant-garde style, not because I am confident in my memory, having made a conscious effort to forget such things as flokati carpets.

Different worlds? Different galaxies. Not only regarding interior design but as far as our ways of looking at life and what we hoped to get out of it were concerned. My parents never accepted Hannelore. Almost the opposite, in fact.

What was it that interested me in this relationship, in which football played no part? Art and music, which lay at the heart of what was soon being called the counterculture, were important. Looking back with a bit of care, there are clues that I was never exclusively interested in football, as I had assumed myself to be. For example, in spite of disliking them, I carried on uncomplainingly with my studies until the bitter end. In the final year it became clear that I was not really contemplating a future as a clerk, sitting at a desk. It is true that if I had a serious injury, a position at Mannessman would have provided security – but what twenty-year-old bargains for the worst? On the other hand, sticking with my vocational training, at the same time as I was embarking on the then very suspect career of a footballer, was not determined purely by practical considerations. If, rather than staying at home with my parents, I went out in the evening, it was with friends from business school, never with my teammates who, for me, remained colleagues in a common enterprise, limited to the training ground and matchday. As footballers we shared the same goals and the same points of view, but I never considered my companions to be friends. Instead, we formed a marriage of convenience which, at its best, without any need for words, was also one of perfect understanding for ninety minutes.

None of my teammates were with me when, pre-Hannelore still, I drove across the Rhine to Düsseldorf, then headed into the Bilk district and my destination: Merowingerstraße, home to Wilhelm Becker's car showroom. There she stood: the E-Type OTS model … Open Two-Seater, the salesman explained to me. A roadster that, as far as I was concerned, was the best-looking car of the time. That was the one for me … *the* most beautiful car … and I think that's an objective fact. Everything was as *Autoquartett* described: a 6-cylinder, 4.2-litre engine generating 265 horsepower; maximum speed: 240 km/h. My charcoal grey Jaguar cost 26,000 marks, a fair price for the realisation of my childhood dreams.

It had not occurred to me that this car might be seen as anything other than a handsome vehicle; that it might represent something deeper. So I found it hard to understand why I was suddenly on the receiving end of criticism in Mönchengladbach, and why my teammates dismissed me as crazy. Why should I be considered suspect on account of the car I drove? Was it such a bad thing not to be driving a Daimler or a BMW, like every other notable in the city? My life, I think, was essentially that of a petty bourgeois. But the idea that I was crassly materialist, or, less superficially, something even worse, began to take hold. It did not occur to me that a Jaguar E-Type might jar with ordinary middle-class habits. Rebelling against these had not even entered my mind.

A year later I was hoping to sell the Jaguar. Neither for materialist (financial) reasons, nor because the criticism was getting on my nerves. I was not bothered about it at the time. I was toying with the idea of a Ferrari (, the first), which I had seen in Becker's showroom. Franz Beckenbauer heard that I was thinking of selling and said he might be interested. We had got to know one another pretty well in the national squad. In fact, I advised him against buying a Jaguar. I found it hard to picture the meticulous Franz enjoying the taut, almost jerky ride or, in a storm, appreciating a bit of rainwater making its way through the soft top. His mind was made up, though. I drove the car down to Munich. Franz seemed delighted, while I was free to buy the Ferrari. Two days later, back in Mönchengladbach, the telephone rang. An indignant Beckenbauer was on the other end of the line: "That is a piece of trash you have sold me".

The story ended like this. After Beckenbauer, it was Wolfgang

Overath who fancied having something gingery to drive. On the pitch the highly talented Overath was ready to undertake any risk; off it he was a little less bold. I cannot remember how long the bird of prey, Wolfgang Overath clung to his perch but I imagine it was until the final moment of our test drive. I have not seen him in a sports car since. Personally, I do not find the challenge they might represent disturbing. They unnerve me very little. If they did, the fascination would not be worth it. There is no point getting screwed up on account of a beautiful car. Beckenbauer and Overath had no conception of such matters.

Things did not go too well with my first Ferrari, either. It was temperamental from the moment I bought it, for 40,000 marks. To be handled with caution. One day I was driving on the autobahn with Herbert Wimmer – Hacki. It was raining hard. What happened I am not sure; in any case, it happened very quickly. One moment we were cruising along, the next, we went into a skid. The car flipped over and we smashed into the crash barrier. Though shaken, we were both able to get out of the car unscathed. Had Franz Beckenbauer been there, commenting, "What a piece of trash," I would not have argued with him.

There was another occasion when I got off lightly. The thought of what might have happened can still give me a shudder today. If not quite like 'a pig on fire', as the saying goes, my driving in those days was still pretty quick. It could annoy other road users. One was an HGV driver, who came close to attacking me. After being stuck behind him for a good two kilometres, the overtaking manoeuvre I made involved braking in front of him brusquely, I admit. But did it justify his excessive response?

He got right on top of me, as if he wanted to flatten me with his big truck. At the very last second, he reconsidered. As he braked hard, the trailer jackknifed into a bus shelter. Luckily no one was waiting there.

That was another day when Norbert Pflippen needed to intervene. It was before the time he became one of the most sought-after players' agents, once, I suppose, I had provided him with his entrée into the Mönchengladbacher football world. He was still working as an official at the city's traffic control centre. Thanks to him, one or two tickets, from amongst the impressive tally I accumulated, were, how shall we say, waylaid. My fines, as far as I can remember, were never too steep. Not even when I entered the old town's shopping district doing 80 km/h. Pflippen's unorthodox attitude was no cause for shame. We got to know each other well and, since then, he has rendered what might be called high service. Thanks are due to him for his leniency.

But, to get back to the question of what drew me out of football's orbit, and towards art and music and Hannelore Girrulat's way of life: my propensity for out of the ordinary cars perhaps played a part in this. An aesthetic appreciation of them may have helped in my encounter with Hannelore's world, even if it was entirely novel to me, bearing fruit instead of falling on barren ground.

Music was suddenly a big thing. Before, it was off my radar. It had never been a part of our daily life. We may not even have had a record player at home; I can't remember. If Aunt Triene had a music system, then no doubt it was top of the range. What music did I listen to? Nothing that comes to mind. As it was played and valued so little in our house, the

36

radio could remain silent all day long. And then along came the Rolling Stones and Bob Dylan, blasting out of Hannelore's speakers. Nothing to get excited about? Maybe not from today's perspective, but in the sixties the Stones' anti-establishment notoriety was immediate. In the world I grew up in the word 'music' was not used to describe the sound of these longhaired, almost apelike guitarists. It was 'noise'. The same for Bob Dylan, even if his music was very different. I liked both. It was love at first hearing.

Several years later, Hannelore bought tickets to see Dylan at the Dortmunder Westfalenhalle. It required all of her persuasiveness to get me to go. I am still not sure if the hesitancy I felt can be entirely explained by my fear of crowds. This was real enough, despite stepping out in front of thousands every Saturday. On the pitch, my heart racing, I would sometimes avoid duels and physical contact, if possible. Whenever I could, I stayed clear of the goalmouth congestion when free kicks and corners were taken. At a concert there was no choice but to join the crowd. I felt anxious as we entered. By the time Bob had performed 'All Along the Watchtower' and 'Like a Rolling Stone' my concerns had vanished. Part of my hesitancy about going may have also been due to having to overcome, with Hannelore's help, the scepticism of those I had been brought up amongst, for whom attending a concert by apeish longhairs was unimaginable. All the same, it was magnificent. Dylan knew how to make an entrance.

She had to give me frequent prods. Music was one new direction she opened up for me. Another was fashion. I have never been a big shopper. Then, as now, I left buying clothes to my loved one. Hannelore's taste did not correspond in the least with Aunt Triene's and my parents' idea of what constituted chic. My girlfriend with the long black hair was strongly inclined towards this all-purpose colour, which I liked too, putting us at the other end of the spectrum from Lilo Weisweiler. If black is common currency now, for a long time back then my preference for black trousers and jackets was met with suspicion. My teammates' reaction was fairly predictable. Whenever I seemed to waver, Hannelore would stiffen me with the assurance that what mattered was not what others thought but what I myself felt comfortable with. Mind you, I did not always feel comfortable with all of her suggestions. We had one or two major disagreements over my outfits – though not as many as I had with myself, given that I still kept my floral wallpaper side from my parents, as well as the Stones side I now shared with her. Even as I wore suede slacks, I swung back and forth between the two. Fast cars, the Stones and new fashions were not intended by me as signs of belonging to a particular confession. When it was occasionally pointed out to me that black was the colour favoured by French bohemians and philosophers, I probably responded with an, "Aha".

Part of the reason I felt torn was that it was never my goal to be dissimilar to everyone else and set myself up as an outsider, even if I suspected more than just a difference in taste was involved when Franz Beckenbauer made it clear that, actually, my Jaguar was not for him, and Wolfgang Overath's reticence was greater still.

Did Hannelore Girrulat turn me inside out? I don't think so. I never felt as though I was being steamrollered into her way of life, nor that I was getting taken over by her circle against my will. It was just the latest instance of someone else being able to unearth something in me that until then I had not been aware of myself. Right place, right time. I gradually became less concerned if I appeared different to others. I wanted to be thought of as a footballer – a good one, if possible; the apparently burning question of my clothes, cars and the company I kept was, for me at least, secondary. In other words, I grew my hair long because I liked it like that. If that was regarded as a sign of the cultural revolution, so be it. I wasn't going to start wearing it short again as a result.

Hair. Hannelore undeniably had something to do with the development of my mane. She, and the group of friends amongst whom we moved, for whom long hair was significant at the end of the sixties. In what way, I did not fully understand. As the conversation revolved around how wearing long hair, Andy Warhol and Mick Jagger, the APO and Rudi Dutschke represented a new age dispelling anything that lingered of the fusty fifties, I would most often remain silent in the corner. These were not the kind of things we talked about in the training ground hut. It was a level of conversation which I found it hard to keep up with. I also failed to notice that I was the first German player to have, first, ear lobe then, later, shoulder length hair. I felt comfortable with it that way.

I enjoyed listening to their conversation. Very occasionally the topic of my football was touched upon. Then I listened even more intently, as they expounded on how my natural game and ball passing ability were to serve as the channel by which the avant-garde would be extended onto the football pitch. The 'aesthetic of the diagonal ball' and the 'visualisation of the bisecting pass' were ways of looking at the game that had never occurred to me. I was receptive to them all the same. Until then I had played football instinctively. Now that the game was being elucidated to me so attractively, I found no real reason to disagree. Nevertheless, I suggested, on the pitch my thoughts were limited either to finding a way through the opposition or shooting at goal. This was when Markus Lüpertz made a wonderful comparison. "Do we understand a painting by narrowly focusing on each brushstroke, or with the appreciation of the connoisseur looking at the finished work? Can the composer tell how his piece will be as he sets down each note, individually?" Yes, I enjoyed listening to these observations – without fully understanding the relation between art on the one hand, and me and my football on the other.

I had already known Lüpertz for a bit. He had grown up in Rheydt and used to go to the same bars as I did. He had a sponsor, the industrial equipment manufacturer, Weller. This did not prevent him from being frequently broke and requiring occasional, quite large, loans. I helped him out with two hundred marks once. Although I was not, unfortunately, a knowledgeable art enthusiast, he nevertheless bailed me one of his paintings for this. Nowadays a Lüpertz original is worth a packet. I don't think I have mine any longer, but his debt was paid in full.

At the centre of this circle stood the Cologne gallery owner, Michael Werner, who soon developed an outstanding reputation with these young artists. Prominent amongst them was Sigmar Polke. Then there were A.R. Penck, Georg Baselitz, Lüpertz, and others too. Neither Lüpertz nor I were well known when we first met. His parents had headed west after the war from their native Sudetenland, to make a new start in Rheydt. He stood out in this group as the only one who knew anything about football; he could even have passed for one of the lads. The others' response to me was much the same as Hannelore's had been at the bus stop; the name Netzer meant very little in this company. I did not impress them. It was the other way round, which was fine. Sitting there quietly, I was absorbed, eager to learn what I could. How naive was I? It certainly took me a while to realise that not just tobacco was being smoked. For them hashish and marijuana were also part of the new liberation, whereas I tended to think it was a case that, every now and again, these guys had had one too many to drink.

It must have been sometime in the early seventies when I received the call. At the other end of the line was the Düsseldorf Art Academy. They wanted to involve me in an idea of Joseph Beuys', their star professor. I had never met Beuys. Regardless, they had a proposal to make in connection with his masterclass. I was somewhat bowled over: how about, they wanted to know, my becoming a professor myself? I, Günter Netzer from Gasthausstraße in Mönchengladbach, high school dropout, was being invited to become applied arts professor. That seemed to be the idea, anyway. My immediate reaction was that they were pulling my leg. They were stubborn however and repeated the invitation several times.

Finally though, there was to be no Professor Netzer. I managed to resist the temptation. Had I accepted, I would have found myself venturing too far into this other world. The scene excited me. It fascinated and impressed me. But, in the course of many conversations with Hannelore, one essential fact became clear to me: I was a footballer, and that is what I wanted to remain. There was nothing for which I would exchange my sport. The danger that I might muddle my priorities and gradually drift away from it did not exist, because I would not allow it to. I already knew, from the fuss caused by my involvement with cars, that I ran the risk of blurring my identity. The only way I could maintain my life with Hannelore and her circle was if I took good care of my essential activity, continuing to improve as a footballer.

The risk of making a fool of myself was not to be underestimated. Nor was the danger of appearing arrogant. For example, in an interview I had recently given to *Kicker*, I said that there had always been an aura of dumbness surrounding football. My intention was not to cause offence either to other players or to the fans who came to watch. At the time though it just happened to be true. Nowadays, a league game is a great social event. More than just being an occasion everybody wants to join in, attendance is almost *de rigueur*, if one wishes to avoid appearing eccentric. At the end of the sixties and beginning of the seventies football was for the masses, too but it was frowned upon – because these were proles, rowdy barbarians even, while players were stereotypically stupid. To be frank, one or two fellow professionals – there is no need to mention names – did not have much of an idea when it came to anything besides scoring goals. So, the *Kicker* interview was not completely wide of the mark. The stir it caused was off the register.

I caused a further outcry with the observation, "Forget all the clichés about teammates being great mates: that's cobblers". There was no doubt in my mind that by then the ethos of a professional side ought not be confused with that of football teams in general. The model which was still being advanced was the one of the 1954 World Cup winning squad

42

in Switzerland. It is plausible that the 'Spirit of Spiez', where its training camp had been, had brought cohesion and victory and, for most, this spirit remained the key to success. But fundamental changes had taken place since then. At the same time that there was still a practical advantage in forming a team spirit, so as to win, being professionals, we now had a commercial outlook, too. Was it really necessary to be friends in our everyday lives? Obviously, a good team spirit can help produce good football. My point was that it cannot, or should not, be forced in to being. I was the first to say this publicly in West Germany. That I might be striking at the very basis of the game came as a surprise to me.

A couple of days later, Hennes Weisweiler drew me aside following training. "Herberger will be coming to speak to you soon. Take him anywhere you choose but, please, not to your discotheque." He was referring to 'Lovers Lane', the English name I had given the Waldhausener Straße disco I opened in April 1971, in Mönchengladbach's bar district. This was the point at which Weisweiler nearly had a heart attack. When I told him of my plans and invited him to come to the opening, he stammered, "No, this is the final straw! The final straw!" I realised that 'Lovers Lane' was a topic best avoided with him. The idea that his old mentor, Sepp Herberger, who was now seventy-four, might be willing to come and talk to me in this den of iniquity must have made him shudder even more.

I had got to know Herberger a little in 1964, shortly before his retirement as the national coach, when I attended one of his last training camps and played in a selection match at Augsburg. It was an amazing experience, as a nineteen-year-old, to find myself face to face with the man responsible for letting the boy sitting in front of Aunt Triene's TV set realise his wildest football fan dreams. So sincere was my admiration for him that the first time I met Herberger my heart was beating fast. I, for one, had not lost my respect for older leaders like him, on account of the rebellious mood that had taken hold in the intervening years. When I thought of Sepp Herberger, the world cup winning manager, it was as someone occupying another, unapproachable, sphere. So, the fact that this gentleman wanted to speak to me, and that it was he coming to see me, in my disco … it was not just Weisweiler who no longer understood the world; I was astounded, too.

Our meeting was set for after the home game against Hertha BSC. The place, as usual following a match at the Bökelberg, which we had won 4-0, was packed. People who only saw our generation's stroppy, loud defiance should have been there to witness the moment Herberger set foot in 'Lovers Lane'. Those sitting stood up, drinks were put down, the dancing paused as everyone joined in a round of applause for the old man. You could tell that Sepp Herberger was moved.

This was not surprising. He could not have known what he would discover on entering. It was the first time in his life he had been in a disco. The place was unbelievably loud. We were shouting to each other so as to be heard. As we did so, I had the feeling I was in the company of a hero. We got talking about football in the old days, when a player would hardly dare to go out in the evening and drink a glass of water, so to speak, without the trainer's permission. And now? An international like me was permitted to open a disco as a sideline, without fear of being flung out of the West German side. We talked about my business; the ideas that I discussed with Weisweiler and put into practice on the pitch; everything. I explained that it was not me who had to turn the lights out at the disco at 4 am, or who, two hours later, was required to go to the wholesale market to buy provisions. All I had to do as owner was to stop by every now and again, or have somebody drop by for me if I couldn't make it myself. People probably thought I was there a lot more than I actually was – which was precisely the point of parking my Ferrari outside the entrance. It drew the punters in. The nightclub environment may have been strange to Herberger, but I think he understood my motive for getting involved in it. "Herr Herberger," I said to him, "I am a professional footballer; that makes me a sort of businessman. But, if I were a real businessman, I would have gone to another club long ago. Borussia just doesn't have the kind of money to pay what my teammates in the national side earn at theirs." I like to think he enjoyed his cocktail and our talk as much as I did. He was a big man, this little man.

Borussia's finances were, for sure, only one reason why I opened the disco. The other was the fascination which the lifestyle, music and clothes of that era exerted on me. From the outside, it may even have looked as if I had become besotted with glamour and the jet-set. Up to a point, I probably had, but when 'glamour' turned out to be not so glamorous after all, that was no problem for me. At a party given by the director, Michael Pfleghar I was introduced to the Hollywood actress, Elke Sommer. Elke divided her time between the Chicago suburb where she lived and visits to her mother in Erlangen. After we had become friends, I joined her in these visits – secretly of course, because Weisweiler must never know. And what did the three of us get up to in Mother Sommer's flat? She brought out a pack of cards and we sat down to play. Just like ordinary people. So much for glamour.

A lot of what went on back then was just a pose. As part of an advertising campaign, I was photographed outside 'Lovers Lane', dressed in suede trousers, leather jacket and white rollneck sweater, sitting languidly on a barstool, my eyelids drooping. I had my hands full: in one was a glass of champagne, while in the other I held the bottle. Pure fantasy!

One evening, driving a little too fast once more, I was stopped at a police checkpoint. The officers on evening duty's main concern seemed to be to talk football with me. Our chat carried on in a friendly manner. So much so that we decided to play a practical joke on their colleagues in the cabin. The previous driver they had pulled over had failed his breathalyser test. Supported by one of my new friends, I mumbled and stumbled my way inside. The officer behind the counter gave a start when the indicator showed green: "That can't be right … Impossible! … Netzer has not been drinking. That means we must be playing Bayern Munich on Saturday." He was right on both counts. The champagne bottle in the advert, as can be seen if you look closely enough, was still corked. The glass had been filled with nothing stronger than water. But even if I did stick to sipping water in the bar, I was always entertained by what was going on around me. You can learn a lot just by observing.

As to the financial reasons which persuaded me to start this business, when we met for international duty the conversation would often turn to our respective wage packets. Nowadays, players do not tend to discuss their pay as much, probably because footballers' salaries are already such a hot public topic.

But I knew what Franz Beckenbauer earned at Bayern, and Franz knew what I was getting at Borussia. This caused him to laugh. All the same, I was doing alright. The end of the sixties and start of the seventies was a very good time for me financially. It was a while since I had overhauled Aunt Triene. The difference between a Bayern Munich player's earning potential and our own could not, however, be ignored. Returning from a week spent with the international squad, I went to talk with Helmut Grashoff. Grashoff had once been king of the Mönchengladbach carnival. In spite of knowing next to nothing about football, he had talked the club chairman, Hans Beyer around into promoting himself to the post of deputy chairman. Since 1966 he had been general manager, responsible for the non-playing running of the club. This was a novelty in the Bundesliga. Grashoff was a businessman and, God knows, he knew how to count. "Listen, Herr Grashoff," I said, "this cannot carry on. I am going to have to make a move to Bayern where they make 450,000 marks, 400,000 minimum. You only pay me 160,000. That is not correct."

"And what should I do?" asked Grashoff. "I understand what you are saying, but you have to consider our point of view, too. With only 2,000 seating capacity in the Bökelberg, where are we going to find the money?"

It was hard to argue with that. In which case, what could be done? Nowadays, the answer would be to seek a transfer. This was also what I, in keeping with my view that as professionals we ought to take care of our financial interests, considered to be the logical step to take. Was it feasible though? What about my artist friends, my life with Hannelore? Or my family ties, and the status I had attained in Mönchengladbach? I led a fairly extravagant life here, after all. There was also Weisweiler and the team to think about. He had convinced us that this, and nowhere else, was where we could put our vision of the game into practice. The idea that we were a group of eleven friends was only strengthened by the nickname given to us by the *Rheinishchen Post* football correspondent, Wilhelm August Hurtmanns; 'Foals' was a name which had stuck. My conclusion was that, if there was nothing in my original contract suggesting I could later ask for an increase, the time had come, if I was to stay here after all, to inquire about other ways of making money with Borussia.

"Look," I said to Grashoff, "I appreciate what you are saying. Just give me the opportunity of earning more money some other way."

"Good. And what are you proposing?"

"Let me take over the matchday programme."

Klaus Matischak, whom I had known growing up, when he played for VfB Bottrop, had made a success of it at Bremen.

"Yes, alright, give it a go," said Grashoff, allowing the project a chance, even if he was not really listening.

Until then the 'programme' had been little more than a couple of loose sheets listing the line-ups. It had a name though: the *Fohlen-Echo*. I suppose I was its new publisher – a grand title, seeing that my sole task was to sell the advertising space. While one journalist wrote the copy and another took care of the layout, I went knocking on doors. It was undemanding work. Those I spoke to at the beginning nearly fell off their chairs: having me stood in front of them, going into detail about the cost and design of an advert, was not what they may have expected as they ate breakfast that morning. It was the shock effect which got many of them to place an advert. My wage increase was not long in coming.

Nor did it take long for me to develop a taste for business. The idea for a disco had its origins in a bar called the 'Spinnrad', a place I used to go to after most home matches. I liked to stand in the corner and people watch. Having said that, I attracted my share of attention, too. Whether we had played well or badly, the question I was always getting asked was, "Günter, it's your round isn't it?" Which it always was. At the end of the month the barman presented me with my tab. There were some months when I handed over more than 1,000 marks, sipping only orange juice and mineral water. I told this to the barman in another pub, Picco. His advice was, "Günter, if you are going to have people get their drinks off you, there's only one thing to do – make sure it's in your own bar!"

"And you can be my manager," I responded. And so it turned out. Hannelore was responsible for the interior's design. The result, by Mönchengladbach standards, was revolutionary. Black and white were the two colours employed. The only evidence of the owner being a player was a football shirt on the wall. It was an old one of mine which I had given to the Düsseldorf artist, Walter Klinzing. He then cut the back and front apart and placed them side by side, pasting geometric forms and matches onto the ripped shirt and calling it *The Reality of Man*. This did not seem to cause any problems with the fans; the hardcore 'hoodies', who may have taken offence, tended to stay away. The disco was a hit.

Soon after, Hannelore discovered a top-end restaurant, 'La Lacque', which she did up beautifully. Maybe even too beautifully, so that, in a strange way, people were put off coming.

Ten years later it might have been a success. At the beginning of the seventies it flopped. Some of the money I had earned in my effort to reduce the Borussia / Bayern pay differential sunk with it.

Still, it was a fantastic time. Hannelore was simply carrying on her life, with me joining in. Frontiers which I had never looked beyond before ceased to exist. I got to know people from whom I could learn. Even today, I continue to feel the benefit.

The down side was that my parents, who felt they no longer understood the world or even their own son, began to turn against Hannelore. It was she who was supposedly to blame for the new path I was following. On the other hand, I cannot remember a single time when they took exception to the way I dressed, my long hair or to my taste for modern art, whose existence they knew about from reading the papers but which was wholly alien to them. Father was still happy with my success, and I was happy that I could provide him with this pleasure. Mother was not really interested in these things. She was just glad that her husband and son felt the way they did.

As a man I changed during this time; that was obvious. Not always for the better, I admit. And as a player? Had I started to hit long balls 'out of deep space' because my horizons had widened? They were undoubtedly broader, but I believe the development of my game towards a specific style, and the courage I needed to play this way, had more to do with Hennes Weisweiler than they did with the avant-garde. "Listen up," Weisweiler would often say, "there is no shortage of players who can hit a long pass. In training, without the whistling and jeering of a crowd, it is not so hard to get the ball to land in the perfect spot. In a match you need courage." After one of my poorest performances – against Fortuna Düsseldorf of all teams – a very grim-looking Weisweiler headed straight towards me. I anticipated one of those stormy dressing-downs he was renowned for, followed by the latest of our drawn-out debates, for which we had become not just renowned but notorious. "Listen to me," he began, "when you have made thirty poor passes and you have nothing more to give, make a thirty-first." That was all.

For that kind of moral encouragement, I shall always remain grateful to him, just as I will to Hannelore Girrulat. However, there was the other Hennes Weisweiler to take into account too, which is what Herberger and I did during our legendary evening at 'Lovers Lane'. I went straight to the point: "Herr Herberger, I can't take it anymore. Weisweiler makes us play an inhuman kind of game. High tempo football. Without a let-up. Running for ninety minutes, up and down, until we are dead on our feet, scarcely able to haul ourselves off the pitch when the final whistle blows." Sepp Herberger, this big little man, looked at me intently. I could sense what he was thinking amidst the din of the disco. Should he put the knife in the back of his old favourite pupil, Weisweiler? Finally, he said, "I see. You are right, Günter."

4

Offside

It was being naturally lazy which gained me the reputation for rebelliousness. That is one explanation at least, perhaps debatable, for what happened one Saturday in Bielefeld. Hennes Weisweiler called a team meeting for 10 am the following day. He was particular about it being held in the Mönchengladbach stands. Why he wanted to talk to us outdoors was not clear. Perhaps so he could vent his rage more freely. What was clear, before the boss had spoken a single word, even before we could make out his expression as he approached – in fact, before he actually appeared – was that it was not going to be a cosy encounter. Hennes Weisweiler was in a furious mood.

The day after our match against Bielefeld, Weisweiler was not referring to me as "slowcoach" or "Günter", but as "Herr Netzer". Mostly he would address me as "slowcoach". He also liked to use the familiar "*du*", rather than the more formal "*ihr*" or "*Sie*". Whenever the tactical talk grew deeper, I would frequently become "*du*, Günter". "*Du*, Günter, what do *du* say about that?" he wanted to know, in his unmistakable Cologne accent. For Weisweiler, the world and his wife were "*du*". The only exception to this was the world champion, Sepp Herberger, who always remained both a Godlike figure and "Herr Herberger" for him. Nothing patronising was intended by "*du*"; Weisweiler was a big-hearted man who meant to be affectionate, just the same as when he spoke roughly. For example, the occasion when he greeted a photographer, who we all knew well, with the words, "*Do kütt ja dä Arsch mit Finger*," and nearly fell over laughing at his own crudeness. There was also a remark he made to me, which has been preserved for posterity: "We get caught offside the whole time thanks to that slow asshole taking his time jogging back". Did I get angry with him over that unkind remark? If I did, it was not because I took offence at being called a "slow asshole".

Once, in the training ground pavilion, we were entertained by Hacki Wimmer – I think it was Hacki, or it may have been somebody else ... it's not important, whoever told it, the story cracked us up. This was pure Weisweiler. In the course of talking to the radio reporter, Kurt Brumme, Hacki – or whoever it was – got to hear about a game of skat Brumme had played with our trainer and with Willy Thelen, a journalist on the *Kölnische Rundschau*. Obviously, it was a no-holds barred contest compared to my sessions with Elke Sommer and her mother. When the final hand was dealt, Weisweiler received an unbeatable combination. On top of four jacks, he held four aces. He bid high. Brumme and Thelen, both crafty players, raised him all the same. Weisweiler naturally re-raised them. At this point the game suddenly accelerated: *Bock* (– double), doubled *Bock*, redoubled *Bock* (... the three of them seemed to have their own rules). "Come on Hennes, it's your turn, you can play," cried Brumme, hurrying along Weisweiler, who slapped a card on the table, at which point Thelen and Brumme threw in their hands in rapid succession. In fact, Weisweiler had played out of turn. Our trainer sprung to his feet and upended the table, sending glasses crashing to the floor in the process. A fortnight passed before his indignation towards his two card playing mates died down. When the memory of the painful defeat was finally banished, they remained good friends.

I have never discovered if the story is actually true, but it is certainly in keeping with Weisweiler's character. He did not like to lose. Nor did he like gamesmanship – other than his own. This contributed as much to his success as did being a gifted tactician. He liked straight dealing. Those who engaged with him in such a way he called real men. In our good moments I was considered to be a "solid guy". When he wanted to be really disparaging – although this did not apply to Herberger, whom, by contrast, he addressed formally as a mark of his respect – he called you simply "*Sie*". Those were the bad periods, in which I would also be addressed, not as "Günter", "slowcoach" or even "that slow asshole", but as "Herr Netzer". This Sunday morning meeting in September 1970 in the Bökelberg stands was a Herr Netzer moment.

Our game the day before was an away fixture at Arminia Bielefeld. For a team that had only just been promoted, they were incredibly strong. Their Alm stadium was a fortress, where they had not lost for years, while we were German champions for the first time since our own promotion, in fact for the first time in the club's history. The praise we had received owed a lot to our energetic brand of attacking football. During the run-in, Weisweiler had threatened resigning if we did not pull it off this time. But now everything was looking good. Everything, that is, apart from the ongoing issues between the trainer and me.

"We get caught offside the whole time thanks to that slow asshole taking his time jogging back." This was what our dispute boiled down to. It was what I would talk to Herberger about in my disco and also what Weisweiler and I would return to during outdoor training sessions, or in tête-à-têtes afterwards, each of us perched on a football. He called his tactics, 'Up-and-Down-the-Pitch' or 'Hurrah! Football'. They were the context for the debate we carried on.

There was not much in principle which could be said against them, since they were responsible for an 11-0 home victory over Schalke 04 in our second season in the Bundesliga. Borussia Neunkirchen were comparatively lightly let off: we limited ourselves to a 10-0 win against them. When everything was running smoothly with our 'Up-and-Down-the-Pitch Football' we provided a groundbreaking spectacle. Its fluidity rested on the technical ability to keep interchanging positions, and its focus on attack on the pace of the forwards: Jupp Heynckes, who had just returned after a few years with Hannover 96, Herbert Laumen and Ulrik le Fevre. Their only goal on the football field was the opponent's goal. They did not let anything that lay between them and it detain them unnecessarily. Our tactics would tire opponents until they had nothing more to give. For example, Hacki Wimmer, living up to his nickname, would swerve past their increasingly desperate attempts to hack him down, continue on his way down the wing and out of sight. Spreading the passes which set the forwards off on their runs, my role in the middle of the pitch was key. I was expected to avoid loose passes into empty space. There was seldom any need to worry about that, since the high balls I floated forward into the opposition half invariably had Jupp, Herbert or Ulrik running onto them. Our battle cry might have been "Forward! ... *En avant!*" This was the avant-garde style of football my artist friends spoke about. But who needed the cool avant-garde? With our crazy tempo we burned instead.

I was convinced that this 'Up-and-Down-the-Pitch Football' was a shallow concept. With justification: there were too many times when we failed to preserve the lead our early onslaught had obtained and when we lost, in spite of our exhilarating play. This approach had nearly cost us the title the previous season. Against Hamburg SV we raced to a 4-0 lead before being pulled back to 4-3. At the end of the game, there were the usual backslaps; once more we were told how fantastic and invigorating we were compared to dreary Bayern. Meanwhile, boring old Bayern kept on winning titles. That is why I had had enough of the tirades.

In the newspapers one could now read that the likelihood of failure was inherent in our style of play. Maybe. On the other hand, perhaps we 'Foals' were destined to become legends. What was clear to me was that glorious failure was to be avoided. I wasn't playing to win all the plaudits but end up second. What I wanted was for us to develop a more measured game. Apart from corresponding better with my notorious languor and sub-optimal fitness, to be more calculating was simple common sense.

We argued over this the whole time. The team listened as I gave my opinion, all of us aware of Weisweiler grinding his teeth. We didn't only argue – otherwise we would not have succeeded in developing various fundamentals of the Mönchengladbacher game together. Originally, a designated minder played alongside me in some games, accompanying me wherever I went on the pitch. This made our play predictable. Even if I was playing well, the guardian system was not entirely set aside over the ninety minutes. It disturbed me and disrupted our attacking momentum. So I suggested to Weisweiler that it would be better if I dropped deeper and my double – usually this was Hans-Jürgen Wittkamp – was positioned further forward. "OK, let's try it," said Weisweiler. Which we did, with considerable success. But he would never forsake his 'Hurrah! Football', that I, with equal stubbornness, continued to criticise.

At least, the previous season, Weisweiler had made the concession of buying two central defenders, Ludwig Müller from 1. FC Nürnberg and Klaus-Dieter Sieloff from VfB Stuttgart. For him to do so was fairly sensational. We had kept at him about the need to plug the holes in our defence. "Get us the kind of players who are a bit of fun to play against," we requested. Both Müller and Wolfgang Weber, who was at 1. FC Köln, fitted the bill. Once Weisweiler finally appreciated that we would not win anything without a solid defence, he and the manager, Grashoff, worked together to sign Müller.

They pulled it off in style. In the last game of the season 1. FC Köln and 1. FC Nürnberg faced one another in a game that was to decide which of the two teams would be relegated. We were aiming to sign the top defender of the unlucky side. Within an hour of 1. FC Nürnberg's defeat, before the fact of their relegation had sunk in, Müller had signed the transfer papers. Not sitting at a desk, or in a suitably upmarket restaurant or even over a beer. This was a day on which Weisweiler had no time for formalities. After his long courtship of Müller, he finally had his agreement. He got the manager to bring the papers over to where they were in the stadium car park. Müller signed them on the bonnet of the nearest car. Like the others, I would have been glad if Weber had joined us, but Köln's 3-0 victory meant they stayed up and he remained in the cathedral city. Even without him, our defence was now a lot stronger. It was a key factor in becoming champions for the first time.

It was not initially obvious to us what Weisweiler saw in Sieloff, no longer VfB's Stuttgart's first choice. He arrived overweight and neither strong nor fit enough. Our two preferences, as we made clear, were Müller and Weber. Perhaps it was because he feared that agreeing with us would be seen as an abdication of authority, Weisweiler decided to assert it instead. After the signing was made, I did not talk to him about it again. Stubborn like me, he then worked at getting Sieloff up to the necessary level. The time and effort paid off. Sieloff turned out to be a good investment. He played as big a part as Müller in helping us to win our first title.

Neither the addition of two centre-backs nor winning the title were enough to dissuade Weisweiler from making us self-combust with ninety minutes of 'Hurrah! Football'. The danger that at this point it could be the other side shouting "Hurrah!" had not been averted. Not even against Bielefeld. And so our quarrel escalated.

If I remember rightly, it was Horst Köppel who had given us the lead at half-time. In the dressing room Weisweiler demanded that we carry on running, running, running. He wanted goals, goals, goals! "Keep it up, keep going," he insisted. And I said, "No!" At least, under my breath I did. Then, as we went back onto the pitch, I spread the word to Berti Vogts and Peter Dietrich; to Ludwig Müller too, I think. There could be no question though of inviting Hacki Wimmer to join this would-be cabal. He did not understand the way I felt, being the kind of player who put his foot down as soon as the kick-off whistle blew and left it there until his tank was empty. Then the game was over for him. Putting a foot on the brake, which is what I now proposed, was not something he did. "Let's slow it down ... knock the ball about a bit," I said. But there was no immediate reaction. The team preferred to stay out of my dispute with Weisweiler, if they could.

However much they may have agreed with me that particular Saturday at Bielefeld, their hesitancy to go against Weisweiler was greater. They all said the same thing: "Yah, yah, you're right, but what can we do? How can we confront the trainer like that?" The trainer in those days was a figure you did not contradict as you might today. For better or worse, I was going to have to stand up to him by myself.

It was not something I particularly wanted to do, but if I was unable to organise a collective go-slow, then I would have to set one in motion myself. That meant making myself the absolute fulcrum of our game. If its pace was to be made bearable, I had to get hold of the ball. Wherever it went, I must be in the vicinity, so as to redistribute it. I don't think I have ever run so much in a match. It was worth it though because, at some point, my teammates cottoned on to what I was trying to do: make our high tempo game more sophisticated by introducing different phases, in place of flat-out attack.

Knowing full well what was going on, but unable to do anything about it, the coach stood by. A Herbert Laumen goal allowed us to win the game 2-0. Returning to the dressing room we could already sense that Weisweiler would have been happy to forsake the victory. He trudged in, looked around for a few moments and trudged back out, pausing only to bark: "Tomorrow, 10 am, team meeting at the Bökelberg". The expression on his face was probably the same one he had worn when he found himself gulled by his card-playing friends.

The following morning he roared and railed that the lack of discipline shown was an outrage and that the best footballing traditions were at risk if tried-and-tested methods gave way to improvisation, and so on and so forth. Throughout this harangue his eyes remained fixed on a certain object: myself. He finally came to what for him was the heart of the matter: "Herr Netzer, I will not let you ruin my reputation!" These were the last words he spoke to me for several weeks. If he had something to communicate, he would say, "Berti, tell the slowcoach ..." Once more, Berti Vogts found himself playing the role of intermediary.

It was an uncomfortable moment. I felt as though Weisweiler had abandoned the method we had developed, of talking through tactical issues. Yes, he encouraged discussion, and even controversy but, when it came to me questioning his precious attacking football, he closed himself to all argument. The matter was not discussed again; he never offered a reply to what we – or rather I – thought. Why not? For me it was obvious: the trainer who was probably the most open to debate there had ever been in German football was not so open-minded after all.

I was cast as the rebel, in spite of having no past history as a troublemaker. It made sense though that I was the one being prodded into this kind of role by the team. Firstly, I was already notorious on account of what was considered to be my crazy lifestyle. No other reputation could have made me appear more dangerous and dynamic. Secondly, this life away from football had not sapped my morale. Instead, it had provided a means for me to develop more quickly than the others. Even if I might often crouch on the edge of Hannelore's artistic circle, hardly speaking a word, as if I did not belong there, I was proud to be leading such a varied life. I felt confident that I was more, rather than less respected around town having decided not to belong exclusively to the tight, somewhat self-satisfied world of professional football. Did you know there were countless christenings I attended as a godfather? Or that, when I was not being asked to act as best man, then it was to lead the bride to the altar? And did you know my sack of fan mail was bigger than the others'? Occasionally, I liked to meet up with my business school friends at the 'Suntan Lotion Bar' in the old town, where we would go through it, paying particular attention to the female correspondence. I promise any of you who wrote to me then that we were not laughing. I simply felt proud, and wished to share that feeling with my friends.

It was with this growing awareness of my abilities, and because I wanted to make the most of them, that I stood up to Weisweiler. The team not only accepted but encouraged this, keeping out of the way themselves. That might sound as though I am suggesting I was surrounded by a bunch of wimps, which was not the case. It is just that in a team a hierarchy establishes itself. Both then and later one or another of them looked up to me. I was leader of the pack. Berti Vogts would go on to say that he had admired me almost as if I were a supernatural being. I think he was going a little far there. Berti was incredibly important for the team. Whatever the situation, he was plain speaking. If Weisweiler and I were starting to have a go at each other once again, it was not unusual as he gave a training talk, with the team gathered in a circle, where I was clearly within view and earshot, that, rather than speak to me directly, he would address Berti instead. Berti then repeated what I had just heard perfectly well. My response would take the same roundabout route. There were also conversations between Berti and Weisweiler alone in which they spoke about me. I know that during them Berti never undermined, deceived nor did the dirt on me.

Some of the things I got up to around then were admittedly questionable. At some point I got to know the director, Michael Pfleghar. We became friends. In the seventies he was responsible for bringing the extremely successful show *Klimbim* (*Odds and Ends*) to the TV screen. For the time, it was also an extremely chaotic show. Ingrid Steeger and Elisabeth Volkmann featured regularly, a lot of cake throwing went on and the proceedings were freely punctuated by pyrotechnics. Michael had an English name for this anarchic comedy that was so popular. He called it "Physical Humour". Through him I got to know not just the stars of *Klimbim* but, since he produced the 'Elke Sommer Show' as well, this leading lady too. Michael put together a sketch for Elke, me and the football-mad British comic Marty Feldman – the beginning of another close friendship.

I remember an evening spent with Steeger, Elke Sommer and Michael in 'Krützche', a bar in Cologne. This turned into a typically boisterous *Klimbim* occasion. On the way out, Michael wrote some fitting words in the visitors' book: 'Full to the brim. Thanks, Wendlandt,' a reference to Horst Wendlandt who was responsible for financing not just the series of Karl May films but this entire evening. 'Full to the brim' was another way in which I risked having my reputation called into question.

Then there were my trips to Erlangen, where her mother lived, when Elke Sommer visited West Germany. Berti and one or two of the others had known about these journeys, burning down the autobahn, for a while. The trainer only learned about them when photos of my Ferrari, parked conspicuously outside the Sommer home, appeared in the papers. This was also the moment when I found myself with some explaining to do to my girlfriend, Hannelore Girrulat. It was the first crack in our relationship.

All in all, my life outside football had become a little erratic. What was predictable about it was the frequency with which Pfleghar and I would head off to Munich. Once a month I drove across the Rhine to Düsseldorf Airport to catch the flight to München-Riem, where Michael would be waiting. Then off we went to bars, hotels and discotheques. These included 'Why Not', *the* hip Munich disco then, where one could be sure to meet new people, new girls. It was a thrilling, happy period: a satisfying meal followed by a fun time at the disco, with good looking women swarming around Pfleghar – and perhaps me, too. The night would often end in a hotel room, or still in the disco, coming up for 6 am and closing time. Then came the rush to avoid missing the 6.30 am flight back to Düsseldorf. The only problem for me in this carefree existence was making sure that I got back in time for training at Mönchengladbach. Most knew about this monthly itinerary of mine. It was not until another photograph appeared in one of the papers that Weisweiler was alerted. I was lucky to be around at a time when there was less thirst for gossip than there is today.

I liked the dual life I was leading. On the one hand, Mönchengladbach, decent, rather staid, where glittering society belonged to the realm of fantasy; on the other Sommer, Steeger and the various beautiful women populating Munich's nightlife. Is it so strange that, in order to broaden my horizons, I would look beyond what the Lower Rhine's left bank had to offer? In Munich Franz Beckenbauer chirruped a little ditty, 'Good Friends Never Shall Part' and developed excellent relations with his future mother-in-law; when I went there however it was to dance the night away with the beautiful people. I even appeared in *Klimbim* with *la* Steeger, who was never afraid to bare her breasts – a real provocation in those days.

A nasty little trick of Michael's was responsible for one of my appearances on his show. Without playing it he would not have succeeded in persuading me. He had casually invited me to drop by while they were shooting. "You'll have the chance to see how it's done; it will be something a bit different for you." I lightheartedly replied that I had nothing against learning something new. When I arrived, Pfleghar came up to me in an agitated state, as the filming of a sketch went on. "Günter, I've got a big problem. We've planned a Heino parody for tonight's show, but the impersonator has not showed up." I suspected nothing. "There is no sign of him at all."

"OK," I said. "So, what are you going to do now?"

"You have got to help me," said Michael.

"Sure, OK. Do you want me to go and fetch him from somewhere?" I still suspected nothing.

"No, no," he said, "there's no longer time. But there's a simple solution: you be Heino."

A month later, Michael came clean about the non-existence of this impersonator who had failed to show up. Knowing me well, he understood the only way to get me to submit to his idea would be a surprise attack. He also knew that he could count on me in an hour of need. This was a moment when I was not so happy to help. "Me as Heino? How do you expect me to manage that?" Michael gave some vague advice and I continued to fend him off. "I can't do it," I said, "the guy will turn up soon," which seemed perfectly reasonable to assume.

Michael tried a new approach. "Yes, yes, of course; I understand, theatre is not your line of work. I guess all these people who have come to shoot the scene today will just have to be sent home. We'll reschedule for another day. It's going to cost me a crazy amount of money, but what can we do? Jesus, all the ordinary production costs, and now this." He was becoming increasingly worked up and melodramatic. It might have been doomsday. I did not even know the words, I told him. A weak argument. "The words are a piece of cake, believe me; for a footballer as much as an intellectual: "Karambo, karacho, one whisky, karambo, karacho, one gin, Jesus H Christ, Dolores, Dolores … (*repeat*)"." And, in the end, the words were not a handicap to me appearing on national TV impersonating Heino.

At the next training session, it was not hard to tell from Weisweiler's expression what he thought: 'Barmy … he's lost the plot … needs to be locked away'. But he didn't say anything. Perhaps he allowed me a long leash because he was not exactly a worthy, stolid type himself? Since we never talked about it, I cannot be sure. It is possible he appreciated, like me, that, in order to perform well on the pitch, I needed this other life too. I also realised that it would only be accepted so long as my football did not suffer.

The Borussia team of the early seventies was a curious mix. The fact that such different personalities could perform so well together was fairly extraordinary. The teammate I was closest to was Jupp Heynckes, my opposite in many ways. For me, he is one of the greatest footballers Germany has ever produced. We usually shared a room on away days and during training camps. Our relationship was typical of Borussia. The completely different lifestyles and tastes in music and clothes we had were forgotten the moment we got onto the pitch, where he converted my through balls with shots on goal. It would be fair to say that I was the one who knew how to make him run, which is what he liked doing. But if he enjoyed running around for me, he remained his own man.

Jupp was one of eleven. His father had originally been a blacksmith. Like my parents, he then set up a grocery store. Having ten brothers and sisters marks you. From an early age, Jupp was used to sharing and to exercising self-control. You could tell when we roomed together. No sooner had we stepped into our new accommodation than he unpacked his bag and hung his shirts in the wardrobe. His carefully folded socks were placed in a drawer. So that it would not get creased, his training gear was put away too. In other words, Jupp was neat and tidy. My own kit bag lay on the floor. I would burrow out whatever clothes I needed, whenever I needed them, ejecting other items across the hotel room floor. Amazingly, we accepted one another as we were. I cannot remember Jupp ever laughing at me for my slovenly ways, while I know that I never smiled facetiously, not even to myself, at his orderliness.

That was the Borussia way: in our private lives we might all be different – or I might be unlike all the others – but as footballers we marched to the same drummer. This was Hennes Weisweiler's, whose strengths as a motivator compensated for any tactical shortcomings, greatest achievement. He brought the players together by getting us to subordinate our differences to the higher interest of the team.

The team were not close friends though, nor were we necessarily faithful Mönchengladbachers. I certainly never considered myself to be one, even if I stayed when a couple of the others left. In fact, when Herbert Laumen and Peter Dietrich moved to Werder Bremen, I almost went with them. Bremen wanted the entire Mönchengladbach midfield; we were a unit. I was definitely part of the package.

In comparison to what other members of the national team were receiving, my salary of 130,000 marks was low. I was living beyond my means, in spite of having sidelines. Because of my inexperience and occasional gullibility these were not an automatic success.

Puma involved me in the development of a new boot, which I tried out for them. Adidas already had a successful partnership with Beckenbauer. My pairing with Puma was portrayed as the alternative. But was it necessary to go as far as a blue boot made of kangaroo leather? The problem was the colour. I may have been thought of as a bird of paradise but this was an embarrassment.

Another less than famous venture was the purchase of a property in Hindenburgstraße in Mönchengladbach's old town, the idea being to use part of the premises for a second-hand car dealership. With my knowledge of cars, it seemed like a good investment. In fact, it was not. There might have been enough street level space for a showroom but I failed to take into account Hindenburgstraße's poor access, an obvious handicap in the motor trade.

Finally, along with 350,000 other West Germans in 1970, I lost money placed in an investment fund. We were all taken in by Bernard 'Bernie' Cornfeld, the founder and director of an American company called Investors Overseas Services Ltd. In my case this was to the tune of 90,000 marks. Like most of the other savers, I had no idea what stocks were being bought. I simply followed my business school training that investing in shares was, on the face of it, a reasonable way to manage one's finances. A reassuring factor was that the chairman of IOS-Deutschland was also a former leader of the FDP and onetime vice chancellor of the country, Erich Mende. Why would one distrust an eminent politician like him? In 1970 such a figure was still deferred to, at least by someone as apolitical as myself. The next thing I knew, I was 90,000 marks worse off, thanks to these fine gentlemen making poor investments and incurring heavy losses. In other words, I got burnt.

At least the matchday programme venture was ticking over nicely. The editorial running of it was now in the hands of a young staffer at the *Rheinischen Post* who had not yet finished his schooling, Otto E. Schütz. We had shaken hands on it in a counter café in Hindenburgstraße, 'Tchibo'. He was to get sixty, rising to eighty, marks for each number. Although a laughable sum by today's standards, he was soon able to buy himself a Beetle with it. Having discounted the possibility of expanding the Mönchengladbach programme, I instead started a second magazine with Peter Meyer, the Fortuna Düsseldorf forward mentioned before, who later joined Borussia. This failed after two numbers, because nobody at the club could be bothered tidying up the programmes which littered the stands after the match.

I was not on the breadline; footballers were already getting extravagantly paid. All the same, why should I turn down a better offer when it was made? During the initial talks, Bremen offered more than double what I was on. As I had stressed to Sepp Herberger in my disco, players' loyalty was now balanced by commercial considerations. This obviously applied to me. I was ready for a move, too.

It soon became clear that the Werder representatives had not done their sums correctly. Maybe they reckoned that the negotiations with me would be the hardest part of their plan and so, to begin with, concentrated on Herbert Laumen and Peter Dietrich instead. It was when they both signed that Bremen saw they had overreached themselves financially. They no longer had the half million marks that I was going to cost them. Laumen and Dietrich went, while I stayed.

To my surprise, I was now regarded as Gladbach's orchestrator and star attraction. I got praised and mobbed. Besides being a member of the national team, I was seen, and not only in the rose-tinted perspective of the Mönchengladbach press, as its future hope, no less than Wolfgang Overath and Franz Beckenbauer. Only the Bundesliga's governing body held back.

Was this on account of my reputation as an egotist who did as he pleased and would not stay in line, who for a while now had openly subverted authority? So long as this notoriety, for which I knew I was partly to blame, was based on my ostentatious lifestyle I didn't mind. But if this was how I was considered as a footballer, then I did. I am thinking particularly of a night in Liverpool – the Goodison Park drama, in which, like a cheat, I had allegedly left the team in the lurch.

Following our first Bundesliga title we were in the European Cup. We had made a brilliant start, with all due modesty. Against the Cypriot champions, Larnaka, our executioner-in-chief in two flawless victories was my roommate, Jupp Heynckes who had just returned after three years with Hannover 96. OK, this was only a Cypriot side, but the scorelines, 6-0 in the first leg and 10-0 in the second, tell their own story. In both games, I have to say, I was outstanding.

Against Everton we lost. Their manager, Harry Catterick, whose strong point does not appear to have been German geography, wanted to know where exactly on the map he could find this backwater with the unpronounceable name, Mönchengladbach? We were admittedly newcomers on the European scene. By the time of the return leg in Liverpool, they had got to know us a bit better. The first game had ended 1-1. This was also the scoreline after extra time in England. Time for penalties. As captain, I went over to Horst Köppel and told him he was to take the first one for us. I then made my way to the touchline. Later it was written that I had disappeared down the tunnel into the guts of the stadium because I was unable to bear watching the shootout. Not true, but it was to become a key part of the controversy that built up around this night at Goodison Park. Horst scored; Herbert Laumen, who had not yet gone to Bremen, and Ludwig Müller both fluffed their lines. This was reported as me chickening out. Really? Even though my name was not on the list of our likely penalty takers? Beside the point, apparently. The central question being asked was, is it not the captain's duty to show leadership at such a moment?

Where was the famous self-confidence, now that it was needed? Maybe I was not so confident after all? In spite of the fancy cars and the beautiful women who surrounded me, didn't I actually still live at my mother's, in a bare little room with a folding bed and a formica table? In other words, I remained shy little Günter from Gasthausstraße.

It was later suggested that I would not allow myself to be goaded into taking responsibility; I would only assume it if I decided to do so, myself. There was some truth in this.

There was also a practical reason for why I did not step up in the penalty shootout. A few days before, against Hamburg SV, I had collided with Willi Schulz. After the match I was diagnosed by the Cologne specialist, Professor Schneider as having sustained bruised ribs. During my career I had my share of injuries. Challenges which would get penalised today were part and parcel of the game then. I got targeted by opponents. This is a quick inventory of the consequences: a broken nose, concussion, shoulder nerve issues, metacarpal bruising, hip bruising, countless hamstring and knee problems, broken cartilage, chronic pain in the achilles, lacerations, scratch marks … and on and on.

My bones in particular had taken a lot of knocks during the season, including in the Bundesliga encounter before our big match in Liverpool. I had a punctured heel, now a blue-green shade. Once more an injection was needed to ease the pain in my achilles. Accompanied by Professor Schneider, I went through agonies as we flew to England. He prescribed a strong painkiller. Weisweiler and I agreed that I should play for as long as I felt able, but that I was definitely not to take part in any penalty shootout. My breathing had been affected. Maybe I wouldn't be able to play? As we got ready for the game, a bandage, acting as a corset, was wound around my chest.

Within minutes of the whistle blowing, I was on the floor. I received the first of several treatments. Nevertheless, I managed to carry on, even having a very good game. This did not alter my view that, if it came to penalties, I could not help the team. I had already given everything I could.

It was a tired and dejected band which took refuge in the away side changing room. Berti Vogts wept bitter tears. He, not I, the captain, stood up and ordered us all to form a circle in the middle of the room. On his instruction, we joined hands. "Lads," he insisted, "we are going to be champions again."

Wasn't it my job to boost team morale in this sort of situation? The pathos of such moments though was foreign to me, in fact a horror. It was the old tale of the eleven friends, all for one and one for all, that I found so schmaltzy and false. The others embraced this camaraderie with enthusiasm. I joined in reluctantly, to avoid being the odd man out. For example, before a match, in the habitual team stroll through the woods to a spot where one of the players had previously buried a stick in the ground. The next part of this ritual came when whoever unearthed it must be touched by each of us. The whole procedure was performed at a slight distance from the trainer who stood by himself, pulling on a lucky duffel coat. The stick oath bound us to never again pull on shirts in which we had been defeated (, something which had scarcely happened since the tradition began). We swore to stand by one another through thick and thin …

It wasn't for me – until this tragic Goodison Park night, down in the condensed atmosphere of an English dressing room. Even I was affected by the emotional charge of the glances we exchanged. If Sepp Herberger had walked in at that moment and returned to the topic of team spirit, I would have had to grant him that, yes, eleven professionals can have a soul.

Later that evening, while most of the team sat glumly in our Southport hotel, I went out for some fresh air with Berti Vogts and Hartwig Bleidick. We walked for a while, mulling our dull thoughts. Then we went for a drink. Weisweiler's reaction was to shrug his shoulders, as if to say, what else would one expect from our diva with his introverted, self-pitying and egotistic ways? The question on this November night back in 1970 was whether I was still not so developed as I considered myself to be? The hero who hailed from the provinces, brilliant, proud and dominating – sure, but only in Mönchengladbach, a small city tucked away on the left bank of the Lower Rhine. I was still not ready for the really big stage. That is what passed through my mind as the wind blew in sharply from the Irish Sea.

5

"Do as you Please, then!"

Events proved Berti Vogts right. What he prophesied and the team swore to that night came to pass: we retained the title at the end of the season, the first side to do so since the founding of the Bundesliga. Was team spirit at the heart of our success? Or was it the team's reaction, prompted by myself, against Weisweiler's unsophisticated single tempo tactics, which set our campaign on the right track? I did not think the 'Spirit of Everton' had much to do with it; the need for cohesiveness in order to achieve success is a given in team sports.

We were no unit, something that probably had more to do with me than anyone else. In keeping with the Weisweiler method, he once gave us a questionnaire to try and gauge how much of a team spirit we did in fact possess. One of the questions asked which teammates you would be happy to go on holiday with; another, who you would not choose under any circumstances. Ninety-nine percent, I believe, named me as the one whom, if they were to find themselves in this predicament with, it would be like receiving a maximum sentence. On the other hand, ninety-nine percent also mentioned me as the player they would prefer to pass the ball to if they were in a tight situation on the pitch.

I can see better now that there were plenty of times when I was uncooperative almost on a whim. I would take time off in a way that is unimaginable today but, back then, was even more astonishing. I did it for my sanity and for the sake of my game. For instance, I might turn up punctually to training, only to tell Weisweiler that I could not stay because I had autographs to sign. On other occasions I did not show up at all. I may have genuinely intended to, but could not finally force myself to make the effort.

Once, the team made a trip to Bulgaria. It was probably for a friendly, although I can no longer remember if this was the commitment explaining why we had to travel there. I do recall that I failed to last the course. I had had enough of hanging around in anonymous hotels, my foul mood exacerbated by the bad weather. The others were no more enthusiastic than I was but stayed on, as I flew home. During a Central American tour, the situation repeated itself in Venezuela. I did not see why I should spend my free time with the same people whom I was already wedded to professionally, performing in the Bundesliga and the European Cup. I would not have been a very good companion in Switzerland, let alone in Venezuela's heat. I flew home ahead of schedule again. Weisweiler and several of my teammates were left fuming one more time.

Such behaviour today would be considered untamed egotism. I probably was extremely selfish. This impression will be reinforced by my next bombshell: not all my 'injuries' were genuine. It was a matter of granting myself some time off, for example if I had strained a muscle. Because the team doctor had a more limited role then, this type of minor injury would often go untreated at the club. On one occasion, I let Berti Vogts know that he had recommended sun as the best cure for my latest injury and that I had therefore decided to go to Barbados. Berti's response was, "You're crazy". He was shaking his head, but then he nodded, acknowledging that this was simply the way I was. My trip to the West Indies would be unthinkable today. In fact, it was unthinkable then. But, without taking an occasional break, I would have been unable to carry on playing football.

These escapades had a polarising effect. It was certainly not the case that the team all lined up behind me. I could sense an opposition forming, and from Berti I knew something of its ins and outs. A sauna was invariably part of Monday's training programme. Beers would be drunk after stepping out of it. Three players – Peter Dietrich, Klaus-Dieter Sieloff and Luggi Müller – three cooling off sessions and three beers got the revolt going. "We're not playing with Netzer any longer," they repeated with growing conviction. Other players, such as Berti, Hartwig Bleidick or Jupp Heynckes, would join the debate. "OK," said Berti on more than one occasion, "then play without Günter. But if that's what you're planning to do, you can play without me too. We will not win anything without Günter." Each time the matter would have to be resolved by my fulfilling some demand they made. Once this was carried out, we were a team again, with my latest naughtiness almost forgotten.

If this unity was initially brittle, outside influences could then play a part in strengthening it, by putting it to the test. Unjust defeats were especially effective in bringing about the improvement. Sometimes all it took was a piece of rotten wood.

Having gradually overcome the dejection we felt at being knocked out of the European Cup, we were at the top of the table. It looked a safe bet that we would still be there when the season ended. I have never been big on statistics, so to recall our scorelines I need to consult the newspaper archives. These record a 5-0 win against Eintracht Frankfurt, a 3-0 defeat of HSV and a 4-0 victory over Hertha BSC Berlin. The XI included Berti Vogts, as well as Sieloff and Müller cleaning up at the back. Rainer Bonhof had recently joined us, though he was not yet the force he later became. My man Hacki Wimmer ran in areas of the pitch I hesitated to while, at the front, Jupp Heynckes and Herbert Laumen unhesitatingly shot at goal. We were no longer foals, but young racehorses whose principal pleasures remained playing exciting football and scoring goals. We could not score enough. I remember an insignificant friendly we played against one of the local sides, FC Linken, which we won 30-1. At 27-0 Bernd Rupp casually wasted an easy opportunity for another. As though stung by a tarantula, I went over and bellowed at him for his carelessness.

On 3 April 1971 we were neither wasteful nor careless, just unlucky; particularly Herbert Laumen. Ten days later we defeated Bayern 3-1 at their stadium. It was a decisive victory but they still had a chance of catching us, as a result of what happened at the Bökelberg at the beginning of the month. Our guests that Saturday were Werder Bremen. A victory against them would have kept us on course for the title. As the ninetieth minute approached the score was 1-1. Herbert rose to meet a cross I banged in. Their keeper, Günter Bernard just got a hand on it. Instead of the ball hitting the back of the net, it was the flying Herbert who was clinging to it. Next, the goal collapsed.

The left post was so rotten it had snapped a few inches above the grass. Decades later, when Borussia Dortmund came up against Real Madrid in the 1998 Champions League, history repeated itself, leaving the respected match commentators, and winners of Bavaria's television prize, Günter Jauch and Marcel Reif, doubled up with laughter. Our doubled-up goalpost was the cause of both a lot of derisive laughter from others and of anxiety for ourselves over the following weeks. It left us with the bitter recognition that, for all our swashbuckling renown, we were a smalltown club playing at a dilapidated stadium.

Probably it would have been a comfort at the time to know that the same thing can happen to the mighty Real Madrid. In the immediate aftermath of the goal collapsing, chaos reigned on the pitch. The groundsman tried fixing the post with a hammer and nails. Bremen wanted to continue, and gain an unlikely away point. Their substitute volunteered to hold the post in place for what remained of the game. Not a great idea, I thought. What I wanted was for it to be abandoned and for there to be a replay, which hopefully we would win. I went to the referee and asked him to halt the game. This turned out to be an even worse idea. He did as I asked, and so brought the comedy to an end. Rather than a replay however, three weeks later the DFB's adjudicating body decided to award Bremen a 2-0 win, because replacement goalposts should have been organised in case of such an incident. Besides forfeiting the match, we Mönchengladbachers were put firmly in our place, when the council's chairman, a Dr Otto Rückert, concluded, "After all, a Bundesliga club is not a village team". A 1,500 mark fine was hardly excessive; the bigger picture though was that we risked missing out on the title.

Did the incident bring us closer together? Maybe. Maybe it awoke in us a keen sense of righteousness. We felt unjustly punished. A length of rotten wood was the city council's or the club's responsibility, not the players'. It could never happen at Bayern, where everything was perfect. They might not be pretty to watch, but they were always effective.

What were Duisburg's thoughts about Bayern on the last day of the season? Was it regional pride which made them play so grittily against Bayern, as if they were fighting for the title themselves? Actually, they were out of the running; but they did us a favour all the same. Bayern lost 0-2 in Duisburg, while we won 4-1 in Frankfurt. We were champions again. Hail Berti the prophet!

Life was pretty good. I remained fairly indifferent to the football world, success and my reputation. It was recognised that I could live contentedly with all the chatter. If one or two other details were known more widely, I would have been happier still. For example, about our trip to Israel.

The tour we undertook there was the first by a West German side since the war and the mass murder of the Jewish people. I do not remember whether the idea for it came from the players or was proposed to us. Looking back, it seems natural that we were the team who should travel there with a message of reconciliation. If commentators wanted to see us as the footballing extension of Willy Brandt's expansive politics then they undoubtedly would. As apolitical sportsmen, we found this second guessing of our motives, a lot of which was drivel, overblown and even a little crazy. All the team wanted to do was score goals. I shared this desire, but was also happy to be able to help a little in paving the way towards the broader goal. That does not mean I took the talk of Borussia "daring to play more football" being the equivalent of Brandt's vision of "more democracy" any more seriously than I did that of my long ball distribution being "visionary". Without going so far as to contradict these opinions, there was no plan, concept or ideology that we were following. We found most of the connections made between our football and Brandt's new politics hard to grasp. And yet … Borussia Mönchengladbach *was* the team standing for a new style of football, where it was not the ends which justified the means any longer, but the means, or style, that determined the ends. During this period, we changed the German game. Maybe we did play a small part in changing West German society too. In which case, it made sense that, with our brand of football, we were the team making the trip to Israel, as representatives of this other, evolving West Germany.

These are just observations, which I am able to make today. Even at the time though we knew that we held a special place in the game. One or two of us probably suspected that this position extended beyond football. I am not sure I was one of them. The memories I have of the Israel trip, which went very well, are more specific. In the match against Israel, which we won 6-0, we were applauded from the stands. "Vivat Germania!" they cried. We had flown on an air force plane accompanied by uniformed soldiers, because of the fear that we might be attacked by an Israeli aircraft, and now the people were shouting, "Vivat Germania!" It was extraordinary. The win had some positive consequences for our opponents too. Their coach, Emmanuel Schaffer belonged to the Weisweiler school. He tweaked the side's tactics and, not long afterwards, they drew 0-0 with Italy. This unexpected result was another sign of a worthwhile trip.

One night, together with Otto E. Schütz, my editor at the *Fohlen-Echo*, I climbed over the fence that circled the hotel grounds. Our destination was a beach disco in Tel-Aviv, which I had heard a lot about in Mönchengladbach. The owner was Mandy Rice-Davies, a very well-known Englishwoman then, who was best friend, at the time of the spy scandal involving the Defence Secretary, John Profumo, of Christine Keeler, with whom she shared a dubious renown. I would not say that our little adventure was the main inspiration for founding 'Lovers Lane' but, like other accidental or inconsequential events it contributed, as I looked to add variety to my footballer's life, to the decision. My immediate concern that night was a bit of unauthorised fun; business was far from my mind.

It was not so bizarre back then to go on a nighttime excursion and bring a journalist along for company. You could still expect to avoid having to read about it in the Press the following day. Three years later though this same Otto E. Schütz did the dirt on me. That is how it felt like at least. He was my ghost writer for a column that appeared in the *Rheinischen Post*. It is fairly standard for the famous name in bold type above a piece not to belong to the person who actually wrote it. All the star does is provide a few key phrases, which the journalist then joins together to produce a more – or less – readable story. Not always when Lothar Matthäus' name appears has Lothar Matthäus picked up a pen; likewise, the presence of the name Günter Netzer does not necessarily mean I have been busy writing. Technically though I was a *Rheinischen Post* contributor. So I thought it was poor form when, on some slim pretext, my own ghost writer took a dig, in the same paper, at the commission I was receiving, before going on to make a number of cheap references to my recent displays. I have not changed my view that he was being openly disloyal, even if it is true I was in poor form in 1973.

Maybe I was too sensitive to criticism during my playing career? Perhaps being pulled down a peg and having his shortcomings laid bare made Netzer the player unhappy? I think I am being honest when I say that I had no problem with thoughtful, pertinent criticism of the kind we were used to as members of Weisweiler's debating club. There were periods though when my football was only seen in the light of my long hair, my lifestyle and the people I socialised with. That made me unhappy.

I once had a big row with Ulfert Schröder, one of the top sports journalists of that period. I knew about him and he knew who I was, but we had never talked before. Schröder was a big fan of Wolfgang Overath, my main competitor for the midfield role in the national side. Whenever it came to writing about the West German team, he praised Overath to the skies. That was reasonable enough. Tearing me down was not. This lay behind us almost coming to blows at the time of an international in Zagreb when, a day before the match, we found ourselves together in the hotel lift. I was a little out of order to grab Schröder, who was a head shorter at least, by the scruff of the neck and start yelling at him that, before he next lay into me, he should at least try speaking to me. Schröder was visibly taken aback. In the match against Yugoslavia we played sluggishly and lost. I was particularly bad. It gave me another opportunity to get worked up about the criticism which, inevitably, followed.

The Zagreb game was in November 1970. Eight months earlier we had played Spain in Seville. In between these two dates I had some heated conversations with Helmut Schön. It looked as if my international career might already be over. You could say the national side and I had not been a success story for a while or, perhaps even, for a long time. Without being able to put my finger on the problem, I assumed that it was mostly my own fault. Now it is clear to me the issue was simply that I did not feel at home in this setting. I was not receiving the trust I needed to be shown, either from the other players or from the coach.

It is striking that my best run as an international came when Helmut Schön seemed to almost withdraw into the shadows, making very few tactical or team selection decisions. That does not mean he was no longer doing a great deal of work behind the scenes, just that he had the sense to leave us on a long leash. I remember a match against the USSR which, according to the records, took place in Munich on 26 May 1972. The day before, Schön stood in front of a blackboard on which he had chalked up the Russian formation. As he was about to begin giving us our instructions, he noticed the expression we all wore and stopped. The attitude he picked up on may not have been an uninterested one, but it was enough to tell him that a team talk was not required, would in fact be pointless. He raised his arms in feigned exasperation and, with a dismissive wave of his right hand, said, "Do as you please, then; just as you please. It's alright by me." How could a trainer show more trust in his players than that? We repaid it by winning 4-1. Another significant aspect of my most successful period in the West German squad was that I was in the company of club colleagues: Wimmer, Vogts,

Heynckes, the goalkeeper Wolfgang Kleff and the Kremers twins were all in the squad too, if not on the pitch.

I had no personal problem with the national team. The issue was somewhat different and indirect. At Borussia I was the commander, playmaker and frontman, who just happened to be a little bit crazy. The side stuff did not matter if I was at the centre of the game. With the national XI, some of the Press coverage represented me as the eccentric and man-about-town who, it was grudgingly admitted, happened to play pretty good football as well. I do not see myself as having been the self-important anarchist in the midst of behind the times conformists. That was not the case at all. But I can see now how I must have rubbed others up the wrong way with my attitude and lifestyle, not to mention my egotism. I also understand better the way in which I was presented as the footballing herald of intellectuals' and the political Left's views. Nowadays, my taste for Pfleghar's *Klimbim* world and weakness for handsome, wickedly expensive sports cars can be seen to have symbolised anything but the Revolution. But, because football was no more than the core, rather than the whole of my life, and since, in spite of Berti's inspirational moment at Everton, I balked at the 'Eleven Friends' theory, my face did not entirely fit in the West German XI. Helmut Schön's view, which he liked to repeat during our difficult periods, was that, "Netzer is incapable of tailoring his game to our style of play". This was fair comment.

But it was not the whole story. The same Schön who deplored my reluctance to integrate into the team structure would have a word with me before a match: he wanted me to produce one of my Borussia Mönchengladbach performances. After such a display would come the criticism. Contrary to what has often been said, though, I liked Helmut Schön. We had at least one thing in common: he did not entirely fit in either. Football may yet to have become as brash as it currently is but, even so, Schön was a quiet man. He was cultured, an interesting conversationalist and a good thinker. I am not sure at all where he would slot in in the contemporary game. (Mind you, I don't know what niche I would find, and which players I would rub along with, myself. Probably one or two of the Jack the Lads, whose rough spots have yet to be ironed out – the reader can insert names here.)

The game in Seville was a low point. I played badly, as did the rest of the team, now in crisis. The Spaniards won 2-0. Franz Beckenbauer was not playing, because his young son was ill and he wanted to stay at home. Overath was out injured. Nothing was right in the team. A particular issue, that had gone unresolved for a while, was whom to play up front: Gerd Müller or Uwe Seeler, or the two of them together? In Seville they got in each other's way. There were only three months left before the world cup in Mexico. We were clearly not in the right frame of mind for it. All the same, I was confident that I would be on the plane.

I had not been selected for the England World Cup four years earlier although, following my debut in 1965 against Austria, which ended 4-1, I received plenty of praise and was selected for the next match. The climate in Cyprus was more testing than in Stuttgart; it was hot, dog day hot. We won 6-0 on a concrete hard pitch that was painful to play on. I did what I could but was weak. In the final game before the tournament, against England, I was muted again, as the hosts defeated us

1-0. From this moment Schön made Ulfert Schröder's friend, Wolfgang Overath his regular choice. I was in and out of the team, sometimes playing a minor role, on other occasions shining, such as on tour in South America, in a 2-2 draw with Brazil. It was a situation that favoured neither consistent performances nor long-lasting enjoyment.

Following the defeat in Seville, Schön gave an early morning press conference at the airport. The first we knew about it was from reading the newspapers. Unlike on previous occasions, he named names. Schön's judgement of myself was particularly unsparing. "Schoolboy errors" was the term he employed. Helmut Haller, who shared midfield duties, avoided censure, even though he had been at least as ineffective as me. Willi Schulz, after producing a blunt performance as libero, was spared. Nor was there any mention of Karl-Heinz Schnellinger, the defender whom the Spaniards had run by time and again. All criticism was targeted at the sluggish player who had provided no creative spark in midfield, Netzer. That pissed me off, to the point that I effectively announced my retirement. I said, "If Herr Schön thinks that I do not belong in the West German side, then he should dispense with me".

Was I being oversensitive? Had I overreacted? Perhaps. Maybe though my outburst was not such a bad thing to have occurred at this point. It finally brought my hesitant beginnings as an international to an end. Unlike Wolfgang Overath, I did not have a burning ambition to establish myself in the team. Which isn't to suggest that there was a dark side to Wolfgang's drive. He never aimed to gain the particular favour of the trainer; nor was he deceitful, going behind his teammates' backs. His ambition was limited to the pitch. Even if it may come as a surprise to many, we got along well. At any rate, I had no real difficulty in accepting my exclusion from Helmut Schön's Mexico squad. I was supported by Hennes Weisweiler, who was in Seville. What annoyed him most was that Schön should come down so hard on the least experienced member of the team. A key principle of Weisweiler's was that the coach ought not to pick out the most vulnerable member of the side for special criticism. Because to make a sacrifice of the one least able to defend himself is cowardly and spiteful, suggesting a fair amount of contempt for the idea of camaraderie. Helmut Schön's condemnation was all the more unexpected given that such motives were foreign to him.

While I do not think I was being oversensitive, my choice of words was not always good. There are a few wild remarks I have to own up to, such as, "Herr Schön doesn't exist as far as I am concerned"; "Herr Schön wants to stab me in the back"; "I will never wear the national team jersey again" … the kind of inappropriate words that are always better left unsaid. I am not usually someone who bears grudges; on this occasion my anger took a few days to subside. Anger is a poor counsellor. I did not spare Schön, accusing him of bad tactics, treachery and spinelessness. Today, I really do not know why I got so carried away.

An event I had not anticipated was a coffee and biscuits get-together in Frankfurt, which the DFB thought it was necessary to organise for all the players likely to be travelling to Mexico. Although I had announced my withdrawal, I was invited too. The idea was to thrash out the Seeler / Müller problem, as well as other tactical issues which I had not been alone in raising, at the same time as trying to do something to improve the overall mood of the squad and reduce the tension that had taken hold between Schön and the players. The real issue, however, was Netzer. My teammates, with Beckenbauer and Overath in the vanguard, and with even Uwe Seeler joining in, tried, with a combination of flattery and disapproval, to make me change my mind. West German football needed – really needed – me, they said. The idea that I might not want to play for the national team was almost incredible. It was also unimaginable that I could develop into an international star unless I was in it, delivering eye-catching performances.

To have such praise heaped on me was fairly extraordinary. Up until then I had only ever been looked upon as a component, not as a driving force of the team. All this attention did not make me feel in the least proud or flattered. It made me even more indignant. Inside I churned with the feeling that I had not made myself understood. Their wooing seemed to relate to the caricature which had built up in the public mind around myself: the cosseted star who expected to be garlanded with wraiths and carried high on a litter and who took offence like some shallow diva if he was not shown sufficient respect. It was probably because I was being manoeuvred into a role which I neither cared to play, nor knew how to, that I was so livid. Guilty maybe of frequent stubbornness, I was no diva, expecting to be courted.

Borussia understood this and stood by me. Both Weisweiler and Grashoff gave their support. A draft agreement forming the basis of a compromise was prepared. I handed it to Schön. In it I indicated my willingness, 'current concerns notwithstanding', to play for the national team in the future. Schön signed, and so, for now, ended an unedifying episode. It had been a storm in a teacup, the kind of drama that would never take place today. One can only ask why everyone allowed the situation to develop as far as it had? Was there nothing more important to discuss in the Republic than a row centring on a football player? I had taken a stand against what I considered to be unjustified criticism. At Borussia such disagreements were almost a daily occurrence. This one had escalated almost into a (minor) affair of state.

The saga of my bust-up with the national coach had an amusing epilogue. Not that the groin strain which I suffered at Malente, our training camp before leaving for the world cup, was especially funny. It may have been neither dramatic nor unusual but it was painful and slow to heal nevertheless. The continuing jibes of a section of the Press was 'humour' I could have done without. Still, I was not that bothered by the accusation of self-pity, made in the context of an apparent rapid backtracking from my initial revolt. I probably could have travelled to Mexico and, with the help of a few painkilling jabs, had a part to play in the tournament in the end. But would I really have helped the team that much? And, if I did not, the whole controversy that surrounded me was bound to have flared up again. Schön would come under attack, for having been persuaded to reach this accommodation with me; so would I, for not delivering performances which justified the rebellious stance I had taken. A week before the departure date I withdrew from the squad.

What state of mind did that leave me in? Did it pain me to be missing out again on a world cup, the high point of a player's career? No. All that hurt in the aftermath was my groin, leaving Borussia to start the season without me. I avoided spending the recuperation period, which dragged on for a while, yearning for my lost opportunity in the summer. Looking back with regret is not something I indulge in these days; nor was it my habit back then.

As for the final part of this story … I did go to Mexico – as a contributor for the newspaper *Bild*. In a radio interview I gave following the opening match, against Morocco, an unconvincing 2-1 victory for West Germany, I rounded on Schön's timid tactics. The following day we encountered one another in the West German compound. He was swimming in the hotel pool; I was standing above him at its edge. What, he scolded me, had got into my head, criticising the team in such a fashion. His own manner must have been extremely condescending for me to answer back, "Herr Schön, do you think a swimming pool is really the place for this kind of discussion?" With which I left. Today, I still find it hard to believe that relations between us had reached this point.

At the tournament there was plenty of speculation surrounding me. Once again Ulfert Schröder, whose paper, incidentally, had run the story that my 'groin strain' was only a tactical ploy to attract pity, took the lead. He suggested that, even in the stands, I had suffered like a dog. Having missed out on the special experience of a world cup, he continued, I could not expect to see my market value soar as the others might. It is true that because of the unbearable heat in Mexico, which rose to over fifty degrees on the pitch, I was feeling as wretched as a dog. My urge to go beneath the stands and have a good pant grew.

As to the others making more of their talents, it is also true that I did not experience Beckenbauer's or Overath's kind of career. Maybe I could have done, if I had always maintained top fitness levels. Maybe, but I am not sure how. Beckenbauer had ferocious willpower; Overath's dedication came close to fanaticism. Mine was not much less strong, but channelled in other directions too. My body had to comply with the demands I made of it in pursuit of a life outside football, particularly the endurance required on nights out with Pfleghar. Most footballers are not so different from chess players who, years later, can still recall every move of a match they participated in. They have total recall of certain moves, goals and missed opportunities. For whatever reason, I do not. I have to browse through match reports to jog my memory.

That is with the exception of three matches: the big three. For these I do not need to consult the archives. The dates are safely stored in my memory.

The details are clear, too. In game number one our line-up consisted of: Kleff, Sieloff, Vogts, Luggi Müller, Bleidick, Bonhoff, Wimmer, Kulik, Heynckes, le Fevre and Netzer. Our opponents were Vieri, Oriali, Giubertoni, Burgnich, Facchetti, Fabbian, Corso, Bedin, Mazzola, Jair and Boninsegna. Eleven legends. Taken together, the Inter Milan side of 20 October 1971. The previous evening, as we ate together at our training ground, we whispered these names with respect, though not fearfully. We were West German champions. We knew what we were capable of, even as we appreciated that our chances against Inter were, realistically, slim. Up until shortly before their arrival, the Milanese, we had heard, believed that Mönchengladbach was a satellite town of Munich.

Two weeks earlier I had sustained ligament damage. This is the type of injury which must be allowed to heal very slowly, doing almost nothing, or at least only moving about cautiously. But what if the leg in question belongs to a wheeling and dealing twenty-seven-year-old who has grown accustomed to hopping in and out of fast cars? Having set my right leg in plaster, the doctor cautioned me to take proper care of it. Unfortunately, the good sense which he wanted me to show has never featured amongst my many excellent qualities. Somewhat bruised, I hauled myself into the Ferrari and roared off. After a few days the plaster seemed to have performed its job. Besides, my leg was stiff. If I was to run around a bit against Inter, I needed to do some fitness routines. We were playing them in mid-week. On the Monday the cast came off.

Two hours before kick-off our manager, Grashoff was still arguing with ARD's Ernst Huberty. At the time, broadcasting rights were negotiated on a match-by-match basis. Huberty proposed 60,000 marks, to which Grashoff replied he would accept the offer if it were increased by 11% – an additional 6,600 marks. Once more: 6,600 marks. Huberty however was not prepared to pay this ridiculously small sum. With both men refusing to budge, the TV screens went blank. Italian television showed only the briefest of highlights. Jupp Heynckes owns a copy, but I have never seen them.

As captain, I exchanged club pennants with Mazzola. The kick-off whistle blew. Those were the last two moments that resembled an ordinary football match. What followed was magical and tragical, a game described afterwards as a 'successful rebellion', an 'eyeful of protest and pop, mixed up with rage, radicalism and religion'. That's fine by me ... one can interpret a great deal from football, which is perhaps part of its fascination. Beneath its surface lies who knows what ... Luckily, the players themselves do not need to get involved in all of that; it would probably be detrimental to them if they spent too much time considering what reaction their performance might produce amongst the game's followers.

On eight minutes, I hit a long ball, the sort that can easily go astray but which can also come off to within an inch. This one hit the mark. Wimmer collected it and moved it onto Jupp Heynckes who did the business. A signal of our intention that tonight nobody nor anything could resist us? That's right. The craziness had just begun. From this moment, the stadium spotlights shone on us alone. Boninsegna's equaliser after nineteen minutes was against the run of play. It did not threaten to stem the Borussia tide at all. We kept coming, playing like we had never played before, on the kind of European night when fantasy football becomes reality. Ulrike le Fevre made it 2-1, then 3-1. I scored. Heynckes scored again. HT: 5-1.

It ought to have been a joyful dressing room. It would have been only natural for us to be sitting in a daze as we tried to get our heads around what we had, nevertheless, just achieved. The look on Hennes Weisweiler's face is not hard to picture, and one can easily imagine his big heart brimming over. It would have been no surprise if, tears welling up, his eyes became moist with happiness, knowing that what he had witnessed in the last forty-five minutes was for real. But the scene in the dressing room was not one of blissful delirium. Some even seemed to be slipping into dejection. Weisweiler and I were on our feet, agitatedly moving in all directions, trying to impress a matter of urgency on Grashoff: we wanted the official doctor to go to the Milan dressing room to examine Boninsegna. But when he arrived, it was in vain:

the door was locked. Behind it, lay / sat / stood Boninsegna, letting out theatrical whimpers of pain and smirking with schadenfreude. He might even have been dancing, knowing that he had robbed us of our moment.

At 2-1 there had been a harmless touchline tussle between him and Luggi Müller, a difference of opinion about whose throw-in it was. We were in full flow at this point; unplayable in fact, as Boninsegna must have realised. I was in an advanced midfield position, waiting for the throw-in, when he collapsed onto the ground. An empty coke can thrown from the stands had lightly brushed the midfielder. From his reaction you might have thought he had been swiped by Muhammad Ali and was on the brink of losing consciousness. He made a big performance of calling for the Red Cross, who stretchered him off to the changing room. Pure theatre. Poor quality drama, too. As soon as I saw Inter's coach, Invernizzi protesting to the linesman, however, I knew that Boninsegna's disgusting performance was intended to achieve a purpose.

Its full consequences were not suspected by any of us. Otherwise, we would not have resumed from where we had left off at forty-five minutes. What can one achieve in an exhilarated frenzy? Everything that good sense rejects and which logic says is impossible. Shortly after half-time, I scored the most beautiful goal of my career. The move began with a long – thirty, forty metres – ball I played to Jupp Heynckes. I ran after it myself, proof that I was not in fact myself this night, but in a state of exultation. Jupp passed back to me. Although I was ready to shoot with my left foot, I took the ball on the outside of my right boot and fired from a tight angle over the keeper into the top corner. I saluted the heavens, my eyes shut.

In the eightieth minute an appreciative Weisweiler pulled me off. With a penalty converted by Sieloff, the game ended 7-1.

The excitement took a while to die down. Sitting in the stands, and also at the top of the Bundesliga table, were the Schalke XI, our next opponents. After the game, a reporter wanted to know what they thought of our performance. Were they trembling at the knees with fear? Apparently, they had failed to grasp what they had just seen. They said they would not let themselves fall behind against us – they were not Inter. That was true. Three days later we scored seven more goals. The only difference in the scoreline was that, unlike the Italians, Schalke failed to score themselves.

A further two days later the spell was broken, giving way to an unpleasant reality.

This was crouching, ready to pounce in the St. Gotthart hotel in Zurich. Being captain, I travelled as part of the Mönchengladbach contingent to UEFA's arbitration of the can throwing incident. On arrival, we sat in reception, without anyone taking much notice of us. The idea occurred to me that we were taken for passersby who had stopped for a coffee. The welcome given to the Milanese by the UEFA personnel was different. It was as though they were old acquaintances; which, in fact, they were. The Inter vice chairman, Prisco chatted with evident enjoyment to Sergio Zorzi, chairman of the UEFA committee. Our bad luck stood in stark contrast to the fun he was having. Zorzi delivered his judgement: the 7-1 result was voided because, "while not guilty, the club was responsible". The first inroads into our fantasy had been made.

It was further encroached on by reality when we travelled to Milan for the return match. Our keeper Kleff, Berti Vogts and

Hartwig Bleidick were all in plaster after a 2-4 defeat. Before it, Weisweiler read out his team selection in the dressing room. It was a much too offensive formation for my taste. Inter, in my view, were not only going to be motivated to win but would be determined to efface their 1-7 defeat. Therefore, it was pretty clear to me that we needed to be braced for the kind of storm we might never have encountered before. Weisweiler did not want to listen. We had one of our more heated disagreements. Eventually I shouted at him, "You have not got the first idea about football!" In front of the whole team. For the following week Berti Vogts had to once again act as go-between. "Berti, tell your captain …"; "Berti, tell your head coach …"

Reality had not done with us yet, when the re-match of our home game against Inter got underway in the Olympic stadium in Berlin. 'Game' is perhaps not the right word. Rather than play, Milan's intention was to step on anything that moved. Sieloff missed a penalty. Plenty of other fouls went unobserved. A particularly obvious one was Boninsegna's scything down of Luggi Müller as both the end of the game and our elimination, with the score standing at 0-0, approached. We had been taught a lesson because of our naivety, a nasty masterclass during the last two encounters in the linked subjects of hard-bitten cynicism, street smarts and professionalism.

The second of my unforgettable matches came six months later. It was the first leg of West Germany's European Championship quarter-final against England, which took place at Wembley on 29 April 1972. Our line-up was Sepp Maier in goal; Georg Schwarzenbeck and Horst-Dieter Höttges in central defence; in front of them Franz Beckenbauer; Paul Breitner and my mate Hacki Wimmer were the full-backs, while Jürgen Grabowski and Siggi Held played on the wings; Gerd Müller was in his accustomed position as centre-forward; I joined Uli Hoeneß in midfield. The German national team had yet to beat our hosts on their soil. Berti Vogts was out injured, as was Wolfgang Overath. It is true that the experiment of playing Overath and me together had not worked. The latest attempt, in a recent international in Copenhagen, had made that clear once again. As soon as the whistle blew, we were both trying to get hold of the ball in midfield to direct the game. The confusion became embarrassing. On the other hand, the combination of two systems, FC Bayern's and ours, worked well. It was the melding of two mature and successful teams. The players from each club carried on playing in their habitual style, rather than experimenting unnecessarily out on the field. With the Borussia boys I knew who I was dealing with; the role I had to play was clear; everything contributed to an elevated degree of self-assurance. Bayern provided the rest, not least Franz Beckenbauer and Gerd Müller, two outstanding players.

All the same, not long before the Denmark fixture, Franz and I nearly came to blows. Not much more was required for me to have taken a pop at him. The ongoing debate at the time concerned who was the boss out on the pitch: Beckenbauer, Overath or even myself? That does not mean that we and the other players openly discussed the subject. Instead, it could be sensed, via gestures and minor details, where the power within the team lay. There was nothing unusual in this. At some point during a match against Norway, which ended in a 7-1 victory for us, we were awarded a free kick. At Borussia and, I thought, for West Germany too, free kicks were my preserve. Slowly and deliberately, I would place the ball just so. Some thought this ritual was pure theatre. They found it affected, almost vainglorious. In fact, I needed the moment of quiet, poise, concentration. While it lasted, the grass may or may not have stirred. I knew that no rustling blades could give the ball a gentle nudge, since I had made a small clearing around it. If someone had spoken to me, I would not have heard them. Beckenbauer said nothing to me. Oblivious to everything outside my bubble, I was stepping back from the ball, still inclined, when, moving in the opposite direction, Franz took two steps forward and virtuosically stroked it into the back of the net. Whoever wants to see symbolism in this little scene will no doubt find it.

Meanwhile, though, we Mönchengladbachers began to count for something in the national team. There were one or two matches in which our influence was decisive, for example a majestic 3-0 win against Turkey.

Beckenbauer pilfering my free kick was what you might call a throwing down of the gauntlet. Fortunately, we did not take the matter any further, just as the question of hierarchy was not one which ever came out into the open. I was aware that, in order for us to achieve success as a team, an accord was necessary. We were competing in the European Championship and we wanted to win it. The Wembley display was to be the consequence of our historic compromise – perhaps too grand a way of describing the agreement, that hardly required day and night long sessions to work out, which Franz and I came to on the basis of our mutual talents and achievements. He no longer played in midfield. For a while now he had operated from a deeper position – that of the libero, a role to which he brought considerable refinement. The danger was that, when he roamed upfield, we would end up getting in each other's way. The solution had already been worked out in those endless discussions with Hennes Weisweiler, mentioned previously, about how I could operate best within the team. Every side Borussia came up against had a player whose sole instructions were to stick with me. There were many matches in which I had the impression that my marker, being so intent on performing the task he had been set, of observing and keeping up with me wherever I moved, did not really appreciate what was going on in the wider game. In order to shake myself loose of these attentions, not least because they made playing the game quite oppressive for me, I suggested to Weisweiler that we should mix our game up. With Hans-Jürgen Wittkamp this is what we did. For periods of the game he would fill the libero role, while I kept the ball moving around in midfield; then we would swap.

During the preparations for our encounter with England I talked this over with Beckenbauer. "If it worked with Wittkamp, then with you it will be even better." Far from me to criticise Hans-Jürgen Wittkamp, who is a very good footballer – but not in the same class as Franz Beckenbauer.

Franz agreed. So did the coach. It was the time when Schön more or less let the team decide what it considered to be right, the period when my relationship with him was at its most constructive. "Do it," he said, and we obliged.

The probability of defeat to England, nevertheless, seemed high to us. In the final minutes before the game began, Franz and I were sitting next to one another in the dressing room. "If we concede less than five, we can count it as a success," I said to him. His view was no different. Then we ran out into this wonderful stadium, onto this wonderful pitch, and from the word go what we had talked over, worked in practice. Without words, telegraphed gestures or mishaps. Uli Hoeneß put us in the lead, as I produced a dazzling performance, 'ably assisted,' wrote one English newspaper, 'by Wimmer and Beckenbauer'. This was probably the only occasion when anyone has described Beckenbauer as being my right-hand man – I appreciate it.

England managed an equaliser. Not long after, in the eighty-fifth minute, Siggi Held was fouled just inside the box and we were awarded a penalty. Now it was Müller declining to step up to the spot. "I am not going to take it. You take it, Günter." I could tell that the saga of the Everton penalty shootout still clung to me. The suspicion that I had run away when the pressure mounted was not true, as Weisweiler, my teammates and I knew. But I was not thinking about that. One does not think much at such intense moments. I had played a big game; I was feeling as sure of myself as I ever have. I took the ball. My shot went past Banks into the bottom left-hand corner. The joy I felt was beyond words. A substantial part of it was shrugging off the tension that had accumulated with years of criticism. The final score, thanks to a Gerd Müller goal four minutes later, was 3-1. We had beaten England at Wembley! I had not just played my part, I was the star of the show. Beckenbauer's and my pre-match chat had been a major exercise in self-deception.

There are worse moments in life.

6

Deputising for Christian Kulik

Being a man of culture, Helmut Schön felt the national team should visit the theatre. His suggestion of such an extracurricular outing met with a typically mixed response at our training camp. While it is always good to get away from its confines, within which you see the same old faces and your existence remains rigidly focused on football, a trip to the theatre would not be a professional's automatic choice as the way to spend his free time.

In early 1973 mine was hardly a haven of peace already. I was torn in fact. Hannelore Girrulat and me were, how can I say, hanging in there. To try and maintain my equilibrium, I would frequently spend time at the very basic self-contained apartment I had at my parents' house. Or I would stay out late with friends, which did not help my relationship with Hannelore either.

At the same time, the successful side we had built at Borussia was heading off in different directions. Horst Köppel returned to Swabia to play for VfB Stuttgart again, Ulrik le Fevre went to FC Bruges, while Peter Dietrich and Herbert Laumen had both completed their moves to Werder Bremen. At the start of the season, I felt sore at having finally been left out of the package. Things were not right amongst those who had stayed. I was frequently injured. When I did play, my performances were well below par. As before, my non-footballing pastimes received the blame. Relations with Weisweiler had taken a new turn for the worse. In short, nothing was really right anymore, with one exception, about which nothing was yet known – or so I thought until this Thursday night we spent at the Berlin theatre, before playing Brazil.

During the interval I noticed Helmut Schön and a journalist holding an animated conversation, from which the coach soon disengaged himself. He wore a menacing expression as he tramped towards me. "Is it true, Günter, is it honestly true that you are moving to Real Madrid?" he fumed. Naturally, he was concerned about his team. Wolfgang Overath, the protégé, had been sacrificed so that he could organise the side around me. We had just won the European Championship playing soccer of a kind, it was said, that had never been seen before in Germany. It was a light-footed, rhythmic football having little to do with the traditional virtues of the German game, repetitively drilled home down the years. Reporting of our stylish achievements was not confined to the sports section; the op-ed pages were full of it. This did not mean so much to the players, but to Schön, cultivated man that he was, it was a source of delight. And now everything appeared to be placed in jeopardy by my prospective move to the Spanish capital.

Schön's fears were not unfounded. Football had yet to become the global game it is today. Even within Europe, awareness of the other national leagues was minimal. Spain seemed far-off.

In West Germany television coverage of La Liga was almost non-existent – a segment on 'Sports from Around the World' lasting a few fleeting seconds, that was all. Whether or not a foreign club would grant an international player leave to turn out for the West German side remained unclear. Schön had not forgotten his battles with the Italians, fought over Karl-Heinz Schnellinger and Helmut Haller when they were playing in Serie A. He now feared having to fight them all over again on account of myself. The situation had been provided for in my case with a clause incorporated into the contract, which applied to all West Germany fixtures – apart from those against Spain. At this point though Schön was unaware of it.

There was another aspect to his anger towards, or, rather, disappointment in me. Being the last to find out about my plans must have counted as a snub to him. Slowly but surely, we had become more confident with one another. I was grateful to him simply because he granted us his trust. It was not always the case that footballers were treated like adults. I had also received the benefit of his advice at the beginning of my career, when I asked him whether or not I should join Limoges. He was sad that I decided against confiding in him on this occasion. I understand that, although I was innocent of any breach of trust. Madrid, Borussia and I had agreed that the transfer should only be made public once the cup final between Borussia and 1. FC Köln had been played on 23 June. Without telling me, the two clubs had since then decided to leak news of it – with the result that Schön held me for a 'gentleman' whose actual, untrustworthy nature was revealed.

Today such a situation would be passed off by the parties with a laugh, as simply a minor irritation between coach and player.

At the time it implicitly gave rise to a sacking. Given the status of the national coach – almost that of a national institution – he expected to at least be informed of such far-reaching players' decisions. I had failed to do this. Even if it was the clubs rather than I who had brought the situation about, it corresponded with the idea people had of me. Back at the training camp from the theatre that evening the atmosphere was not good.

For a while now, Berti Vogts had been privy to my Real Madrid plans. Even before, he could tell that I would not be staying at Borussia for much longer. Two weeks ahead of the theatre trip, we drove to Eintracht Braunschweig for a Bundesliga encounter. I trundled along behind the team bus in my Ferrari. My reason for travelling separately was that I wanted to make a quick getaway after the match, in order to return to Mönchengladbach as rapidly as I could for the opening of my new restaurant at 8 pm. As I later heard, this solo journey was the main topic of conversation on the team bus heading back after a poor showing, myself included, against Braunschweig. Beer was drunk; the tenor mounted. The turn the discussion took, until Berti got up to tell the others they were mad, was that the team would be better off without me. In which case, he prophesied, (a) dark days lay ahead; (b) if they kept on like this, I would indeed be on my way. He still did not know the deal was being negotiated; talks had in fact only just begun. He could sense my restlessness though. When the transfer was settled, I told my trusted friend. So, as the news of it broke during the theatre interval, he already knew.

The next day in Berlin came a call from Mönchengladbach. It was an emergency call from my father, telling me my mother was close to death. A stroke. There had been no prior warning.

She had seemed perfectly well. In the family we talked about my departure for Spain. Typically, my father was proud, and I could tell that my mother was happy too. Any remaining concerns she may have had about her boy going away were lessened as Hannelore was coming too. She may not have grown any fonder of Hannelore; the important thing was that I had some female support, not who the particular woman providing it was. About the difficulties in our relationship, she knew little or nothing. Her attention was more focused on planning visits to Spain. The first, which would take place in the summer, had already been sorted out. The prospect of flying for the first time excited rather than alarmed her. She was in fine health when I set off for Berlin and the training camp. My mother was sixty-one. That evening she died. Fortunately, she did not have to suffer too much.

One of my characteristics, and I do not know whether I should be glad or disappointed to possess it, is that I soon recover from life's blows, too many of which I have been lucky enough to avoid, and turn to the future. Maybe this is a way of protecting myself from giving too much away, or of lingering too long over my feelings. If this is considered emotionally detached or excessively rational by others, I don't mind. It is the way I am, which has served me well whenever I have had to deal with sorrow and hardship. What shocked and angered me though, in the days after Mother's death, were the newspaper headlines and articles claiming that my move to Spain lay behind it. What cheek and presumption! Those with whom I had yet to exchange a single word, or others, who knew me only superficially in my capacity as a player and from interviewing me on television, without any knowledge of the relationship between me and my mother or of her happiness about my plans to move, offered their analyses. It is only because they knew nothing regarding medicine that they could invent such far-fetched explanations. I think it goes without saying that feelings of respect were foreign to such people.

A week later came the cup final at the Düsseldorfer Rheinstadion, the third game there is no need for any rustling around in the archives in order for me to remember. I took a couple of days off training to be with my father. We both agreed that I ought to play in the final. I wanted my farewell to Mönchengladbach to take place on the pitch. I know that is what my mother would have wanted too.

In the middle of the week I began training again. That is to say, I wanted to begin training again. When I returned to the practice ground however, Hennes Weisweiler barely paid me any notice. Rather as if I had ceased to exist for him now. The others trained; I was sidelined. It was Geroweiher all over again, only this time I had no ball provided for me by Mother. I made a few circuits of the pitch, went through some conditioning and exercise routines and ran up and down the stadium steps. Weisweiler cut me. Not a single word from the man with the big heart, who could be extraordinarily insensitive when he wanted. I asked myself whether he considered I was incapable of playing because of my mother's passing away? Or, could it have been his way of handling the anger, and maybe even the sadness, he felt at my leaving for Real Madrid – 'Let's just get rid of the 'slow asshole' and take it from there'? Or did he actually believe the vindictive headlines which suggested my departure was the cause of her death? Many years later he confided to me

108

that he wanted to shield me. But from what? I did not have the feeling that the fans had turned against me.

For several weeks I had not been in the best physical shape. Now there was a psychological factor to take into account as well. This meant there were objective reasons for leaving me out of the cup final. I can appreciate that. But in this way? Weisweiler knew by now that I was capable of handling difficulties. Drastic situations tended to bring out the best in me. Some of them were ones he himself had put me in. He should have appreciated that since that long-ago night at Everton, when I had been accused of ducking my responsibilities, a change had taken place. I had grown into the role that was expected of me, playing my part in the development of a new Borussia team, as the old one dispersed. From time to time, I even orchestrated the national side's performances. So, my ability to cope with stress had been tested, and never more brutally than by Weisweiler on the occasion we travelled to Italy for a friendly against AS Roma.

Because of the anticipated takings, friendlies were frequent. Having broken a tooth a few days earlier, I was not going to be able to take part in this particular one. Two days before travelling, Weisweiler summoned me to his office. "This is a bit silly, Günter," he said. "OK, you cannot play, but you can come along with us all the same. It will give you something new to see. Rome is always worth a visit." I was surprised by his friendliness; there was something a bit odd about what he was proposing. Would we have time to be tourists, or even get the opportunity to drink a cappuccino in the Piazza Navona? Still, I happily accepted.

A few hours before the kick-off Weisweiler asked me for a word. This time he wore a serious expression. It looked as though he was carrying the weight of the world on his shoulders. A contract for the friendly had been signed. One of the terms was that I should be playing. Besides, the Borussia Mönchengladbach line-up, Günter Netzer included, had now been announced in the Roman press. Well, he wanted to know, could I play?

With my broken tooth, the idea was alarming. But Weisweiler had taken this into account. The doctor had assured him that a numbing injection could be administered. "I am afraid there is no choice," the coach told me. "You must play or we get no money." The failure of the contract to mention the possibility that I might pick up an injury made me defiant. I was boiling with anger, knowing that Weisweiler had been planning this from the outset. The anger motivated me to play one of the best games of my entire career.

By half-time the pain was too much. When the whistle blew, I crept carefully towards the dressing room, in an attempt to soothe it. This made no difference. Still, I felt confident that Weisweiler would now show mercy and pull me off. I was mistaken. As I entered the changing room, the doctor was ready waiting with his syringe. The violence with which he jabbed it into my skin got me swearing like a sergeant-major. At least it killed the pain. My second half performance reached the same heights as the first. The following day the *Rheinishchen Post* journalist, Wilhelm August Hurtmanns, who had been a prisoner of war in Italy, translated some of the match reports for me. The praise was unanimous. One of the pieces bore the headline, 'The White Pele'.

What has this story got to do with Weisweiler's disregard for me in the days leading up to the cup final? The answer is

I resented not only that he was no longer interested in me, but that he deliberately ignored the hard sacrifices I had made for the team and the club. His curtness was not merely a response to my poor fitness but a means of brusquely signalling that, as far as he was concerned, my time at Mönchengladbach and our shared adventure were now both consigned to history. I had no appetite for scenes nor for a battle of wills. In spite of all our differences, I knew then, as I do today, how much I owed to Weisweiler. I sincerely wished to have a peaceable parting of the ways. Instead, I was burning with rage.

A final training session took place on the Friday. It was during the Saturday team stroll before the match that he eventually plucked up the courage to tell me what I already suspected: "I will not be playing you in the final". Earlier in the day there had been a bit of a stir. It involved Berti Vogts rather than myself. We had all had breakfast together. I sat next to Weisweiler as usual, without him addressing a single word to me. At about 11 o'clock he called for Berti, to tell him that he would be captain. Berti obviously realised this meant I was not going to be playing. He protested vigorously. Under no circumstances, he declared, should I be denied the opportunity to play my last game for Borussia after so many years and after so much success, for which I was not just jointly, but chiefly responsible. The good and trusted Berti Vogts, in other words, refused the order. An announcement was immediately made that Hacki Wimmer was to captain the side. My response when, walking together, Weisweiler told me of his solitary decision, was that it was not what the fans wanted. I also said I felt it was a very courageous decision. He did not reply. He forced the pace instead and left me in his wake.

On returning to the team hotel, I went up to my room to pack my bag. Downstairs, the others sat at a big table in the hotel restaurant, the same as before any match. Some played cards, a few chatted amongst themselves, while those who needed a moment of calm before such a big game sat silently with their thoughts. Weisweiler's decision had not yet been announced when I came down. "Well, then, I am off now. All the best. Good luck today, and in the future."

I was honestly ready to leave the Mönchengladbachers that unceremoniously. It is what Weisweiler wanted.

There was a great commotion, everyone talking at the same time. I did not detect any sympathy for Weisweiler's decision. Someone said I could not simply steal away like that. "We have spent almost ten years together. At least sit on the substitutes' bench. Even if the coach doesn't, we may need you." Berti Vogts and Jupp Heynckes persuaded me to return upstairs, where the three of us carried on talking. Berti said that in such circumstances he understood this abrupt manner of parting. Jupp, however, stubbornly repeated: "Just take your place with the other substitutes. Please. That's all you need to do. The coach might not need you; we do. Please." I began unpacking.

When the team lined up before kick-off and the PA announcer introduced each player, there was a near riot in the Rheinstadion. The fans started chanting my name. A camera crew parked itself in front of me. It recorded every reaction of mine throughout the first half. With such an unbelievable spectacle being provided by both 1. FC Köln and Borussia – still my Borussia – out on the pitch, they were not short of material. We were playing in the same exhilarating fashion as against

Inter; the difference was that on this occasion we were matched by our opponents. The action was hot, red hot, a relentless drama provided by perfectly balanced adversaries playing at a flat-out tempo. Wimmer gave us the lead. Fifteen minutes later, shortly before half-time, Neumann equalised. At some point Heynckes missed a penalty. That first half particularly stands out as some of the best, perhaps even the best, football I have ever seen. Nevertheless, the anti-Weisweiler – and pro-Netzer – mood in the stadium continued to grow. This did not escape him. The thing was it had become impossible to justify taking any player off. Each had given everything and surpassed himself in the process. If any were substituted at this point of the game, he could consider himself, with justification, to have been treated shabbily.

Regardless, Weisweiler came over to me at half-time. "Now you can play, Netzer," he said. 'Netzer': our dispute, the last ever, had brought us to second name terms again.

"Me? No … really, no. I cannot help you in this game. Better to make do without me."

I was giving a spontaneous, unreflected reaction but even now I think it was the right one. A substitute joining in the game would have needed a long while, perhaps right up until full-time to adapt to its tempo. Every player was in a state of almost indescribable euphoria, on a different stratosphere, adrenalin pumped to the max. I would be gatecrashing. At this juncture, Weisweiler's notion was plainly absurd. Not least because of my poor physical condition. What could I hope to contribute in a match being played at such a blistering pace? It was not hard to tell what Weisweiler's motivation was in making his volte face. Rather than being based on a sound tactical judgement, it was, albeit subconsciously, dictated by anger and the desire to take revenge. His suggestion was fair neither to me nor to the others. As for the fans, it was a populist sop in their direction. "No, I am not going to play, coach," I told him.

I will not, however, accept that Weisweiler deliberately wanted to make a sacrifice of me, that he was prepared to risk defeat in order to pin the blame for it on Günter Netzer, traitor to the fatherland. Not only won't I, I cannot accept it. He was neither disloyal nor a hypocrite; such treachery was foreign to his character. But concerning this game, first in the preparation for it and now at half-time, he was acting not only out of character but also at odds with all of his footballing know-how. He must have been very unhappy with me.

As the teams came on for the second half, and the crowd could see me taking up the same position on the touchline, the whistling chorus broke out again. Weisweiler was huddled on his bench; I was huddled on mine. Six feet separated us. Out on the pitch the game resumed where it had left off. Had it not already existed, the well-worn cliché that there are certain matches which neither side deserves to lose would have had to be invented to describe this one. Köln had a string of chances; so did we. But the ball refused to go in the back of the net for either side. Up above, the sun shone brightly.

At the end of normal time, I circulated amongst the players. I was not thinking anything. My only concern was to offer a little encouragement as I handed around drinks. While I was doing this, Christian Kulik wandered – or staggered – over in my direction. Recently turned twenty, he had run out of gas. The unremitting sun had parched him. He stumbled and fell down directly in front of me. "I cannot go on, cannot run any more, I just cannot," he sighed. At the same time, the crowd's roar grew louder: "Netzer! Netzer! Netzer!"

The sequence of events which followed took place in a fantastic daze. As fiction, it would have seemed so incredible, that a screenplay adaptation could expect to be dismissed by studios throughout the world as pure kitsch. I pulled off my tracksuit top and trousers, tossing them down on the substitutes bench. "Now I will play," I said, as I passed by the squatting Weisweiler. I can no longer recall the exact emotion I experienced as I headed towards the pitch. There was no triumphalism. Perhaps it was just satisfaction to be playing. Weisweiler did not react. He continued looking out at the pitch where the players were already lined up. Not a word, nor any other token of acknowledgement. The whistle was already blowing for extra time.

I do remember the prolonged barrage of noise as I emerged onto the playing field and into the opposition half. The next instant I had the ball. I dribbled it forward and passed to Rainer Bonhof, continuing my run into the channel where I automatically knew he ought to play the return ball. For a year now we had been practising this move in training, but the wall pass with Rainer had never come off. He must have been waiting for the right moment, because he could not have played a more perfectly weighted through ball, to arrive at the precise point I was galloping to. One, two strides and I was inside the Köln penalty area, onto it. When I hit the ball it was with offspin; it was not a perfect strike. But if I had connected with it any better, it probably would have barrelled forward within easy reach of their keeper, Gerhard Welz. Or, alternatively, it would have soared over the goal, out of the stadium and plopped dolefully into the Rhine. Instead, it ended up in the top left corner, far beyond Welz. Goal! Of the phenomenal kind which cries out for an exclamation mark and earned me the Goal of the Year award, to accompany my second Player of the Year trophy. It was my farewell present to Borussia, delivered as the final credits rolled.

It had been a happy ending for me – but not for Hennes Weisweiler. I felt genuinely sorry for the coach. A volley not only of criticism, but of malice and mockery, was spewed all over him. He did not deserve any of it. It was he, after all, who had led the club to the cup final, just as he had led it from provincial insignificance on the Lower Rhine to the heights of West German and European football. It was his vision of how the game ought to be played that lay behind our new, celebrated status.

When the final whistle blew, he disappeared down the tunnel, without saying a word to me, nor, I believe, casting a look in my direction. I do not know what he said down there in the dressing room, nor whether he began celebrating with the others. Because I had to give one interview after another, by the time I was able to go and shower, Weisweiler was on the team bus heading back to Mönchengladbach. Nothing personal was intended by this. I had driven to Düsseldorf by myself. I only mention it to make the point that we never had the opportunity after the game to speak directly to one another. Mind you, whether he would have taken advantage of such an opportunity is another matter. I'm not sure he would have. In the evening came the traditional celebration in Mönchengladbach's Kaiser-Friedrich-Halle with the team and fans, civic dignitaries, Weisweiler and I. Still, no communication between the two of us, nor between him and anybody really. My teammates then came along with me to 'Lovers Lane' to carry on celebrating victory over the *Kölner*, always a special occasion for Borussia. My departure was treated no differently to that of any other player.

The next contact I had with Weisweiler came two years later, when he was coach at Barcelona. There was still no mention of the cup final. And nor was there on a memorable evening, long after my retirement, spent with Berti Vogts and Weisweiler at his Düsseldorf local, the 'Walliser Stuben'. He invited us to address him as '*du*'. Some may find it strange, but neither of us could do this – after all these years, our respect for him remained too great.

Such a cosy trio was never in the offing on the night of the cup final. Weisweiler did not choose this moment to visit 'Lovers Lane'. My father was there. No Mother, of course. A few tears were shed. Three days later I flew to Madrid.

7

The Monarch's Club

"Your passport, please," the customs official at Düsseldorf Airport requested. The plane taking me high over Frankfurt to Madrid was scheduled to depart in forty-five minutes. After many years of Spanish isolation, I was to be officially presented there as the first foreign footballer to perform in La Liga again. On top of which, I was the first German footballer to be heading abroad since the founding of the Bundesliga. No wonder it was a media event. Hundreds of journalists awaited me in Madrid. "Herr Netzer, your passport, please," the customs official asked a second time. But however much Herr Netzer rustled around in his jacket pockets and hand luggage, he would not find his passport – which had got left behind in Mönchengladbach.

There was no time remaining to go and pick it up. I had my driver's licence on me, which should be enough, I considered, for Customs to let me out of the Federal Republic. "We know who you are. That is not the problem. You will not be allowed into Spain," said the man behind the counter. This meant I would have to cancel my appointment with the Press and

Real Madrid's hierarchy. I did not see what else I could do, embarrassing though the situation was.

For weeks the news had been full of my move. My supposed treachery was widely discussed, as, in a more shameful way, was my alleged blame for Mother's death. Another aspect was the extravagance of the Spaniards' big money move for me. And now, when it came to actually making it, it appeared Herr Star was not capable of travelling by himself. So, straightaway, I was going to be pigeonholed as a pampered diva all over again … fantastic!

I called Madrid, where I was put through to one of the club's English-speaking officials. I hemmed and hawed, stammering something about cup final related stress. My unveiling in Madrid would have to be put back twenty-four hours, I suggested.

There was laughter at the other end of the line. "Listen, old boy, who do you think we are? And who do you think you are, playing a prank on us?" I couldn't help feeling that I was about to receive a serious ticking-off. But when the official resumed, he seemed more amused than angry. "Regarding us: we are Real Madrid. That's right. Real Madrid. Different to Borussia Mönchengladbach. Not a provincial outfit. There is no way that Real Madrid is going to call off its appointment with Günter Netzer." Those were his words. Still, what was I to do? "Yes," I accepted, "but I am not going to be allowed into your country." There was more laughter down the line. "Come on now, we are Real, you understand? Real Madrid. Just make sure you get on that plane out of Germany. One call from us will be enough to avoid any problems at this end, just because you have not brought your passport." Now I understood.

This is what Real Madrid, the high and mighty of the game, is like. First and foremost, mighty. Not just within the footballing sphere, either. In 1973, Franco's dictatorship was still in place. It may have been the year when, for health reasons, he had officially designated Juan Carlos to succeed himself; that did not mean Spain had become a free country. What counted was power. And, as I stood in a telephone booth at Düsseldorf Airport, although I still knew precious little about politics, I could sense the power which emanated from Real Madrid. It did not matter that the club was going through a lean spell on the pitch, it retained the mythical status which allowed it, with either the stroke of a pen or via a telephone call, to place itself above even a dictator's laws.

The flight was uneventful. At the airport a club deputation was waiting to greet me by the customs cabin. I was asked about how things were in West Germany, what the weather was like – just small talk, nothing concerning my passport. We drove to the stadium where I was led to the reception room in which post-match press conferences were held. Quite some press conferences too, compared to those at Mönchengladbach, which were attended by a small core of journalists, most of whom showed up on an almost weekly basis. There was a commotion as I was guided in. Snappers snapped. The noise created by a hundred or more reporters rose. I had, without doubt, ended up in an entirely different environment once again.

This was the result – how else was it likely to be with me? – of lucky circumstances, chance and, especially, the help of a married couple I had never met before. Manfred Wengert was working for the Bayer Group, I think it was, in Barcelona where, he emphasised to me, he had close contacts with the club's directors. He was probably just a straightforward businessman who happened to appreciate, before such a broker existed, the role a player's agent might play. Borussia Mönchengladbach had taken part in plenty of tournaments in Spain. In Zaragoza for example and, a couple of months before, in Barcelona. These performances ranked amongst my best. The local press was highly appreciative. For a while, as my name became known in Spain, the admiration I was shown there could only be matched back in West Germany in Mönchengladbach itself. The Barcelona board were so enthusiastic that, as soon as the tournament ended, they wanted to sign me without further delay. Soon after we had got back to Mönchengladbach, I received a call at 'Lovers Lane'. It was Wengert, wanting to know, as he moonlighted from his Bayer job, if I would be interested were he to organise a contact with Barcelona. Provided, of course, that I could envisage a move to the Mediterranean? I could. In fact, I would have happily started packing my bags there and then. I wanted to get away from Mönchengladbach, Weisweiler; from my relationship too, perhaps. I also wanted to leave West Germany, where I had gradually become tired of struggling against my ambiguous reputation as a partying playboy / rakish man-about-town. Barcelona appeared a very tempting spot to escape to. I had got to know the city a little during our visits there. I thought the lively atmosphere was wonderful and I had grown familiar with the Nou Camp, where the passion of the supporters was obvious, too. The sooner talks began with the club, the better. The coach, Rinus Michels however was not so eager. Having only recently arrived from Holland, he had other ideas than to build a team around a German, of all people. The player he had in mind was the Dutch inside-left and captain,

Johan Cruyff. But Cruyff was coy about the move and his club, Ajax, frankly uncooperative. So, the talks with myself dragged on. I scarcely knew those who were representing me. In the end I broke off negotiations.

Fortunately, the German couple were not about to give up so easily. I do not know why they were so keen to act on my behalf. Presumably, there was a healthy commission at the end of it, if they succeeded in bringing me to Spain. Without mentioning anything, Wengert telephoned Real Madrid. The club directors did not hesitate to issue an invitation to fly down as soon as I could. That meant the Bundesliga would have to get along for a little while without me. A light injury picked up the previous weekend, against VfB Stuttgart, came at a good moment. Weisweiler was already unhappy with me when I told him about it. We were pacing around the training ground, with Berti acting as intermediary again. Weisweiler told him, "Berti, ask your friend how long he is going to be off injured this time". In turn, I instructed him, "Berti, tell your trainer I do not know. At least a week." An absence of forty-eight hours would probably pass unnoticed. For this first flight to Madrid I did have my passport with me. Very few people in Mönchengladbach knew of my plans: Berti, my parents and Hannelore Girrulat, that was all. And they all kept quiet about them.

These days it would be impossible to try and keep such a trip secret. Someone would recognise the prominent player at the airport, then one of the check-in attendants would reveal where he was flying to. Anybody could then pass this information onto their pick of the tabloids. Speculation would take off from there. Teammates would be contacted. There are always one or two who know what is going on, or at least like to think they do, and who consider that spilling news to the Press will make them look important. What an outcry would have ensued if my flirt – that is all it remained – with Madrid had leaked out at this early point. It does not require too much insight to guess the subsequent reaction. I was the most controversial, criticised player in West Germany. It is quite likely the transfer would have been called off, with my career then following a very different course. No one at the airport though was taking any notice of me. If I was recognised by anyone their reaction is likely to have been no more concerning than, 'Oh, there's crazy Netzer, off to Madrid this time, on another of his little jaunts'.

A couple of years later, Franz Beckenbauer was contemplating a transfer to The New York Cosmos. A helicopter waited at JFK to whisk him off over Lower Manhattan. Later he confided how impressed, even overwhelmed he had been. If he had not already made his mind up over the move, this introduction to The Big Apple would have done it for him. My welcoming party consisted of a pair of club officials standing at the airport exit, ready to usher me into a mid-range saloon and take me, without ceremony, straight to the club's training complex. "You will be dining tonight with two of the club's representatives," I was told. "It is still not known if Chairman Bernabéu will be there." The sub-text was evident: this is not a club that needs to throw itself at foreign players. Real is Real, and that is that.

It was not long before we arrived at our next stop. Nothing had prepared me for the stadium. Not even Wembley. Its immensity commanded respect … with a hint of intimidation. Eventually one gets used to it. Walking out into the empty stadium for the first time a shiver went down my spine. I imagined the roar, the howling and the concerted cheer of a crowd of 100,000, maybe 120,000, booming out over the pitch from the ramparts, and I tried to comprehend that soon this phenomenon might be the natural reaction – at least partly – to Günter from Geroweiher entering the arena clad in white. All the disagreements with Weisweiler had not caused me to become so hard-boiled that this moment should leave me unmoved. The experience was probably enough for one day, as Real Madrid no doubt understood. "Tomorrow," they said, "we will talk."

So here I was, in an anonymous Madrid hotel room with two hours to kill before dinner. Up until now, I had not really pondered this move abroad deeply. Certainly not all the difficulties involved. There was the language barrier. If need be, I could make myself understood in English, though not yet in Spanish. And other day-to-day considerations? I knew very little about the Spanish or, indeed, any foreign way of life. The footballing aspect? How would I fit into and maybe even subordinate myself within a team full of stars? This was something else I had not thought through; nevertheless, of all the cherished local traditions I would need to get to grips with, it might be the one that ended up causing me the most trouble. What counted was Real Madrid – champions fifteen times, cup winners on eleven and European Cup winners on six occasions. Di Stéfano, Puskás and Gento were famous names I had become familiar with growing up.

And wages? I had no idea what one was likely to earn playing for a foreign club, nor for that matter what I was worth. Speaking in very general terms, Weisweiler had mentioned that a German footballer could expect three times what he was accustomed to in the Bundesliga.

The following morning, I was collected again and driven to the club's offices. Now I did get to meet the onetime centre-forward for the club and its chairman since 1943, Santiago Bernabéu. As he sat there in the flesh, what was striking about the seventy-eight-year-old was his strength and vitality, expressed by his lively eyes. He was Real Madrid through and through. Bernabéu was the overseer; he did not intervene. He left the negotiating to his vice chairman, Raimundo Saporta. Besides greeting and taking our leave of one another, no words were exchanged between the two of us. He spoke neither German nor English and I did not speak Spanish. Nevertheless, I was impressed by the man and liked him straightaway. I also got the feeling, and so it turned out, that these powerful first impressions were reciprocated.

Saporta asked what annual salary I had in mind. Based on what Weisweiler had told me, I responded, "350,000 marks". He gave me an astonished look. The minute taker laid down his pen. Bernabéu did not react. For a few, drawn-out seconds it looked as if Saporta was struggling to maintain his composure. He then asked me to confirm whether what he thought he had just heard was correct.

"350,000 marks," I repeated.

Although a big man, this was too much for Saporta. In a near shriek he exclaimed, "That is what we pay half the team put together. Our star players – who are Spanish – only get a third of what you are suggesting."

I had come into the meeting without any real plan and so I was not prepared for the situation I now found myself in. Was Saporta bluffing? Or was Weisweiler's broad estimate one that he had plucked out of thin air? It was impossible for me to say, but some instinct told me to stand my ground. "Very well," I said, "then this discussion has been based on a misunderstanding. I appreciate your invitation. Now I will be going." I stood up. Complete silence accompanied me as I made my way, unimpeded, towards the door. I had just placed my hand on the handle when Saporta yelled, "Come back here!"

I turned around. "What is it worth," he bellowed, "to you to play for Real Madrid?"

In retrospect, the question strikes me as presumptuous. They wanted me, they had flown me here for talks and now they were acting as if one ought to pay for the privilege of pulling on the white jersey. At that moment, however, the self-assurance that goes with being the most successful and powerful club in the world made its impact. So, I did a trade. "If I am to play for Real Madrid, it will cost you 300,000 marks."

Saporta was still not happy. He looked at me for a while before saying, or, rather, groaning, "The '3' needs to go".

"Why is that?"

"A question of appearances. A question of appearances."

Neither before nor since have I ever surrendered 55,000 marks so lightly. "Alright, 295,000."

With this, Saporta regained his composure. It was now the minute taker whom he directed imperiously: "Go and draw up the contract". The poor man exited without ceremony. Bernabéu stood up and, extending his hand, murmured a few words of farewell. He then made his own way out of the room. The rest of the negotiations could be left to the vice chairman and scribe.

The 'rest' included the small matter of the transfer fee, which until now had barely been mentioned. Perhaps because

I had not yet calmed down from our heated exchange, I gave the unusual assurance that I would take care of this. It was all very different to the elaborate transfer negotiations of today in which both sides are represented by legal teams.

I went into an adjoining room to make a call to Helmut Grashoff, Borussia's general manager. "Listen, Herr Grashoff," I said, coming straight to the point, "I am in Madrid at the moment for talks with Real. They want to know what my transfer fee will be." This was the first he had heard of the move and he took it, as he did most things, calmly. "Ah, something to do with the knee?" he asked, but that was all. It was a spontaneous reaction to hearing that I was in Madrid; he had already guessed that I had gone off somewhere for a few days' convalescence. As for the fee, at some point in the past he had mentioned a figure of just under a million marks for a transfer to another Bundesliga side. In a calm and matter-of-fact fashion, he told me he could not give an immediate answer. He would have to think it over. That did not help me. I said, "Herr Grashoff, we have shared many years together. They have been enjoyable. We have known success. Now it is time for something new. The fairest thing, but also the most appropriate, would be if you could stick with the same sum for Real Madrid." For a short while there was no response from the other end of the line. Then, as I wanted, but did not realistically dare hope, Grashoff agreed, "Yes, good, let's do it like that".

One must take into consideration that I was a legend at Mönchengladbach and had recently been instrumental in West Germany's European Championship success; even if I was not in peak condition, as my critics in spring 1973 were quick to point out, there is no question that I could have fetched more than a mere million. I thought it was good of Grashoff not to try and secure a better deal, or maybe it was just that he lacked the necessary experience.

Since it was laughably low by international standards, when I named the asking price to my Spanish counterparts there were once more exclamations of shock. First there had been the extravagant pay demand, now came this bargain-basement fee. And yet, even if I had entered these talks unprepared, combined, the two amounted to a fundamentally sound bargaining position.

The following morning came the medical. I was more anxious about it than anything else. The previous week I had visited Professor Schneider in Cologne about my knee. He diagnosed a torn cartilage, a handicap heading to Madrid for talks. Now the Spanish doctor examined me. He found everything to be in good order but wanted to take a closer look at my knee. A lot was riding on his not making any unpleasant, for me, discoveries; if he did, the scribe's contract would have to be ripped up, and the riches I had negotiated forgotten. Instead, I would be staying in Mönchengladbach, where I could expect further strife with Weisweiler, the critics, Hannelore. West Germany was looking more and more like a prison.

He set about kneading it with both hands. I clenched my teeth for as long as I could, then let out a cry of pain. "Just a knock I received last Saturday," I remarked to the doctor. Luckily for me, medicals were less advanced then. Also, the footballing world was more opaque than it is today. Because the Spanish and German leagues were effectively worlds apart, the doctor believed my explanation and declared himself satisfied.

The cartilage never troubled me as a player thanks to a solid musculature. Approaching sixty, it is a different matter. The likelihood of an operation can no longer be ignored.

That evening, thirty years ago, I flew back to Mönchengladbach. I would make the return journey again in a couple of weeks, with all my stuff, with Hannelore and in the knowledge that my future now lay in the Spanish capital, playing for the royal club. I could not have been happier.

8

Real Madrid – Las Vegas

From time to time, I wondered whether Santiago Bernabéu had learned about my passport misadventure. Probably not, I thought, and, if he had, it was too petty an incident for him to have remembered for long. As for the bizarre transfer negotiation, we never discussed it; not even once I was able to speak Spanish and began to have frequent talks with the old man. Bernabéu had actively encouraged me to learn the language. He hoped that a German hotelier he knew would help me. But, whenever the two of us met, my compatriot was more interested in learning about myself and talking football than in teaching me Spanish. It was obviously easier for me to help him with these subjects by speaking German. So we stuck with our mother tongue.

Bernabéu was a man of firm principles. The club rules on players' appearance – specifically hair – were ones he had personally decreed. Moustaches, for example, were not allowed. There was a sharp difference between his ideas concerning the way those representing Real Madrid should present themselves and ours, particularly when it came to my own fashion taste.

I found a dark suit and tie a gross combination. My hair was still shoulder length. When I started to speak a bit of Spanish a couple of months later, I was told that journalists had placed bets on how long it would take before I was told to get it cut. I am not certain what would have happened if Bernabéu had gone ahead and issued such a command. Back in West Germany, there could be no question: I would stick to my guns. But here in Madrid, with so much that was unfamiliar, and where I had yet to earn recognition … I was not so sure. My resolve, though, was not put to the test. He never mentioned my hair, clothes, or appearance. All those journalists who had bet on a display of the chairman's authority lost their money.

For some reason he liked me from the outset. OK, as a prestige signing, I was bound to be held in some esteem. But did that mean he was necessarily going to prepare the suite once occupied by Alfredo di Stéfano for my use? The greatest, most revered Real player of all time. That showed a degree of care. It indicated the expectations Bernabéu had of me and the personal attachment he already felt. But, to be honest, the enormous apartment, spread over two floors and crammed with heavy furniture, was not really my style. I felt flattered all the same.

There were other examples of the club's solicitous attitude towards me. I had been provided with a Mini, all optional extras included. It was the ideal car for getting around Madrid. Parked outside the house back in Mönchengladbach though stood my black Ferrari Daytona. I wanted it delivered and, since I knew the racing driver Jochen Maaß, I asked him whether he might drive it down from West Germany, the next time he was competing in Spain. My instinct told me that even a top professional driver would find the Daytona something special. Maaß' reaction bore this out; unfortunately, however, he couldn't do it. In the end it was with a friend at the wheel that the car headed south to Madrid.

The next morning, I was feeling quite proud as I drove the car, with its Mönchengladbacher number plates, through Madrid to the training ground. Which is where the storm erupted. "Are you out of your mind?" an official demanded bleakly. "Move that car out of sight, immediately." I didn't understand what he was talking about. Next, I was summoned before the club authorities. In an excited state, they all began reprimanding me at the same time, as though I had committed high treason. Little by little, I understood what a serious offence it was to have brought my Ferrari to Spain. Delivering private cars into the country like this was *verboten*. Without an import licence, one could only drive cars with foreign number plates if one was a tourist. Which I was not; I was an employee of Real Madrid. A few telephone calls made it clear that importing a Ferrari by the book would cost more than the car itself. The well of rebukes did not dry up. The conclusion to each had become predictable: "The car must go – now!" Bernabéu then intervened. He agreed it could not stay. What he suggested was that he would get his chauffeur to make the reverse journey to West Germany, leaving Madrid under cover of night. Hopefully he would make it undetected. Three days later the poor guy set off and successfully returned the Ferrari back to its parking slot opposite my front door in Mönchengladbach.

A mutual respect existed between Bernabéu and myself. On one occasion, the all-powerful chairman sought my advice. This was as to whether, a year after my arrival, he should now sign

Paul Breitner. He called me to his office, that was in fact more a reception room with a desk in the middle, into which you could easily have fitted three ordinary sized offices. As he informed me that, "the coach wants to sign this Paul Breitner," his expression suggested that the coach might as well be proposing that the devil himself should pull on the Real Madrid jersey. "Yes, I know," I answered. "It's a good idea. Breitner is a fantastic player. He will strengthen us considerably."

The coach was Miljan Miljanić. I had first met him earlier in the year at the world cup in West Germany, where he was in charge of Yugoslavia. He let me know then that, after the tournament, he was going to be my club manager and that he had his eye on Breitner. He wanted to use him as a midfielder. "Breitner is more than just a defender," he said. "Together with Netzer, I see him setting the tempo at Real Madrid." First, he needed to convince Bernabéu.

The chairman writhed in agony. "The man is a Maoist," he said. It must have taken all of his self-control simply not to have fallen on his knees at this moment to call on divine intervention in favour of his Real Madrid. I had still not seen the photo of Breitner, which was later to become famous, sitting with the *Peking Radio Times* in his hands and a copy of Mao's *Little Red Book* at his side. I must have looked baffled and disbelieving perhaps, that he should be so well informed. "How do you know?"

He showed me the paper with this photo. "He is also a follower of Che Guevara," he said, pulling out another paper. The photo in it showed Breitner in his apartment. Like many another at the time, there was a poster of the Cuban revolutionary stuck on the wall.

"Maybe I have not been very observant," I said. "These pictures are new to me. As far as I am concerned, Paul is a fantastic person. A little bit strange perhaps sometimes, and possibly even more unpredictable when he wants to be than I am myself. I can't recall him expressing any political views though. Certainly not of this variety."

This did not reassure Bernabéu. "Can you guarantee that there will be no trouble with him?" There was no doubt, he was in deadly earnest. I may have been only twenty-eight but he seems to have sensed that, with the experience I had accumulated as a casual observer in various bars, I could be trusted to make a reliable assessment of Breitner. My judgement was that, even if Paul enjoyed being provocative and espoused left wing ideals, he would not be calling for a coup d'état against Franco once he was in Madrid. Nor would he be trying to convert Santiago Bernabéu and Real to socialism. "I guarantee it," I said. This now appears to me a rather grandiose conclusion to the intriguing backstory of a footballer's transfer. It was enough for Bernabéu to rubber-stamp the coach's decision to sign Breitner.

If Bayern Munich had had their way, things might have turned out very differently for me at this time. I had barely arrived in Madrid when the club, in the form of Robert Schwan, came to the city to talk with me. I had no idea why but here he was, installed at The Ritz. Just to have a chat with him there was not, it turned out, an easy matter. It was a brutally hot day; forty degrees at least. I was wearing a short sleeve shirt. When I entered the prestigious hotel, it was pointed out that I was underdressed. Even stepping into reception in such inappropriate clothing, it was made clear to me, was frowned upon. No tie meant no entry, and therefore no natter with Robert Schwan. At the time, opportunities to speak to a countryman were rare. Other than the owner of the hotel where I was staying and someone working at the embassy, I knew no Germans here, so a talk with him would have been pleasant. How though was I to let him know that I was standing outside the hotel entrance, in inappropriate clothes and in a sweat? Mobiles had yet to be invented and telephone kiosks were thin on the ground. Somehow or other, I succeeded in getting a call put through to Schwan. A tie was brought out to me, which I put on. The hotel's etiquette was satisfied. Personally, I found my simple summer shirt more chic and agreeable than a suit and tie.

It was a surreal prelude to an absurd conversation. Robert Schwan came straight to the point. "My proposal is this, Günter: come to Bayern. We will buy out your contract." Had I, sitting in the Madrid Ritz, in shortsleeves and someone else's tie, heard that right? It was only two weeks previously that I signed this contract and two days since training had begun. I had yet to make an appearance for my new team. Now, here comes Robert Schwan proposing something completely different. "Robert, say that one more time."

"We will buy out your contract, and you can come to us."

For a year now I had been waiting for the invitation. I knew what Bayern paid and what I was then receiving. Only with my various sidelines could I approach Franz Beckenbauer's salary. I was conscious too of the constant battle with Weisweiler, the continual pressure to justify myself. Knowing my predicament and the way I felt, Bayern only had to ask and I would have come running. I already felt at home in Munich. Regarding my nights at 'Why Not' with Pfleghar and assorted female company, my

136

flights from Düsseldorf to Riem Airport and back again in time to train with Weisweiler … Bayern knew all this. The gossip columnist Michael Graeter barely let a chance pass to publicise my visits to the city. In the Press, a young woman photographed standing next to me would be described as my girlfriend. Sometimes this might be an exaggeration, on other occasions pure fiction. What was neither fiction nor a secret was that a move to the Bavarian capital would suit me very nicely from both a financial and a practical point of view. Not to mention having the opportunity to play alongside Franz Beckenbauer, and reproduce at club level the success we had already achieved together with the national side.

I had come to accept that Bayern had no intention of making an offer. On the other hand, I knew via Beckenbauer that the club's chairman, Wilhelm Neudecker was not being entirely honest when he said he would have nothing to do with me on account of my appearance. Now he had obviously changed his mind. No doubt he could picture the glowing headlines which could be expected to announce how FC Bayern had gone to rescue the traitor to the fatherland from himself, by bringing him home once more, as the prodigal son. That seemed to be the only explanation, given that Robert Schwan was indeed sitting across from me and this was not a dream, or an hallucination brought on by the Madrid heatwave. "We are bringing you back," said Schwan once again.

"Are you completely nuts? I mean, are you out of your mind?"

Astonished is not really the word to describe how I felt. Anger and rage are closer to the mark. "For ten years I was on your doorstep, without you showing the slightest interest in me and now, all of a sudden, this. You are nuts. I am not interested." As far as I was concerned that closed the conversation. I was not prepared to even think about such a foolhardy scheme.

The ambitious Robert Schwan was not, however, the kind of man to be so easily deflected from his goal. Sooner than anyone else in the game, Bayern had realised how helpful the media could be in creating a national ambience. All that was required was to keep feeding it pieces that would guide this mood in the right direction. In the early seventies Schwan paved the way for a technique which Uli Hoeneß later developed to perfection. The normal practice until then was for transfer dealings to remain discreet, so as to try and keep the eventual price down. Now it was intended that they should be thrown wide open. By leaking to the Munich tabloids, Schwan assured that the story built to a point where he could be confident it would achieve its effect. In one corner stood FC Bayern, which had contributed so much to German football; in the other, myself, with my reputation for not paying it proper respect. Guess who was in the better position. At least I was spared from having to read everything then being written about me in the German press. If I had, the pressure would have become too much.

So, the Bayern deal was eventually completed … without having been agreed to by either myself or Real Madrid. My employers behaved the way you would expect the directors of the world's most famous and powerful football club to: phlegmatically, knowing that if I broke my contract, for the following twelve months Bayern would only be able to make use of me as a mascot in the stands.

I found the belated interest shown by FC Bayern to be at least as absurd as The Ritz's dress code. The only possible explanation, it occurred to me, since there was never a chance that Real Madrid would allow itself to be made a laughing stock of, and because Bayern could not genuinely have expected this offer to be accepted, was that Neudecker and Schwan were far less interested in signing me than they were in obtaining the excellent publicity which any attempt of this kind would result in. I still think this is probably the incident's most likely interpretation.

At least my visit to The Ritz introduced a little variety into an otherwise predictable daily routine. Monotonous is the best way to describe this initial phase of my time in Madrid. In the morning I went from the Di Stéfano mausoleum to the training ground; later in the day I returned from the training ground to the Di Stéfano mausoleum. Same sequence the following day; and the one after. Conversation with the German hotelier was not exactly sparkling. At supper the language barrier was the problem. On the positive side, I suppose, I was at least able to eat a little during this first year. After Miljanić arrived twelve months later it was not so easy. Before 11 pm, at which hour everywhere in Mönchengladbach would be closing, it was hard to find an open restaurant in the Spanish capital. This was the hour when people went out, ideal for a nighthawk like me. Miljanić regrettably imposed an 11 pm curfew on the players, checking up with frequent phone calls to our homes.

His predecessor, Miguel Muñoz was not so strict. With a combined total of thirty-one years at the club, first as a player, then as coach, Muñoz was almost part of the Real Madrid furniture. He was, how shall we say, a little set in his ways. The team was ageing. The time to have made one or two organic changes had passed. Amancio, Grosso and Zocco, Pirri and

Vélazquez were all famous names but their best years now lay behind them. Not all saw it that way. In particular they did not see what this newcomer, a German with long hair, was doing amongst them. The chances of integrating smoothly did not look good.

By giving me the No.10 shirt, customarily worn by the playmaker, Muñoz may have hoped to make this easier. Since he had the chairman's backing, it did not require a great deal of courage on his part. Meanwhile, the Press did its best to suggest there was an issue between us, just because my arrival coincided with a gradual reduction in Vélazquez's influence. For ten years now the '*Cerebro*', or 'Mastermind', as he was known, had led Real Madrid's performances. Now he was being sidelined by a newcomer from abroad. He did not personally have a problem with the new situation; in fact, we got along fine, in spite of the language barrier. The newspapers though wanted to stir things up between us. A clear majority was pro- Vélazquez. The hotelier translated a selection of the headlines for me. There was no mistaking that, while Mönchengladbach may once have lain at my feet, Madrid, so soon after my arrival, did not.

During the course of my first appearance, Real Madrid were awarded a penalty. Almost as a matter of course, I claimed the ball. Wasn't I the one who was expected to assume responsibility after all? Within the tight-knit group of a football side, in which status matters, this sort of apparently minor gesture draws attention. Either the new boy is a little too sure of himself or he is showing admirable self-confidence. Placing the ball on the spot, I sensed that both my teammates and the fans were prepared to give me the benefit of the doubt. When I made to kick it, the keeper dived to his left. Shooting to his right, I cut my angles a little too fine. The ball bounced back off the post. Luck was not with me in my first moment in the spotlight. Judging from the fans' sympathetic applause, however, I ought to have counted myself fortunate. Their reaction was probably a consequence of Bernabéu's known esteem for me and of my reputation, which had preceded me here; or maybe it was just a sign of approval for the initiative I had shown. The Press' reaction the following day was different. Just like in any game I had ended up on the floor a few times. The paper whose photographer snapped me in a heap on the ground captioned the image, 'The Fallen Statue'. Now, in this entirely new environment, I needed to stand up for myself as never before.

At Mönchengladbach I occasionally directed training. The Friday session before a league game nearly always ended with a short game of attack versus attack, in which I stood in the middle distributing the ball. This was football at the highest level, where tempo and technique were both pushed to the limit. It is possible, and Berti once said as much, that the others hated me for taking things to this extreme. But it was good schooling for our style of play, and I was not about to see it abandoned. The only concession to my teammates was to move this practice game to Thursday, so we could have an extra day to recuperate before the match. When I mentioned this to Weisweiler there was an ugly scene. "So," he demanded, "you now want to be the one who decides when we train?" In the end he agreed to the change. What I want to emphasise is that at Borussia we hardly ever trained without the ball. It was almost the reverse at Madrid during this pre-season. For four of the six weeks we scarcely saw one. Muñoz was big on gymnastics and PE. I had never felt so supple before – nor since.

Another area in which it seemed only natural that I should be involved at Mönchengladbach was the signing of new players. Berti Vogts has gone so far as to say that I had the final word on which targets should be our priority. That is not strictly speaking true. It was never a case of a club director coming to me to say, "Günter, the coach wants to sign so-and-so. Are you happy about that?" In practice though my situation at Borussia amounted to something like this. At the time, a Bundesliga player, often from one of the lower divisions, whom the trainer already knew a bit about and was interested in, would come for a week's trial. Those who failed to show the potential to fit in with my game would not be signed.

Weisweiler was well aware of how much responsibility he had handed over to me, but was savvy enough to understand that it was best to establish whether a possible signing had my approval. With a forward this took the form of a practice game in which I would serve up long balls to him, the same as I did with Heynckes and Laumen. Afterwards Weisweiler would ask us what we had concluded from the examination. We – myself especially – were not infallible. There was once a very young man who turned up at our training ground. He had travelled from Zweisel in the Bavarian Forest, on the back of a glowing reference for the promise he showed as an outstanding centre-forward. I saw no talent that day. Klaus Fischer appeared to stand no chance at Mönchengladbach. None of the balls I played to him came to anything; he was not on my wavelength at all. The defenders had a bit of fun nutmegging him. It was hard not to have a laugh at his expense. Weisweiler remained confident in his instinct that he was a special player, but how could we agree, having, in our superior way, given him such a runaround? What a poor assessment of mine that was! Fischer made a good enough impression at 1860 München for Schalke 04 to take an interest in him. Having joined them, he went on to become one of the best centre-forwards West Germany ever had.

We were fortunately spared from having to pay for another, collective, error of judgement. In 1972 Allan Simonsen was brought to Mönchengladbach from Denmark. If Weisweiler had had his way, his stay at the club would have been brief. I would not have argued. Nothing to begin with went right for Allan who in those days looked no more than a lad. He was incapable of asserting himself, this shy, spindly smalltown boy. Put on the transfer list, he attracted no interest. Only later did Allan reveal his full abilities, as he helped Borussia to three league titles and two UEFA Cups, after which he did well at Barcelona too, winning the European Cup Winners Cup in his time there.

No one at Madrid during this first season asked for my opinion. In almost every respect it was a wasted year. At the end of it, Real Madrid finished somewhere in the top third of the table, a disaster by the club's standards. It could have been worse. We even flirted with the relegation zone. I was frequently injured and never really found any form. There were very few moments when I could justify having made the move. With hindsight I can tell I was missing the familiar surroundings of my country, hometown and old teammates. I felt unsettled in Madrid, almost as if I were a wandering spirit, however strange that may sound.

God knows, I was unsettled. Which was when I received an unexpected mid-week call from Michael Pfleghar in Munich. I was injured again – nothing serious, but it meant I was unable to train or play. "Take care of yourself, Günter," he advised me, "and start packing the essentials: toothbrush, dinner jacket … Tomorrow we need to be in London, so we can get a flight to Los Angeles and then onto Las Vegas. We've been invited to Tina's wedding."

"Aha," I went. At some point I had got to know Tina Sinatra, daughter of Frank. She was part of Michael's circle. The groom was Roxy Music's producer. The band and its singer, Bryan Ferry were making waves in 1974. Tina, like Raquel Welch and Elke Sommer, and one or two others, had been romantically linked with me. As I mentioned earlier, some, but not all of the stories were true. Together with Michael, I had done some fairly bizarre things, both in Munich and elsewhere. His latest plan was without doubt the craziest yet. Too crazy, in fact, for me to believe.

"Yah, yah," I said, "good idea. The only problem is I don't own a dinner jacket."

"Then pack your toothbrush. We'll meet in London tomorrow and sort you out with clothes there." He sounded serious.

"Michael, try to be sensible. How do you think that is going to be possible? I can't come. I can't even leave the country." Indeed, without special permission from the directors, players were limited to travelling no further than thirty kilometres from Madrid. Another constraint was that our passports were held by the club. Given my forgetfulness and the frequency of foreign tours, there were good grounds for this measure being taken in my case.

"That's irrelevant," replied Michael, not so easily dissuaded. "I have already spoken to your pal at the embassy. He is going to make sure that you have a temporary passport you can travel with. Tomorrow morning we fly to London. I'll have a private jet come and pick you up."

With any sense, I would have stuck firmly to my original "No". But maybe good sense is not one of my strong points. If this escapade were to be discovered, I would be regarded not just as a player in poor form and prone to injury but as being highly unprofessional. Not fit to wear the Real Madrid jersey. I was worried I could get thrown out. If so, my career, considering the dismal reputation I then had in Germany, and having turned down Bayern, would be jeopardised. It is true that Schalke, knowing that I was struggling to fit in at Madrid, had proposed taking me back to West Germany, but I had declined that offer too.

How could such a trip go undetected? Sure, in Los Angeles and Las Vegas I might be able to move about anonymously. Not many Germans yet chose the United States as a holiday destination. It would be a different matter at Madrid Airport or shopping in London. Since my performance in the victory over England at Wembley, I had a certain celebrity there. My singular face did not help. The whole thing was crazy. Still, I flew.

My contact at the embassy came up with a temporary passport, as promised. He also supplied me with a slouch hat and a broad collared coat. With the first slanted low and the second turned up, I made my way through Madrid Airport. It remains a mystery to me how I did not arouse the suspicion of a single customs official. Arriving in London, there was Michael, grinning broadly. His smile said he knew he had not needed to employ all his powers of persuasion: he could always count on my willingness to come along for the ride. We jumped into a taxi and, hat tilted down and coat collar pulled high, made our way to the shops. Without messing around, we bought everything required for a Las Vegas wedding with the Sinatra clan: DJ, patent leather shoes, dress shirt and bow tie. Safely checked in at our hotel, we drank to this latest adventure.

The next day we were on the long-haul flight to Los Angeles. Besides Tina's wedding, there was, as Michael knew, another major event going on in Las Vegas. Her father had recently had a year's residency at the Sands Hotel. At some point he and a couple of his friends, not for the first time, drank a bit too much. They went on the rampage. Furniture got thrown about and a hotel guest was shoved through a window. After that, Frank Sinatra was no longer welcome at The Sands. Instead, he was due to make his big Las Vegas comeback, coinciding with Tina's wedding, at Caesar's Palace. 'Ol' Blue Eyes is Back' the show was called. Everyone now seemed to be heading in the same direction as Michael and I. All the Los Angeles to Las Vegas flights were full. We were stuck. To think that I had risked my job, stealing out of Madrid incognito, then buying some extravagant gear in London in order to end up like this aggravated me. Michael nevertheless had an objective, Tina's wedding in Las Vegas, and we were going to be there. He occupied a telephone booth making a succession of calls; to whom I was not quite sure. Eventually, he ambled over to where I had been waiting morosely for the past hour or more. He wore a triumphant smile. "Come on, our transport is ready to go," he announced. He did not confide what he had had to pay for a single engine plane with pilot, but I guessed it was not cheap.

I can still recall the distinctly uneasy feeling I had taking off in this crate and then climbing to the necessary height to clear the Sierra Nevada, on the route the pilot took to stay out of the main flight path. It was an overwhelming experience, in keeping with the rest of this mad trip. The sheer pleasure of flying above the mountain range outdid my feelings of apprehension. When we landed in Las Vegas, Tina Sinatra's pleasure was at least as great.

After the ceremony, the wedding guests went along to the concert. They were not any old wedding guests. Michael and I, the German footballer, took our places. Apart from Tina, I knew none of the female company at our table. Sitting diagonally across from me I did, however, recognise Sammy Davis Jr. And, next to him, Dean Martin. On the other side of my neighbour sat Neil Diamond. How strange to be at the same table as the Rat Pack, chatting with Sammy Davis Jr! On hearing that I was a professional footballer from Europe, Neil Diamond wanted to know how far I could kick a ball. When I told him about eighty or a hundred metres it looked as though he might sign me on the spot, being the co-owner of a football team – who nevertheless did not seem to appreciate the difference between football, as the Americans understand it, and soccer. It was Dean Martin who cleared things up for him. Like I say, an extraordinary situation to find oneself in.

The problem was, the concert was being recorded. Throughout, a camera crew zoomed in on our table of celebrities. What if the performance was broadcast in Europe too? And my beaming face got splashed across the newspapers? The crew must have wondered why, at a table full not of camera-shy but of unquestionably photogenic people, one should be ducking in an attempt to hide himself. It goes without saying that I was not entirely successful in this.

The adventure continued the following day when, with Michael and Tina, I found myself in Frank Sinatra's suite. We chatted and joked like old friends. When the conversation turned to his show, which was due to start in an hour or so, just around the corner at the Hilton, Frank asked, "Would you like to go and see Elvis?" Obviously, we would. Sinatra dispatched one of his entourage to go and take care of arranging tickets. He was back before long, empty-handed and contrite. "There are none to be had," he reported. The concert was already sold out. Sinatra did not look entirely convinced by this. He sent his bodyguard, whose assertiveness and organisational abilities he appeared to have more faith in, instead. But he fared no better. "Hopeless," said Frank, "absolutely hopeless." I was beginning, as one of two eccentric Europeans, to feel a little uncomfortable at our immoderate wants. Even without seeing Elvis, we were having the trip of a lifetime, by passing the time of day with Frank Sinatra, for example. Up to this point he couldn't have been more relaxed, sitting in an easy chair. When he sprang up, it got knocked to the ground. "Are you trying to tell me," he bellowed at his assistants, "that Frank Sinatra cannot obtain tickets for two German friends who would like to see Elvis?" The pair shrugged their shoulders helplessly. Sinatra grabbed the telephone.

I have no idea whom he spoke to. It would not have surprised me particularly if it had been the president of the United States himself, Richard Nixon. A quick, two-minute conversation ensued. Sinatra put the phone down and turned to us with a smile and said, "OK, you might as well go now. There will be someone to meet you at the entrance." I may have already mentioned that this trip bore no resemblance to anything that had happened before in my life.

Michael and I made our way without exchanging a word. Outside the Hilton waited two heavyset bodyguards. One of them asked, "Are you the two Germans? Let's go. We need to get a move on." The hotel and the concert hall were both heaving. This was a sell-out alright. In every direction you looked people were standing or sitting, waiting for The King. The bodyguards managed to squeeze out a path within the crush, for us to make our way forward. On this occasion I forgot to panic, my usual reaction to being pressed in in a crowd. Having managed to struggle our way through the standing audience, we glided between the tables, all of them occupied. All except one. This small round table, positioned directly in front of centre stage, and on which stood a bottle of champagne, was waiting for its guests, Michael Pfleghar and Günter Netzer. The show could now begin. Ah! What a trip.

And now the time has come to say a few words about my friend, Michael. Through him I was given an entrée into the world of showbiz stars and performing artists. An even more superficial milieu than football. The term friendship, already misused when applied to the eleven 'Friends' on the football pitch, is resorted to in showbiz after one or two chance encounters. But with Michael Pfleghar, who later married the easy listening singer, Wencke Myhre, I developed a genuinely close friendship. He was, I think, the type of person best described as compassionate. Always taking an interest in those around him. He was there for me after my move to Madrid, where, during those early days, my morale was not so good; he had been there for me before the move, when I was attacked for leaving West Germany and on account of my mother's death. Recently, Ingrid Steeger and Elisabeth Volkmann, leading stars of *Klimbim*, have both had less positive things to say about Michael. Perhaps they saw a different side of him. My memory is of a good man. In June 1991, in Düsseldorf, Michael shot himself. He was only fifty-eight. Why? There were times when he suffered from depression and grave self-doubt. Why didn't I notice it at the time? Why did I know nothing about his problems and anxieties? Why did he not confide in me? Was it because I was too insensitive? Or was I myself a superficial person? It required a lot of time and many conversations before I could finally accept that there was nothing I could have done to help Michael. In looking out for others, he sacrificed himself, to the point of emotional self-neglect.

During our weekend in Las Vegas, seventeen years before his death, we had nothing but fun. The buzz lasted throughout the flight back to London. I felt happy, inspired and proud. It was as if I had rediscovered the bold, instinctive and spontaneous part of myself, which could not help but please me. On the final leg of the journey, to Madrid, a mild hangover set in. How was I going to get through Customs and then back into the Di Stéfano suite unnoticed? I was certain that, once again, club officials would be looking out for me at the airport and that, this time, the greeting would not be warm but boiling – with anger. I was sure Santiago Bernabéu's protective hand would now be withdrawn. As the plane made its late night arrival, it was time for the hat and coat routine again. I went unrecognised. No one knew me; nothing need become known about my time with Frank, Tina, Sammy and

Dean. On the Tuesday I began to do some running exercises. I had recovered from my injury.

The following weekend we travelled for an away game. My roommate during that first year was Zocco. I could now manage basic conversational Spanish. A few nights before, he had been watching television. "There was an amazing Frank Sinatra concert," he said. Bloody hell, I thought, the concert *was* broadcast in Spain. Zocco chatted away. "They were all there. Sammy Davis Jr, Dean Martin. The whole crew." His wife, a well-known Spanish easy listening singer, was watching with him. All of a sudden, Señora Maria exclaimed, "Look, there's Netzer!" Zocco took a closer look at the screen. "You're right. But it can't be. The club has got his passport. It must be his spitting image."

For a couple of years, I kept the story of my trip a secret from him. At the time, I was struggling not to laugh. "Sure," I bantered, "I was in Las Vegas. Sitting at the same table as Sammy Davis Jr. And afterwards we may have gone to an Elvis concert. As one does." Now we were both laughing, Zocco at the vividness of my imagination, me at the absurd truth of it.

Perhaps Real Madrid was a gilded cage from which I needed to make intermittent breakouts? Another mad trip, this time with the express permission of my employers, was to Ghana. It confirmed to me how important it was at this point to get away from it all. The origins of this latest sortie went back to when I was still at Borussia. Amongst the regular visitors to 'Lovers Lane' was a Ghanian businessman from Accra. One evening, probably after several rounds, he extracted the kind of foolish promise one can make in these situations. "Yeah, alright, why not?" I responded to his proposal that, "When you have the time, you must come and play a match in Ghana".

And now, several years later, the phone rang in Madrid. At the other end was the African businessman, reminding me of our late evening conversation. I am not, I think, the sort to pull out of a commitment just because it becomes aggravating to keep. But to have to travel all the way to Ghana on such a slight pretext, to satisfy someone who was not much more than a fleeting bar acquaintance ...

There was a possible, more or less honourable, way out. "I would like to come," I told him, "but they won't let me here." He continued to insist. I do not know what exactly prompted me to ask Real for its permission to go. Was it a sense of duty, boredom during my free time or the attraction of an offbeat challenge? Whatever, I was taken by surprise when the club agreed. There was no equivalent then to the flying missions which nowadays it encourages David Beckham to make to Asia for either an endorsement or as part of a PR campaign. The coaching staff, taking into consideration that at least I was going to be playing a game of football, probably thought to themselves, "Let the loon travel there, it might do him some good".

My old Borussia teammate, Hartwig Bleidick was on the flight with me. His name was being linked with the post of Ghana team coach, so it was a timely opportunity. As the plane came in to land at Accra Airport we could see a crowd, which was maybe two thousand, three thousand strong, close to the runway. My immediate thought was that there must be some statesman, whose face I did not recognise, on the flight. As the two of us descended the passenger stair, the crowd drew nearer. We met on the runway, from which I was carried shoulder-high to the terminal building. The official language in Ghana is English but those who had waited at the airport spoke the local dialect, Twi, which is beyond me. Still, I understood the chant, "Netzer! Netzer!" By the look on his face, it seemed that the world had ceased to make sense for Bleidick, just as it had for me. Who knew me here? And how? Nothing had prepared me for this.

Once inside the building, I was set down. And now I was required to talk at a press conference, specially called for me. A press conference! For me! In Ghana! Why? I was used to being questioned about football in West Germany and at Real Madrid. This was the first time I had been asked for my thoughts on the Ghanian game. Obviously, I had none. In order to say something, I remarked that it was becoming a force to be reckoned with.

For the rest of the day, I was both passed and shown around. In the morning our party was invited by a tribal chieftan, or 'king' as he was called. I got treated royally myself, which was both embarrassing and amusing.

In the afternoon there was going to be a match between an Accra side and some other, unspecified team. Two hours before kick-off I was led to the stadium by my acquaintance. Thirty thousand must have been there already. "Now you can show us," he said.

I had no idea what he meant. "Show what? What's this all about?"

"The people take you for a sorcerer."

I had no response to that.

"Because," he explained, "you can kick the ball round the corner."

The businessman came to the stadium frequently when he was in Mönchengladbach. What he called, 'shooting round the corner' was the technique of side-footing the ball in such a way as to give its flight some curve. I was not the only one to have mastered it. He did not just come to games but, occasionally, to training sessions, too. That is where we would line up at the corner flag and try, with the same enthusiasm as kids might display, to score a direct hit. "And now you can do it here," he said, "it's what the people want to see."

So that was the reason I had flown from Madrid to Ghana – to put on a dancing bear / circus clown performance. I could now see that my businessman friend was counting on me as the means to raise his profile and enhance his reputation. Slowly it dawned on me that it was via him that news of me and my extraordinary feats had spread amongst the people. He was, I thought, taking things a bit far. I was saved by the excuse that, here in Ghana, I did not have the right football boots: my own. "Unless I have my own boots," I said, "the magic will not work." For nearly two hours I kept delivering this sad message, as comfortingly as I could, until, finally, the spectators recognised that no voodoo show was going to be provided today by the white man from Europe.

We flew back. Bleidick did not become Ghana's coach. Rather than my refusal to take the stage, financial difficulties were the stumbling block. Back in Madrid, I simply remarked that I had travelled at the invitation of an old business friend without going into the full story, too embarrassing for me to talk about then.

9

Playing Hide-and-Seek in the Volksparkstadion

When Hannelore visited she would bring the German papers with her. Somehow or other we were still together – not as a couple, but as business partners. She took care of the disco in Mönchengladbach, which continued to do well, and the restaurant, a guaranteed headache. It looked as if all my first-year earnings with Real Madrid were going to be used covering its debts. Things could not carry on this way indefinitely. We were now in 1974, the year of the world cup. I had opened 'La Lacque' twelve months previously, since when it had done nothing besides amass liabilities.

In the meantime, we had moved into a house in the Peña del Sol neighbourhood. I was mostly living there by myself, even if Real had done everything, as part of the transfer, to accommodate my girlfriend. When she arrived in Madrid her cats naturally came with her. Like dogs, cats – hers were strays – did not always get treated as lovable pets in Spain. In other words, security arrangements for keeping ours off the Madrid streets had not been taken into account. Even if they probably thought we were barmy, Real straightaway dispatched a couple of their two hundred and forty employees to come and erect a chain-link fence around the property, secure enough to prevent their escape. There was also no escaping that it was a rather precious measure which, if heard about in West Germany, would cement my reputation as a self-indulgent diva. Real Madrid though were always conscientious in keeping a lid on anything that might cause problems for a player. The problem in this case having to do with a stressed partner concerned for her cats, and the player in question being myself. Anyway, could the issue of cat security make my reputation back home any worse than it already was? In the papers which Hannelore brought with her from Germany there was no mistaking the static I was creating at this time. It jumped off the pages. With the world cup only months away, the old question of who should be given the central midfield role, Wolfgang Overath or myself, was being asked once more.

Being far away was a factor. This was round about the time of Robert Schwan's futile Ritz mission to rescue Netzer and, in so doing, West German football itself. It was followed by a big debate in the media concerning the legitimacy or otherwise of my contract with Real Madrid, and the apparent desire of the Football Association, Helmut Schön – who found himself once more having to deal with my situation – included, to bring me back to West Germany. There was an objection to this, namely that I was neither free nor willing to return. I was determined to stay at Real Madrid and make things work. If my services were genuinely required by the national side then, naturally, I would be available. Only, not at any price. Schön was actually quite relaxed about this. So long as he had Real Madrid's written assurance that they would release me for international duty, other than for games against Spain, he was satisfied. But that is not what got reported. Instead, the Press blamed Real's disappointing season on my poor form.

Their portrayal of it was based neither on sound information nor on coming to watch me play – though what did that matter? What I always feared at Borussia Mönchengladbach, but had largely been able to avoid, was now happening. This was the evaluation of Günter Netzer the footballer on the basis of his lifestyle. So long as I was still at Mönchengladbach there was a possible response to all the mistrust I generated with the way I looked, my friends and acquaintances: every Saturday my football did the talking. Now that I was abroad, I had no perfectly weighted through balls or brilliant free kicks to set against the prejudice and preconceptions. I was reduced by the majority of the Press to this caricatural playboy, who had always been lazy and let others do the running for him and who, as a result of being more interested in business ventures, parties and hanging out in bars, had wasted his talent. All this was rubbish. The proof being that, besides my Las Vegas trip, which no one knew about, I simply did not have the time for dissipation in Madrid. I trained, then went home. Nothing else. Because nobody bothered to check on it, the dreary reality of my existence never got reported in the West German press.

The contrast between its increasingly negative treatment of me and the undue respect I received abroad was striking. Nevertheless, whenever I had any free time, I flew home. Hannelore's overflowing love of pets would often provide the excuse. It was not enough for her to stop and give a little attention to the countless stray dogs one runs across in Madrid's streets. Her mission was to take as many as she could in, nurse them back to health and then transport each back to West Germany and to a home with either a friend or an acquaintance. Norbert Pflippen, for example, who often used to help us out when we received speeding or parking tickets, himself received a mongrel with an uncertain past. Cats were sent home too. I would find myself acting as chaperone on the aeroplane, the cat in a cage and the dog settled on the cabin floor. Not all captains were happy about this. Those who foresaw an in-flight disturbance from within the animal kingdom would occasionally prevent us from boarding. This was not a problem for someone on Real Madrid's books. It only took a phone call for the two of us to be reallocated seats; Hannelore with the dog in business class, while I was upgraded to first class, still an unusual privilege for me back then, shared with the cat in its cage at my feet. Just one example, albeit a bizarre one, of the way in which players were indulged by the club.

If not a dream world exactly, Real Madrid's orbit was one in which it determined the way things were and, also, how it should be perceived. Amongst the fixtures that first year was a friendly against Ajax, the European Cup holders. Such games were a means of boosting players' salaries before TV rights money began to flow into Spanish football. 65,000 came to the Bernabéu on the night. Afterwards, the directors announced there would be no more friendlies if this was the maximum gate they were going to attract. Only at Real Madrid …

The Federal Republic, however, was a part of the world where, even if it had wanted to, Real Madrid could not exert its influence. Back there, the tabloids' campaign against me had reached its zenith. Later, articles in the Quality Press would reflect on how the Republic had entered a new, pragmatic phase with Helmut Schmidt becoming chancellor, following Brandt's fall. I have never known much about politics, and would still consider myself to be more or less apolitical. Still, I think there might have been a parallel between Borussia's expansive style of play and Willy Brandt's hopes. Neither was governed by pure calculation. Suddenly, Brandt was gone, while our footballing philosophy no longer counted for much. As one of the stars of the expansive style and a dissenter from the new orthodoxy, I, in particular, did not count any more. Helmut Schön may have selected five of the Borussia team, as well as myself, for the world cup squad, but we were virtually surplus to requirements. Kleff was the No.2 keeper. My position was by him on the bench, where we were joined after the first group stage by Wimmer. Heynckes was out injured. That left Berti Vogts and Rainer Bonhof as the only team members, obliged to adapt to a manner of playing that was different to the Gladbacher game.

I was back in my country, without feeling at home in it. When we reported to the pre-tournament training camp I was not in good condition. I therefore put in some work with Drygalski, my old fitness coach at Mönchengladbach. Gradually it began to pay off. I was still not included in the eleven. This did not prevent me from being more sought after by the Press than any of those who were. The same journalists who pounced on me as soon as I went to Madrid suddenly wanted to be best friends. Not because they had had second thoughts or felt in some way intimidated by me. No, they were hoping to be there the moment trouble arose. Something they felt they could count on with me. I was, after all, notorious as the rebel and oddball who had shown no fear in standing up to either Hennes Weisweiler or Helmut Schön. Now the expectation was that, following the poor first group stage performances against Chile and Australia, I would rip into the side. Or that at least I would have a go at Wolfgang Overath who, having taken my place, was making a slow start to the tournament. In a matter of a fortnight – although some were changing their minds about me from one day to the next – I had turned, in the Press' eyes, from the petulant one refusing to play his part, into the magnificent maverick, who could once more be expected to stand up against all the timid conformists. In other words, I was being heavily prompted to let them have it full on.

Why though would I do that? I had a good rapport with Overath. It would have been shabby to have intrigued with the Press in order to try and get him dropped. Besides, the mood in the team, not good for a while, would have hardly been improved either by outspokenness or a revolt. As I have already mentioned, I am an instinctive person. My instinct on this occasion told me that silence was the best course. This had nothing to do with practical calculations, such as what would have happened if, giving in to the journalists' pressure, I had gone ahead and caused trouble, but without any effect? The answer is I would have gone from being an endearing oddball to an out-and-out rotter overnight.

Considering the team went on to win the world cup, I did the right thing. But did Helmut Schön do right by me? He could see that, in training at least, I was in better form than ever, now the tournament was underway. The problem was I

Netzer and Beckenbauer. Borussia vs Bayern, early in the 1970-71 season. The matter of who was to end it triumphant would not be settled until the final Saturday

Günter Netzer's game was a combination of languor ...

... and drive: surging forward in the 1972 European Championship final

Preferred means of transport

Hamburg SV's young manager

With his wife, Elvira

did not figure in his tactical plans, including for the last group match, against East Germany. The encounter had political overtones. Chancellor Schmidt himself made the journey to Hamburg's Volksparkstadion. I would have done better to stay at home. The best thing would have been if Wolfgang Overath had joined me. His opposite number, Reinhard Lauck had him in his pocket. The rest were not much better. From the bench I watched our team's blunt attempts to muster itself with a feeling of helplessness. There was no bitterness on my part at being disregarded. If there had been, the feeling would not have lasted. Whether we would have done any better had I been involved from the kick-off is debatable. I did not relish being sent on as a substitute. The second half had just begun, with the score still 0-0, when the crowd began calling out my name. Such moments usually make a footballer proud and happy. My reaction though was one of fear. Helmut Schön came over to me. "Start warming up," he said, taking me by surprise.

Could I have contradicted him, as I had Hennes Weisweiler in the cup final the year before? Neither manager necessarily wanted to send me on. They were both influenced by the crowd. But the previous situation had been fundamentally different. To have sacrificed any of the starting eleven so that I could join that amazing final would have been an insult to him, because each one had raised his game to the highest level. Here in the Volksparkstadion it was the reverse: none of the starting line-up was playing well. My distinct feeling was that it was I who was to be the sacrificial lamb. I literally made a run for it, towards the furthest corner of the stadium, half-hoping that I would not be found there. Schön yelled at me to come back a bit. I yelled back that I needed to settle myself before going on. The strange games people play!

What chance was there of me influencing the match? It was well known that I only played at my best when the team was functioning smoothly, which was still not the case as I came on with twenty-one minutes remaining. Eight minutes later, Jürgen Sparwasser wrongfooted Horst-Dieter Höttges and fired in the DDR's winning goal. Helmut Schön would now have happily pulled me off, so that the crowd no longer sang my name.

His team became world champions, but what did that have to do with me? In the last training session before the final against Holland, I was Cruyff. And I think I can say, without false modesty, that in this practice game I was one of the best Cruyffs there has ever been. At the end of it I needed to build my marker's, a shattered Berti Vogts, confidence back up again. He was fearing the worst for the final. "Berti," I told him, "Cruyff has never in his life played the way I have today." Everything I did came off. For the final itself I was not even on the substitutes bench. But, however strange it may sound, that did not matter. Thanks to this dress rehearsal I felt relieved, even exhilarated. The West German team were world champions. Even today I would not claim to be. I was European champion but never world champion. It is not something that bothers me.

Another probable reason for my good mood was that after the second group match, against Sweden in Düsseldorf, I caught a glimpse, through the pelting rain, of the shape of my immediate future. It did not look too bad. Although still to be officially named as the new Real Madrid coach, after the 4-2 West German victory Milan Miljanić confided this, as well as the plans he had for his target Paul Breitner, to me. I could now look forward to an end to my Madrileño solitude and the anxiety which went with it.

It was hard to guess, during that first meeting, exactly what Miljanić had in store for us. Maybe I got a hint when, at the stadium for the final, he took me aside. Even if he was not yet in post, he gave me his first instructions. They were delivered in perfect Spanish, a sure sign that, like Real Madrid, he had been preparing for this move for a long time. "You have now had a good rest. Training begins in Madrid in three days."

"What do you mean, "rest"?" I asked. "I have spent six weeks of the summer at a training camp. I need a break." Miljanić ignored this. "Madrid," he said, "in three days." On that first day back at the club it was immediately clear that, at the final, he had been giving me a little foretaste of his attitude towards work.

10

Madrid – Zurich

"Slave driver," I shouted. "Oppressor. You sick sadist, taking pleasure in our suffering." I was not prepared to take any more. All my strength had gone and my nerves were shattered. Paul Breitner, the world champion who had now joined us, after I managed to allay Bernabéu's concerns about his politics, was gradually approaching his limit, too. And he was a fitness fanatic.

It was my second year in the mountains for pre-season training. Madrid in summertime is too hot. During the day any sport is impossible. Only in the evenings, and then not until late, can one run around a little. Miljanić insisted on three training sessions a day; that meant the mountains.

How suitable though are they for sport? Coming down on skis might be fun; going up in the opposite direction is another matter. For those who like that kind of thing, fine, but I do not. I hate it. We began at 7 am with a run. You can probably imagine how much the German running machine that I was appreciated heading up there. I had never been Mönchengladbach's answer to Paavo Nurmi. What Miljanić demanded of us was a lot more than I had been used to with Hennes Weisweiler, or Fritz Langner, another taskmaster, or, earlier still, what I had encountered as a youth player at the Duisburg-Wedau Sports Academy. Their training programmes resembled a spa cure, with a little exercise thrown in, more than they did this regime. It was supervised by a fitness coach who accompanied Miljanić from Yugoslavia and who had been the national 1500 metres champion on several occasions. Later, he went on to be head coach at Sporting Lisbon. At the time I am talking about, he did not know a great deal about tactics and training with the ball. Radišić knew a lot about drills though. His first name was Felix, meaning happy. In order to live up to it he must have disregarded his own exercise instructions, which, as far I am concerned, amounted to attempted GBH.

Following some sport in the morning, the midday session was devoted to muscle development – of the stomach. What role though did a muscular stomach play in improving a footballer? Even today I do not have the answer. The exercise involved was mean and nasty. The athlete and his patron, Miljanić had us do never-ending sit-ups, as though a washboard stomach would guarantee more goals in the months to come. Our training was really gymnastics. For four of the six weeks' pre-season preparation we did not get to see a ball. In the evening came another run. And why not? It is always good to discover the mountains.

After two weeks of this torture, I began to go a bit mental and started yelling and screaming at the sadists. The two gentlemen were unmoved. Unfortunately for us, Miljanić also had firm views on day-to-day discipline. There were to be moments when he had me running, for the telephone this time, as I made it back with seconds to spare to answer the 11 pm call that was made to check players were at home. In contrast to Weisweiler's encouragement of debate, Miljanić also made it clear that our tactical views were not required.

The result of my outburst was that I had to show everyone how fit I was by running up the hill again, this time on my own. I was certainly fit. Fitter than I have ever been in my life, and not just physically, but mentally too. Although the first year in Spain had been hard, on account of the hostility in West Germany, the jibes of the Spanish press and the barely concealed scepticism of my teammates, I can now see that it was one of the most important times of my life. Back home, Hannelore Girrulat had been an important influence in helping me to find a life beyond football, while Hennes Weisweiler had left his mark on me as a footballer. Here, for the first time, I had to sort things out for myself.

Without going so far as to say that it was impossible to find an equivalent social milieu in Spain, the circumstances here were very different to those I was used to. Besides the different language, the mentality was more nonchalant. Then there was the pride of my Spanish teammates, who were satisfied they could get along perfectly well without me. Regarding penalty taking responsibilities, which I had assumed in my debut match, they were probably right. I was no longer royalty like in Mönchengladbach. The distinct and novel feeling that luck would not necessarily shine down on me grew. There were obstacles to contend with during the first year. I needed to assert myself. To suddenly be shaken out of old habits is not such a bad experience. If one is unable to adapt then it is a question of turning back, or surrender. But if an adjustment can be made, at the end of it one will emerge stronger than before. I believe – in fact I am certain – that it was this maturity, demonstrated by a new self-control, which allowed me to find my way back into the national side so smoothly.

To anyone who has the opportunity to live abroad for a year or more, my frank advice would be to seize it with both hands. Independent of the work aspect, the experience is worth the trouble. I had succeeded in branching out. Paul Breitner's arrival meant I was over the worst of my expatriate existence. Now it was just Miljanić and his track athlete sidekick I had to survive. By getting to grips with their methods I did.

It is futile thinking about how my international career might have turned out if I had always been at the physical level I had finally attained. I now understand that it is only by being a natural choice for the national side that one can develop into an international star. At the time, I did not appreciate it; nor did I particularly care. I won thirty-seven caps. If I had been fitter, I might have earned more. Or, perhaps, less. The confinement and drilling of six weeks pre-season with Real were so extreme that if I had had to endure them on a long-term basis, I would have been a much worse player. Not having a life outside it, at the same time as taking the fun out of football, would probably have turned me into a nervous wreck. But it is vain to speculate.

With Breitner and – through clenched teeth, I have to admit – Miljanić the persecutor, Real Madrid had become a different proposition. A single look at Paul's bush of hair and handlebar moustache was enough for Chairman Bernabéu to tell that the use of hairnets, introduced in the army for those doing national service, would not be effective here. There were no more rules and regulations concerning what a Real player could or could not wear. But why would they moan about Paul's curls and my mane? In peak condition, we were the guarantee of an upturn in the club's fortunes. Linking and directing play, the two of us ensured there was hardly a side that could touch us. Together we formed a strong unit. We were rarely injured. When others' tongues began to loll, we remained strong. Should the tribute be laid at the foot of the mountain? Looked at objectively, yes. My subjective feelings were hard to dispel though. How I had suffered; how I had cursed the coach …

Our partnership brought two successive league titles. The first, if my memory can be relied upon, was won by a fifteen-point margin over the runners-up, Barcelona. That year we also retained the Copa del Rey. Real Madrid was back where it belonged, occupying centre stage in the national game. It was Breitner, complementing me perfectly in midfield, who made this possible.

And now a couple of words about this man Paul Breitner, whose reputation in Germany is not all that it might be. I got to know him in Madrid, where we had a great time together. Contrary to most of what one reads and hears regarding him – that he is a schemer who only cares about himself – Paul is a man with a big heart. There was not a single occasion with me when he was phony, dropped me in it or thought only of himself.

I was very close to the Breitner family, in whose home I was a frequent visitor. The gaps between Hannelore's visits to Madrid were getting longer. I am not the kind who likes to spend the evening alone in his flat preparing something to eat. It was Paul and his sweet wife who fed me. As a small thank-you at

Christmas I dressed up as Santa for their children. They were all kind enough not to remark upon my limited acting abilities. Nor, just because they were abroad, did they deprive themselves of wholesome Bavarian nourishment. If roast pork, meat loaf, veal sausage and dumplings were unavailable in Madrid, they would have a food parcel sent from home. For Paul, who was able to eat as much as he wanted without it showing, that was not a problem. But, after I had weighed myself the following morning, I needed to go for a run so as to immediately shed what had been put on. This was the price for family living, which I was happy to pay. I now had the balanced existence lacking in my first year.

Better performances on the pitch gradually brought acceptance from both the team and from the Press. It no longer wrote about 'The Fallen Statue'. Instead, after I had played a particularly good game, I was called 'The Blond Angel with the Big Feet'. Slowly, I built a relationship with my Spanish teammates, particularly Amancio, Pirri and Zocco. Conversation was no longer limited to just football. We would quite often talk about Spanish politics too, a subject I had initially taken little notice of. The purring Real Madrid machine sheltered and cocooned its players. In 1974, though, you could hardly fail to notice the signs that a change was coming.

The political stirrings had first touched the football world and become a dressing room topic of conversation with the killing of Carrero Blanco, in a car bomb attack the previous December. This was the former admiral whom Franco had appointed prime minister only a few months earlier. The following morning there were spectacular images in the newspapers showing his car blasted ten metres up into the air by the devastating explosion. Elsewhere in the papers there were reports of the political trial of a dissident priest. The two stories seemed to be of a pattern. The gravity of the situation was brought home to all us apolitical footballers when it became clear that, for the first time ever in Spain, calling off that weekend's La Liga fixtures was being seriously considered. The debate occupied several hours of parliamentary time, before a vote decided in favour of the matches being played. Depending on how one looked at it, the assembly's interest revealed either the special position held by football in Spain or just how radical the changes taking place had become.

Our privileged everyday lives remained largely unaffected by events surrounding the dictator's decline. Every now and again, without knowing what was going on, one would see the Guardia Civil making its heavy-handed presence felt. There were frequent stories of arbitrary arrests, which, unlike Paul and me, the Spanish players were well informed about. Occasionally these involved someone they knew. Bomb attacks and assassination attempts became common. I was advised by one or two acquaintances to take it easy if stopped in the street or pulled over by the traffic police. I wondered whether it was really that bad? The police and the Guardia Civil knew all the players by sight. But, because there was so much tension during this period, I would make a point of putting my hands on the steering wheel or the dashboard when one of the numerous checks took place. Just to be on the safe side. There had been instances of jumpy officers shooting when unexceptional drivers reached into the glove compartment for their papers, because they feared they were about to pull out a gun.

Throughout the country, Real Madrid was regarded as a supporter of the old order. It certainly did not distinguish itself by any attempt to distance itself from Franco, even if it alone continued to bear the royal name during this period. As an uncommitted German, the club's affinity with the regime only struck me when we played in the Catalan capital. FC Barcelona, whose motto was, and remains, '*Més que un club*' – 'More than a club' – had for many years been at the heart of the Catalan resistance. The home fans chant of, "*Madrid, cabrón!*", which echoed around the Nou Camp for our benefit, meant, "Madrid, you shits!" Fortunately, they did not single out Paul or me. Everywhere in Spain, as far as I could tell, we were taken for the footballers – good footballers – we were, and nothing else.

It was Paul who followed the situation more closely than I did. At about 5 am on 21 November 1975 he called to say that the dictator's death had just been announced on the radio. Franco had indeed been very ill. It had taken thirty-two doctors to prolong his life by an extra month. Now that he was dead, Spain was poised to enter a new era. I was in Madrid for eighteen months before and eighteen months following the change. For a neutral its effects were most obvious out on the street. One would have needed to be deaf and blind in the first days after Franco's death not to have noticed a radical lightening of the previously heavy ambience. It was immediately plain to tell that the people were intent on trying to catch up on what they had missed during forty years spent under a dictatorship. The nightlife in Madrid suddenly became livelier and continued later. Not for us, however. Miljanić made sure that his 11 pm curfew was more rigidly applied than ever.

Real Madrid was once again a force to be reckoned with in the league, without having yet returned to European supremacy. In 1976, having made a good start in the tournament, we found ourselves two matches from the final. It was another occasion when a corny scriptwriter appeared to have been at work, this time in plotting the quarter-finals draw, the kind of scenario most serious writers would have resisted composing. That is to say, we were up against Borussia. Hennes Weisweiler had in the meantime left, to manage, of all clubs, Barcelona. Fortunately, this was not a great success and he was soon back in West Germany, where he ended the club's drought by leading 1. FC Köln to the title.

The new coach at Borussia was Udo Lattek. The initial plan, as Berti Vogts informed me, had been to try and find a trainer in the Weisweiler mould. The question was, where could you find such a person? The most obvious solution would have been to appoint the assistant trainer who was most familiar with his aims and methods. Erich Ribbeck fitted the bill but was now under contract with 1. FC Kaiserslauten. Trying to imitate Weisweiler was never going to be a straightforward option anyhow, since he was one of a kind. Because he cast such a long shadow, it was necessary for his successor to choose a different path. Lattek did this by introducing a direct style of play. Even though I had enjoyed the liberty which he placed such value on, I was pretty sure that Weisweiler's football philosophy had been taken as far as it could at the club. Lattek's new method, as the Mönchengladbacher players told me, involved a great deal of discipline, punctualness and order.

It had already brought success. His record was first rate. Out of the old, impetuous Borussia he had created a team capable of playing strong defensive football for the 1975-76 European Cup campaign. So, we knew what to expect in the Düsseldorfer Rheinstadion, which is where Borussia chose to play again, given the Bökelberg's limited capacity. On the other hand, I was not sure what sort of welcome awaited me personally.

I had had a strange feeling from the moment the draw was announced. Playing against the club where I had spent ten phenomenal years was a big deal. I still felt a strong attachment to Borussia. At the same time, my intention was to do everything I could to dump them out of the cup. To swipe them off the mountain. Not that I was free of emotion. This was the stadium in which I had made my triumphant farewell in that memorable cup final. It was where I had made my last appearance in the Federal Republic – I do not count the farcical twenty-one minutes against the DDR. How would the crowd react to me? Two years on, was I still a traitor to the fatherland? Football fans can be forgetful – both of the good and the bad times.

They can also have a fine sense of occasion. As I ran out onto the pitch, the 68,000 crowd began a minute-long ovation. I was deeply touched. For me it remains a good example of those, not infrequent, occasions when there is a big difference between the official consensus and what the public actually thinks. The fans did not regard me as a traitor. They remembered the good times we shared together. Perhaps they appreciated that I was partly responsible for some of the sublimest moments they had experienced in a football stadium. It was a joyful homecoming, both for the people in the stands and for myself out on the pitch.

I felt right. The mood helped me to play at my best. All the same, it was Borussia who took a two-goal lead through

Jensen and Wittkamp. Then, after the break, everything clicked. Martinez scored our opener. The equaliser involved playing a wall pass once again in the Rheinstadion. This time my partner was Pirri. It was he, rather than me, who concluded the movement. Who knows, maybe the atmosphere would have soured a little if I had been the scorer instead? Probably not, but I think it was best the way it was. 2-2 was the final score.

After the game came an embarrassing press conference in the vaults of the Rheinstadion. I was invited along by Miljanić to act as his translator. His remarks posed a bit of a problem for me. Was I really supposed to announce that, "Günter Netzer's performance was world class"? Or that, "Netzer has once again shown that he belongs amongst world football's elite"? If someone else were to say such things, I might feel proud. But they are not the kind of remarks one can really make about oneself. I provided various matter-of-fact observations instead: 2-2 was a fair result, reflecting the run of play; Borussia had the better of the first and Real Madrid of the second half, as our midfield, in which Paul Breitner was outstanding, took control. That kind of thing. Then Miljanić, who spoke at least a little German, butted in to uncover my diffidence. He had said nothing of the kind suggested by my translation. The fulsome praise now began. But at least it was he who was providing it, unaided by myself.

The mood of the return leg was not so good. The fault was neither ours nor Borussia's. Udo Lattek's instructions were to attack. This made sense. Because of the away goals rule, a 0-0 or 1-1 result would see us progress. On the night, Borussia were clearly the better side. But what good did that do them when the worst performance, by far, was that of the referee, Leo van der Kroft? We could not have argued with a final score of 1-3, spelling the end of Real Madrid's European Cup hopes at the quarter-finals stage. Van der Kroft, however, disallowed two Mönchengladbacher goals. One he gave offside, the other he overruled for a handball. I saw no infringements and nor did my teammates. Nor did the 120,000 spectators. TV action replays later confirmed that both decisions were blatantly wrong. How could an internationally recognised referee have messed things up so badly?

The result was that, for the second time, Borussia had been shooed out of the European Cup unfairly. On the first occasion, against Inter Milan, I had experienced this injustice myself; now I was on the other side. Knowing how they felt somewhat marred my pleasure at progressing in the competition. It prompted me to go to the hotel bar, where they were hanging around dejectedly, to express my sympathy to my old mates. Their anger was evident. I was rather put out that they held me partly to blame for the result. Suddenly, I was no longer the old companion but the opponent, the enemy who had profited from an ill-starred performance by the referee. But Real Madrid had done nothing wrong. After both of the goals we had walked back, without protest, towards the halfway line, since we couldn't see anything to object about either. It took a while before the Gladbachers and I were able to have a normal conversation with one another about this night.

In the following days there was a lot of speculation in West Germany as to what could explain Van der Kroft's aberrant decisions. Two theories emerged. The first, without any supporting evidence being provided, was that this was a case of good old-fashioned bribery. However hard I might try, I still cannot imagine that being true. Not when the person involved is Santiago Bernabéu, a man of principle. The other theory related to Holland's defeat in the 1974 World Cup Final, in spite of being the better team. Apparently, the Dutch were still resentful of the Germans' victory, and so Van der Kroft was subconsciously inclined to blow his whistle on these two occasions. Without knowing, that also seems unlikely to me.

The screenplay for our European campaign did not include participation in the final. In the second act, the semi-finals, it was Paul Breitner's old team, Bayern Munich, champions in 1974 and '75, whom we came up against. With Paul out injured, the best we could manage in the home leg was a 1-1 draw. Bayern's game management was simply cleverer than ours. The return match, in the Olympic stadium, showed how different the culture of FC Bayern was to that of Borussia. Breitner had not left the club on bad terms. He had been involved in some memorable moments, including that first European Cup triumph in 1974. Nevertheless, the crowd showed no gratitude, nor any understanding that a player might want to move on from Munich, if only for financial motives. Football fans can be forgetful; sometimes they do not have a fine sense of occasion. Paul was whistled at. So, for that matter, was I. The chorus was maintained for half an hour whenever either of us had the ball, which was frequently. By this point Real Madrid were 2-0 down, which was also the final score. Bayern went on to win their third successive European title.

Our failure meant that the intensity of Felix Radišić, the track athlete's torture went up a notch. As I neared thirty-two, there were days when I felt like giving up, when I had had enough of having to endure this misery. These grew more frequent. With a stronger will, I might have resisted being phased out of Real Madrid, as now seemed quite likely. Long before Manchester United and Bayern Munich began to share the limelight with Real, football was no longer just a sport and a pastime. It was already a show. A show which must continuously provide new attractions. As the club appreciated, every two or three years the public has to be presented with a fresh face. I understood that I was the number one candidate for replacement. That might sound cynical, seeing as old Bernabéu, following Madrid's retention of the title, had automatically extended all contracts, regardless of the views of either the coach or the players themselves.

All except mine that is. Why, I do not know. I frequently talked with my roommate Amancio about how I was keen to stay. As I came towards the end of my career, my ideas were fairly vague. I fancied the prospect of dividing my time half-and-half between West Germany and Spain. I had no real plan though as to how I would actually be spending it, either in Germany or in Madrid. In a way, these conversations with Amancio were intended to signal to Real that I hoped to stay. I was aware that, if my football career ended at this moment, I had no other means of fending for myself. Overall, my feelings were mixed, which is probably the impression I conveyed.

The club, as Miljanić later confided to me, had pondered for a long time whether, contrary to its custom, it should keep me on, so long as the level of my performances gave no cause for concern and my teammates did not grow sceptical. Finally, they decided against doing so. The general manager, Agustin Dominguez, let me know. My reaction indicated that my ambitions as a footballer, never particularly strong, had already been satisfied. There was no display of disappointment or anger. My main feeling was one of liberation. The misery of training and all the daily rules and regulations would soon be over.

I did not have to worry about my playing career coming to an immediate end. For the past six months the chairman of Grasshopper Zürich had been telling me that, if ever I felt like a change, I should pay him a visit. The determination of this man, a manufacturer of BBC equipment, became clearer with each, monthly, call. There was no doubt that, one day or another, he expected me to come and play for him.

Alternative options included America, which did not appeal, or a return to West Germany. Berti Vogts had suggested this should be back to Mönchengladbach. Knowing of my growing tiredness, part of his plan was that I would only be used in home games. Schalke showed interest in me for a second time, and a daring offer came from FC St. Pauli. How serious it was I am not sure. Money though did not seem to be a problem. I would not have been any worse off going there. Apart from lacking the desire to play in the Bundesliga again, the idea that someone like myself, with a weakness for expensive fast cars and reputation as a playboy, should play for the club located by the rough-and-ready Reeperbahn, famous for other things besides football, was not without its amusing side.

Maybe the club's fans sensed that there was a difference in my case between reputation and reality. Several years later I had an experience in St. Pauli which suggested to me I would have been welcome here. It happened following an appearance for the Uwe Seeler Old Boys XI at the Millerntor stadium. A man leaned towards me out of a scrum of autograph hunters. As he passed an envelope, he said *sotto voce*, "On Sunday it is your birthday. This is my present for you." He had got the dates muddled up. My birthday was not until Sunday week.

I ought probably not say this, but neither every envelope nor blessing one receives from the fans should be taken entirely seriously. Not out of either ignorance or arrogance but simply because the attention can often become overwhelming. At home on the Monday, I picked up the envelope again and opened it. Inside was a marked lottery ticket. I had never bought one myself. I inspected it for a few moments and, feeling none the wiser, dropped it into the wastepaper basket. Without thinking anything more about it, I carried on with my day. Later on, perhaps instinctively – looking back, it appears as one of those mysterious moments which occur every now and again in life – I checked for the winning numbers in the newspaper. Again, for the first time in my life. I had the strange feeling that I recognised the numbers. The next two hours were spent searching, before I remembered that I had thrown the ticket into the wastepaper basket, from which I now retrieved it. Five correct numbers and the bonus …

The winning numbers which this fan had provided were not random. They were 6 – 9 – 14 – 37 – 44 – 47. I was born on 14/9/'44. My shoe size is 47. 37 is the number of West German caps I won. I scored 6 goals as an international. The way the numbers were ordered meant I did not immediately see the connection. It was the fan who pointed it out to me. At the time, I was working in the office of the Swiss licensing rights firm run by Caesar W. Lüthi. While the phone number was listed in the directory, to be put through to me required persistence on the man's part. He told me that for the past twenty years he had entered the same number on his lottery ticket. Also, that he had a tattoo on his bicep, 'Netzer 10', after the position I played in. That week he had not only filled out a ticket for me but, wisely, for himself as well. Arriving at the kiosk late, he had to knock at the door to rouse the vendor and talk him into accepting his ticket. The lucky thing was that he had got the dates mixed up for my birthday: if he had given me the ticket a week later it would not have matched the winning numbers. As it was, we had both won 150,000 marks. Was it right, as the well-off man I had become, to accept such a present, I asked myself? On the other hand, I further thought, would it be right to turn it down? The fellow had put plenty of thought into this. He wished me only good. I suggested to him that we divide my 150,000 between us. Fortunately, he agreed, which also made me feel good.

I imagine he would have been happy had I signed for St. Pauli twenty years before. My plan though, if I was unable to stay with Real Madrid for a final year, was to find another foreign club where I hoped to play at a somewhat lower level. A French side, giving me the opportunity to learn the language and enjoy the country, would have been ideal. The only problem was that no offers were made. Servette Geneva, on the other hand, expressed interest, as did Grassphopper Zürich, whose coach, Helmut Johannsen, made no attempt to conceal his eagerness that I should play for him.

The situation I was in was a good one. I was still under contract with Madrid so would continue to draw my salary for six more months, without having to comply with the Yugoslavian 1500 metres champion's regime any longer. The last stage of my career was more or less assured. It would be spent in peace and quiet in the Swiss league. The choice of club was mine. I arrived in Zurich for contract negotiations on a summer's day that began amidst Madrid's big city pace and noise. Being shown around Zurich, through which the River Limmat burbled, I could see the lake stretch out serenely. My face was known, even here in Switzerland, but I was able to move about freely. Partly perhaps because football is not as big a deal as skiing or ice hockey. Besides, Zurich and her inhabitants are unfazed by celebrity. Nowadays, Tina Turner is a resident. Like everyone else, she visits the market. On this summer day Zurich exuded its charm. It was idyllic, promising peace, at the same time as offering the convenience of city living. I was staying a little outside the city in Regensdorf. The owner of my hotel was also Grasshoppers' treasurer. Seclusion, quiet and relaxation: this is what I was looking for. It was Zurich's beauty which swung the deal for me.

What I had not counted on was that Johannsen had other plans for me besides a gentle winding down of my career. He thought I would enjoy the responsibility, as an experienced player, of guiding the team's younger members. His calculation was correct. Still, it was hard work. On the first day of training, I sat with the coach in front of the other players gathered in the hut. When my new colleagues came to shake hands and chat a little, I could not understand a word they were saying. Was this a practical joke at the widely travelled man of the world's, the former Real Madrid star's expense? I can speak German, reasonably good English and am able to make myself understood in Spanish. This though was a foreign tongue. While I would expect to make out the odd phrase in a jovial pub in the heart of the Bavarian Forest, at Zürich's training facility I did not comprehend a word these new teammates were saying.

Thanks to the universal language of football, it didn't take too much time for us to get along. The Swiss league was not as ordinary as its reputation suggested. Some of the players were top class. Köbi Kuhn, the current national coach, Karl Odermatt and Fritz Künzli could have played in any European league. The Swiss one was not about to be a veteran's stroll for me. I was going to have to carry on exerting myself.

This was around the time the great Pele was marking his retirement. Like Franz Beckenbauer, he had chosen to spend the last phase of his career playing for The New York Cosmos, with whom he hoped he might help establish football in the United States. I had been invited to play in his farewell match. Besides being honoured, the trip promised to be a welcome break from the routine of Swiss football. With a Swiss friend, I flew to New York.

We are talking about 1977. The Big Apple was far from a safe place. On the day of the match, it was pouring rain as we stood waiting helplessly for a taxi in front of the Manhattan Hilton. But there were none to be had to take me and Mario Widmer, then reporter for the Swiss paper *Blick*, now the partner of tennis player Martina Hingis' mother, to the stadium. All of a sudden, I heard my name being called. "Hey, Netzer! It's Netzer, isn't it?" The voice belonged to one of two black men sitting in a car that had drawn up on the other side of the street. He was waving excitedly. "Netzer! Hey, Netzer!" To be recognised in football ignorant New York, where even Pele and Beckenbauer were barely known, came as a big surprise. I crossed the street. "You are Netzer, Günter Netzer from Germany!" There could be no doubt about it, he knew who I was. He must also have been aware that I was anxious to get to Pele's farewell match on time. He wanted to go himself. His buddy, if his face were anything to go by, didn't have the slightest idea as to what was going on. "You have arrived right on cue," I said. "It's impossible to find a taxi. Do you have room for me and my friend?"

He happily accepted, and we got in. He mentioned that he had a small errand to run. Widmer grew wary. "Come on. Let's get out. This is becoming a joke." But we were already on the move. I felt relieved. We were out of the rain and on the way to the stadium. We drove for what seemed quite a while. To Widmer, who knows Manhattan well, it appeared that we were heading out of the city. The car then pulled up in front of a bar. This was his bar, the man said. "You must come in with me," he added. "It won't take long." Was I feeling wary? The situation was in fact not entirely new. In Europe it was not unusual for a fan to want to show me off to his friends. But here in New York, in America? How come I had a fan here?

As he led us inside, the busy bar instantly fell silent. No Latinos, no whites were to be seen amongst the staring faces. We were a novelty; this was a blacks' only establishment. Our friendly chauffeur ushered us through the saloon. Feeling a little bemused, we followed him. At the stadium in two hours an enthusiastic 75,000 crowd would be celebrating Pele and, amongst other things, expecting me. The man opened a door to a sort of inner sanctum. We followed him in.

"Here we are," he said. I had already noted the two posters on the opposite wall which he was gesturing to. One of Johann Cruyff and, next to it, one of myself. Standing in this Harlem bar back room with the Dutchman and me staring down from the wall was a strange moment. All he wanted was for me to autograph my poster. "OK," I agreed, "then you can drive me to the stadium." Widmer's face was no longer (completely) white. I had been fairly naive. New York in 1977 was a dangerous town and Harlem was not a tourist destination for whites. Although I knew a visit there could be fatal, I had allowed myself to be led astray.

Pele's farewell was a success. I never saw my Harlem friend again.

Even adventures such as this could not divert me from the realisation that football was becoming harder for me. Every morning I ached all over. I had had enough of being a professional footballer, living alone in a hotel. My image as a playboy with a stream of girlfriends was precisely that: an image. One last year, I told myself ... But the injuries incurred throughout my career were becoming increasingly difficult to ignore, and the willpower required to battle their cumulative effect harder to summon. It was sometime in the summer of 1977 that I went to Johannsen to tell him I was calling it a day. I had played enough football. I had no desire to carry on.

Johannsen and the club realised that. The point was, however, that Grasshoppers' budget was strictly limited then. Compared to a West German or Spanish club they drew very small crowds. So long as I was involved, they could go ahead with plans for a lucrative tour of North and Central America. That, I acknowledged, was not such a bad prospect. It was something for which I could rouse myself.

The club was very keen that, before departing, we should spend a bit of time training in the South. Thanks to my contacts with Real Madrid, this was easy to arrange. On leaving the club, I had provided it with my successor, also from Borussia. Uncovering him took time: Henning Jensen had disappeared back to Denmark, where he liked to live simply in his log cabin during the summer break. Even with a generous offer from Madrid on the table, luring him back into the football world at such a moment had been hard work. Having finally succeeded, Real owed me a favour. Grasshoppers made their base in Marbella, which is where, running the training sessions, I discovered I had a taste and talent for management. In spite of the Ajax experience, a friendly with Real Madrid was arranged.

It was an enjoyable night in the Bernabéu. We lost 3-6. I played like a Gladbacher foal again. There were no aches and pains. Everyone had fun. After the match we all got together for a rowdy time. At 4.30 am the phone rang in my hotel room. "There are three gentlemen here to see you," reception informed me. "Aha, at half past four in the morning," I said and put the receiver down.

Two minutes later came knocking at the door. It was a trio of police officers commanding me to accompany them. They gave no reason. Any opposition or refusal on my part seemed pointless. I had no idea what it was all about; nor did my roommate. All they said, when I asked, was, "You'll find out". It couldn't be anything to do with importing the Ferrari illegally, nor with my unauthorised trip to Las Vegas on a temporary passport. Was exporting rescue dogs an offence? I didn't know. I was taken to the nick.

The crown prosecutor would come, I was told, and present me with the facts of the case. I wondered where they were going to find such a person at 4.30 on a Saturday morning. My nerves were getting a little frayed as I joined others in the remand cell. You can imagine how I felt. I was known in Madrid, after all.

'Günter Netzer in Jail' did not look good. For most of the three hours I was stuck in the cell, I was being questioned about Real Madrid. I don't think the man opposite appreciated I no longer played for the club.

Finally, at around eight, the prosecutor arrived. The mystery of my detention was now resolved. "You left Madrid with an unpaid 14,000 mark telephone bill. And your final month's electricity too." I understood the electricity being unpaid: there had been a mad rush to sort everything out in the last few days before leaving Madrid for Zurich. In fact, for the last six months at Real I was living, as I had at the start, in a hotel. It is quite likely that, when leaving the house I had been renting in Peña del Sol, I forgot to pay the final electricity bill. The outstanding amount came to forty-three marks and I am not sure how many pfennigs. When the landlord read that Grasshoppers were planning to take me to Zurich, he pressed charges. All this fuss over forty-three marks and a few pfennigs plus a telephone bill was a bit irritating.

At least it was clear when the 14,000 mark telephone bill had been run up: a two-month period during the summer of 1974 which I had mostly spent with the national squad, preparing for and competing in the world cup (six weeks) or in the mountains, with Miljanić and his henchman (another week). Neither was hard to verify. The prosecutor obviously realised that the sum being demanded could not be correct. Although he was unwilling to let me go just like that, by a stroke of luck he was a football fan who happened to know Agustin Dominguez. When I asked him if I could phone Dominguez, my learned friend gracefully obliged. A few minutes were all that was needed for Agustin to arrange for me to be set free. During eighteen months of Franco's strict regime I had avoided any trouble with the law. Now this.

Who had caused my phone bill to mount so high remained a puzzle. Perhaps it was the landlord trying to make some money out of a rich footballer? I never learned what had actually happened, nor whether Real Madrid ended up paying the amount to Telefónica. Once freed, I was able to return to Marbella, where my teammates were waiting for me. Completely unconcerned, it seemed. Hell, they must have thought, Günter's been on a bender in his old Madrid haunts.

This was the unusual concluding episode to my time in Madrid. My stint with Grassphoppers was also coming to an end, and my playing career with it. And then what? Looking back today, I am shocked at the insouciance, or even arrogance, with which I was contemplating the future, without having any plans in place. It was certainly not the case that I had no need to worry about money. Players' salaries were still a long way off current levels. A lot had been sunk into the Mönchengladbach restaurant. Compared to most people, it is true, I was comfortably off. But Switzerland, where the cost of living, in a decent property, came to 200,000 francs per annum, was not somewhere I could afford to take a couple of years off, even if I had wanted to. Without a nest egg and not being freelance, I both needed and wanted to find a job now that my career was over. But as to what might be a worthwhile future, matching my talents: I had barely given it a thought.

11

Benefactors and Wide Boys

Mexico were simply in a different class. We stood no chance in a friendly with the national team, which ended 0-6. After the final whistle I went straight to the dressing room, took off my boots and everything else, showered and got dressed. That was the end of my career as a professional footballer. Talking about it with the Grasshopper teammates I had joined on this final tour did not seem worthwhile. No speeches were made, no bottles uncorked. I had always found the rituals performed at such moments to be an unnecessary indulgence. They are much too sentimental for my taste. Matter-of-fact acceptance rather than melancholy is the way in which I prefer to react.

Does that make me strange? Perhaps; but when was I anything else? Football is meant to be an emotional game, I realise. And now the final whistle had blown. It belonged to my past. The time had come for something different, a new phase bringing novel experiences and fresh encounters.

Had Breitner been around, my departure from Madrid might not have fallen so flat. He would probably have organised an extravagant farewell meal, with plenty of Bavarian beer and

Spanish wine. But he and his family were away on holiday, so it took place without either commotion or emotion. We had formed a close bond during our shared time in Madrid; once our paths divided the contact was soon lost. It was not the only case of a football friendship being confined to a particular time and place. Why that should be I am not entirely sure. It probably indicates that the relationship built on the pitch is dependent on that single, shared interest. Our career paths had coincided and for two seasons, during which we played top quality football and were rewarded with trophies, we had been close. But this familiarity was not based on sharing private joys and sorrows, or looking to one another when in extremis, which is how real, long-lasting friendships are formed. Our friendship was about football. It soon faded into the past, where my time as a player now belonged.

It took a while for the next phase in my life to take shape. The carefree period in Zurich emphasised that I was at heart a relaxed person. It could have continued indefinitely. Instead, the challenge I was next presented with was one of those which, when it came, guaranteed I would be under continual pressure. 1 February 1978 was my first day at work as general manager of Hamburg Sport-Verein: HSV.

I had not gone looking for the job. Nor had it ever crossed my mind that I might want to follow in the footsteps of Mönchengladbach's Helmut Grashoff, or of any other manager. Organising Grasshoppers' training camp schedule in Spain had been fun, just as helping with Henning Jensen's transfer had been. But I had never envisaged the possibility of developing this interest into something more serious. Luck played its part again. And, once more, it was a matter of someone else detecting a quality in me I did not personally know I possessed, which he thought he might be able to put to use. It was the leitmotif of my life.

My benefactor this time was Paul Benthien, the chairman of HSV. The story began with a Grasshoppers Zürich sideline, making the odd journalistic contribution while I was there. What such 'journalism' amounted to was offering my views on this or that game; someone else then wrote these up. I can no longer remember which paper it was I contributed to for the European Cup Winners Cup tie between HSV and RSC Anderlecht. The HSV matchday programme however was memorably bad. I had had some experience with the *Fohlen-Echo* at Mönchengladbach. The idea now occurred to me that I might be able to make a start on my post-playing career by offering to do something about the HSV programme. After the game I spoke to Benthien. He responded by saying that we should meet at the next HSV away match, against Schalke 04.

Our conversation began with him accepting my proposal for the magazine. So far, so normal. That could not be said for what he now suggested himself. "On the condition, that is, that you agree to be HSV's general manager." Benthien was a decent man with candidly held views. When I objected that I did not have the slightest qualification for the job, he brushed this aside by saying, "And I don't have the slightest idea about football".

While in Zurich, I had naturally followed what was happening in the Bundesliga. I was reasonably well informed about the messy situation at HSV, accused of being clueless itself. For a long time, the big cheese had been Peter Krohn – Dr Peter Krohn. He had recently been fired. On hearing of my appointment, his distinctly unfriendly comment was, "Netzer? I call him the corner specialist."

He was the club chairman before becoming general manager in 1975. If I was considered a bit flash, what did that make Peter Krohn? Compared to him I was a stolid bourgeois. He was ahead of his time, there was no doubt about that; probably a little too ahead of his time. Before he took over, HSV had become a bit sleepy. It had grown complacent, relying too heavily on the enduring fame of Uwe Seeler. Then along came Krohn to give the citizens of the Hanseatic port city a jolt with both his talk and provocative initiatives. His aim, to make HSV better known and more popular, was realised.

At the same time, there was no escaping that his antics occasionally provoked ridicule instead. The new team colours, a combination of shocking pink and sky blue, were without precedent in the Bundesliga. Before a routine UEFA Cup game against Young Boys of Bern he promised champagne if they won. Showering his players, their wives and girlfriends with it provided the publicity images Krohn was after. So did a training session in which the players dribbled around beer tables and a beer tent to the accompaniment of a brass band. As far as a football team is concerned, these stunts would have been silly if unaccompanied by sporting success. HSV, in fact, had its share. In 1977 they won the European Cup Winners Cup, having won the cup final the previous season.

Another, particularly extravagant coup of Krohn's was the signing of Kevin Keegan. The little Liverpool forward was already something of an international star, whom Real Madrid, Barcelona and Manchester United were competing amongst themselves to buy. Today it seems almost incredible that Keegan should opt to sign for HSV, for what was then a record transfer fee of around two million marks. Krohn was clever enough to take advantage of the comparatively favourable economic conditions in West Germany at the time, which allowed him to pay Keegan's wages.

A further, projected coup, which did not come off, was the purchase of my old pal, Paul Breitner from Real Madrid. The two met in a Salzburg coffee house, Paul later told me, but could not come to an agreement. Instead of joining HSV, he went to Eintracht Braunschweig, the club sponsored by Günter Mast, the Jägermeister distiller.

Krohn's real piece of misfortune though was to succeed in engaging Rudi Gutendorf as coach. By this point, Gutendorf's career as a trainer had taken him virtually all around the world. He stood for a certain kind of circus football, which obviously appealed to Krohn. The team took a different view, lamenting Gutendorf's predecessor, Kuno Klötzer, whom Krohn couldn't stand. Newspaper reports soon publicised the trench warfare now being waged at HSV. The team were against Gutendorf from the start. Their solidarity, according to the defender Peter Hidien, stemmed from a steamy session in the beer cellar one evening. It was clear that the trainer was reticent to stamp his authority on them. Then came a night in Split, following a European tie, when his weakness was fully revealed. The players felt free to behave as obnoxiously as they pleased in front of Gutendorf, who did nothing. Stuffing themselves with caviar and drinking as much as they felt like, the evening ended up with them throwing a double bed into the hotel swimming pool. When Benthien made his proposal that I should be manager in Schalke's Parkstadion, both Gutendorf and Krohn had already been dispensed with. The new trainer was Arkac Özcan. Those who knew the Bundesliga were not surprised when he turned out to be too pliable to get a grip on the players. Benthien's offer was certainly interesting, even if I did not know exactly how things stood. My information was limited to what I read in the papers. Given the context and my own inexperience – actually, cluelessness – I asked him if he wouldn't mind giving me some time to think it over.

I drove to Mönchengladbach to meet Helmut Grashoff. Encouraging me to make the leap from unoccupied retirement to management, he emphasised all the experience I had gained at Borussia and Real Madrid. "The first thing you will need to do," he said, "is to impose some order. If only half of what one hears is true, it seems that HSV is in a mess."

There was a lot to be said for not taking on the job. But Grashoff's faith in my ability to handle it was genuine. I shared his confidence, in fact. All that stood in the way was my cluelessness ... and my image. While it was possible to do something about the first, what could be done about the perception that had formed of Netzer, which was not perhaps as false as it had once been? No sooner than I accepted the post and Hamburg announced my appointment, all the old remarks would be recycled about Netzer the party-going lady-killer who, in his playing career, had always let others do the running for him on the pitch. To say that I received a sceptical welcome at Hamburg is an understatement. Overt disapproval would be closer to the mark. The general opinion was that, following Krohn, Netzer's arrival spelt the end of the club.

My first day at work began with a visit to the training ground. I wanted to introduce myself to the trainer and players, without any club officials hanging around. Kevin Keegan had other ideas. I went over to greet him first, but Kevin had no words of greeting for me. He was shaking with rage. "You might as well know," he told me without any preliminaries, "I am on my way."

I knew Keegan from a match we had played against one another a while ago. Since he had joined Hamburg he had been in wretched form. I realised though that he was essentially a formidable player. Letting him go was not the way I wanted to begin my time at HSV. For the club it would be a sporting disaster. He had yet to fit in and was frequently at odds with the team, which was divided about him. There was friction during games, training and at almost any other opportunity which presented itself. The story was not much different with Ivan Buljan, a powerful defender, originally from Split, who had studied in the Jura. That was enough for half the team to treat him as though he were an outsider.

Anything can happen at a club ... including that it does not stick to its own commitments, even the contractual ones. That is what occurred with Keegan, who ran through all his grievances in my office. Despite having been promised a house by Krohn, he was still, almost a year after his arrival, living in a small one bedroom suite in the Dammtor district's Hotel Plaza. Not just him but his wife, their baby and two big dogs. "HSV," Keegan complained to me at this first meeting, "is the most rubbish club I have ever come across. I want to leave." It was a less than ideal start for me as manager. The immediate future looked like being a lot of fun.

For the next few days I made my way directly to the training ground. What I saw there was hardly encouraging. Keegan was not a self-indulgent, whining diva. The worst thing about his tirade was that it was justified. The word had yet to be used in West Germany, but the treatment he and Buljan were being subjected to was an unpleasant example of 'mobbing'. At the beginning and end of a training session, no one said hello or goodbye to them. During it, they received plenty of rough challenges but not the ball. The senior players also showed no respect for the trainer. Others, for example Felix Magath and Manfred Kaltz, were still too young to have established themselves and be in a position to stand up to all that was going on. Instead, they went along with it.

As a player, I was hardly known for setting an example in training with my industriousness. Now that I found myself on the other side of the fence, my inclination was also to indulge the less keen players, so long as their matchday performances did not suffer. But what was going on here was a different story. Nothing was right. Neither the shifts they were prepared to put in, nor the way in which the senior players, instead of using it for the good of the team, derived whatever benefit they could from their privileged position. Three or four were primarily responsible for setting the bad tone: Georg Volkert, who, since scoring in the European Cup Winners Cup Final, had become the fans' darling; Arno Steffenhagen and Ferdinand Keller, both internationals; Willi Reimann was another. He still had a year to run on his contract. There was a chance I might get him to integrate into the side. I had no doubt about the other three though: they would have to go. Then new signings must be made, and a new trainer found, too. It was no mean agenda for a novice. And, of course, I also needed to sort out Kevin Keegan's housing.

Who relishes having to give somebody the axe? Particularly when uncertainty is liable to result. I had neither identified a new trainer, nor was there any guarantee that I would be able to replace the three players I was discarding with newcomers of the same, undeniably top class, calibre.

I may have been abroad in Switzerland but that did not prevent me from hearing about the second division player who had scored forty-two goals in the season, thanks to which Rot-Weiß Essen were promoted to the Bundesliga's top flight. You need more than just luck, even in the lower leagues, to score that number of goals. It is an achievement, on whatever pitch in the footballing world, for which a highly developed instinct for goal plus the talent to put it to work are required. What astonished me was that none of the region's big clubs – Schalke, Borussia Dortmund or Köln – had come after him. Besides his goal tally, I knew his name, Horst Hrubesch. That was all. I set my mind on him without ever having seen him play. Did he have what it would take to replace Ferdinand Keller up front? It was a risky strategy. All I had to put in the balance, for the three players I was going to move on, was the outline of a hope. It would have been hard for me to articulate what my concrete objection to the three was. I sensed that they were stirring things up in the team. There may have been good arguments both for letting them go or letting them stay; what counted was my gut feeling. My instinct told me that, unless things were changed around here, my image would remain the same too. The soft option was to be avoided. I called Georg Volkert into my office.

Volkert was aware of his popularity in the city. He enjoyed playing up to his crafty reputation. He was sharp and not without wit, as the fans appreciated. What they didn't see was the other side of Georg Volkert, the one that liked to cause trouble with the coach and with Kevin Keegan. As I told him of my decision to allow him and his two friends to go at the end of the season, he regarded me closely. He seemed amused rather than shocked or angry. When he saw that I was serious, he remarked rather haughtily, "Go ahead then, if you think you know what you are doing. Just go ahead and do it." The interviews with Steffenhagen and Keller were much the same. All three thought they could count on the fans.

The way I was treated in the weeks after they were transfer listed showed they were not entirely wrong to do so. In the beginning, it was just verbal abuse in the streets and from anonymous callers. Then came the death threats. Were they to be taken seriously? Although it was probably a case of the dog's bark being worse than his bite, and there are no doubt people who, in my situation, would not have paid much notice to the threatening language being used, I wasn't one of them. The Hamburg police department shared my point of view. I was provided with visible and heavy police protection for the next few weeks. Trying to rationalise what was happening, on the basis that football is a passionate game and hatred can sometimes be a by-product of strong feelings, failed to settle my queasiness. It was my constant state at the time.

While the overt hostility diminished and the death threats dropped off, I was still serving the probation written into my contract by HSV's directors. Even as I received their full backing, and was spared any interference from them, they were prudently hedging their bets. This did not trouble me. It was only natural that they should be guarded. The job had come to me unexpectedly, without my having sought it. I had no strategic plan in my back pocket. Then again, in football, as in most lines of business, it is unlikely a step-by-step blueprint for success exists.

I knew that, when required to, I could apply myself, even if hard work might not be one of my most obvious attributes. If there is a better way, why get carried away, after all? But when needs must, as was now the case … In fact, I enjoyed this time, which was fortunate because otherwise I would not have been able to endure the frantic task of reorganising the team. Seventy-hour weeks were normal, not exceptional. Office, training ground, airports were where I spent all my time. It was a step change for me having, only a few weeks before, been a footballer making the transition into retirement, and getting a little lazy in the process. Kevin Keegan's house was the most straightforward problem, which was soon sorted out. For the time being, the Englishman was happy.

One of the players I wanted to sign was Jimmy Hartwig, from 1860 München. The Lions legend, Peter Gross tried warning me off him. However, I was determined to secure Jimmy for HSV. As things turned out, he was ultimately responsible for all my hard work at this point being generously rewarded: not only did his signing work out well for the club and him but, at a personal level, for me as well. It was my good luck that he played for a Munich club, although it did not seem so fortunate on the day I travelled there for transfer talks, when the flight had to be diverted to Stuttgart, because of thick fog at München-Riem Airport. Passengers were requested to continue by coach. As can probably be guessed by now, not my preferred means of transport. I decided to hire a car instead, once I had picked up my suitcase from baggage reclaim. Also waiting for hers was a young woman with long blonde hair. Earlier, on the plane, I had noticed her, like others, casting a glance in my direction from time to time. Or maybe I was imagining it. Now, as we stood almost face to face, I got the feeling she was not looking forward to continuing the journey to Munich by coach either. "I am going to get a hire car," I told her. "Would you like to drive with me?" She looked somewhat taken aback, perhaps because she was thinking, "Don't I know this guy from somewhere?" Even if she had no interest in football, my face had become so familiar on the TV and in the Press lately that it was quite likely she did. She accepted.

Off we went. We had barely got onto the autobahn when she remarked for the first time that I was starting to drive very fast. The observation became more cutting as she repeated it. She then demanded, "Do you really have to race?" I may have been moving along, I certainly wasn't racing. Nor was I very happy about this back-seat driving, however charming my passenger might be. Halfway to Munich I was ready to offload her at the next service station, where I would phone Stuttgart Airport, so that they could instruct the coach to pick her up. Was I that ungallant …? In the meantime, things calmed down. The topic of conversation shifted from my driving to her sharing that she did have a rough idea of who I was. A couple of days before she had seen something on the television about me coming to Hamburg, something to do with HSV. She also let me know, shortly before we arrived in Munich, that she was married. All the same, we exchanged addresses.

That is the story of how, on the way to meet Jimmy Hartwig, I also met my wife, Elvira Lang.

To return to HSV. Hartwig's transfer was an easy matter. That of the unknown quantity, the second division goalscoring phenomenon, was far from being so. Later, when Horst Hrubesch had become an international, as well as the cornerstone of HSV's success, I could give myself a pat on the back for having had the vision to imagine our right back, Manni Kaltz sending in crosses for Hrubesch to head into the back of the net. Only, in Essen that day, watching him, after he had agreed to sign, for the first time, I couldn't picture it. I was too preoccupied with the thought that this Hrubesch, my first ever signing, might also be my last.

It was depressing. Playing against Bayern Uerdingen he was, quite frankly, a disaster. I finally saw why, after a trial with each, Borussia Dortmund and VfL Bochum had both sent him home. He was incapable of anything. At the age of twenty-seven, he could neither trap nor pass the ball. He was less developed technically than most colts. At the start of the game I sat up with anticipation; gradually, I sank morosely into myself. To make way for this man I had sold Ferdinand Keller, an excellent footballer. On his account, I had been driving three times a week from Hamburg to Essen, then speeding down to Frankfurt at midday before making the return trip back up to Hamburg in the evening. Everyone can have an off day. But Hrubesch had done nothing. Not even a header.

Nevertheless, there had been a big race to sign him. He already had an agent, Holger Klemme. From him I learned early in the negotiations that Eintracht Frankfurt had not only been shocked and awed by Hrubesch's exploits, they hoped he might become a goal goldmine for themselves. Their trainer at this time was Dettmar Cramer, who had once coached me in the West German youth team (– you may remember: "Günter, you need to toughen up"). Although Frankfurt already had a formal agreement with Hrubesch, Klemme had other plans. He saw bigger possibilities with HSV. It did not matter to him that Hrubesch had put his signature to the Frankfurt contract. Nor did it matter much to the player himself. Once HSV came along, he was no longer so keen on joining Frankfurt. Looking back, he must have been very naive indeed in order to have the confidence to reassure me, "There is no need for you to worry, I am going to join you, not Frankfurt". The only thing was, there was no cancellation clause in the contract he had signed. The race for Hrubesch was about to turn into a game of cat and mouse.

First of all, I needed to neutralise Cramer's powers of persuasion. I knew what he liked to get out of players and I also knew the means he could bring to bear to win them over. I suspected, in fact I strongly believed, that he would succeed in softening up Hrubesch, this big man with a big heart, with his promises and prophecies of what the future held. He would end up convincing him that only with Frankfurt was he likely to achieve the success, renown and financial rewards he was aiming for. I knew what I had to do: remove Hrubesch from Cramer's sphere of influence. If the chance arose, I needed to hide him away and begin the job of piloting him towards HSV. Fortunately, Klemme and I managed to cloister Hrubesch in a small hotel somewhere in The Hunsrück Hills.

Then I drove to Frankfurt to begin talks. En route I pondered how I was going to overcome the difficulty that, regardless of whether the player had suddenly had a change of mind, there was a bona fide contract between them and him. They had not plied him with drink in order to obtain his signature against his will. Eintracht could be counted on to be steadfast. The commonsense argument that the player '*nicht will*' and that only a willing player will be an effective one, which might be quite true, could not be relied on to succeed. Until an eventual compromise can be reached regarding a claim for breach of contract, the gatecrashing club only achieves the hollow triumph that the player prefers itself to the other, which is in turn left with nothing besides its sense of righteousness. As for the player, he discovers that he is both unable to play and is burdened with a lasting reputation for being untrustworthy. Where the commonsense argument prevails, it can be at a high price. In our case this was 250,000 marks, the sum HSV guaranteed Eintracht it would receive for a friendly between the two clubs to mark this change in destination for Hrubesch. No gain without financial pain ...

I had done it, and I felt proud to have landed a big fish. The contract was ready. All that remained was for it to be signed, without delay. I would take the flight to Düsseldorf, then onto Essen and finally hurry down to Frankfurt. There was, though, a final obstacle: Chairman Benthien. A Hanseatic chairman does not sign a contract in a hurry, without reflection. He now went through it, paragraph by paragraph, before adding his signature. Meanwhile, the plane had taken off without me. So, for 6,800 marks, I hired a private jet, to arrive at the meeting on time. I had the experience of Bruno Recht, Fortuna Düsseldorf's chairman, not turning up as arranged to remind me of the importance of punctuality in these situations. It made me wonder what Dettmar Cramer and his team of negotiators would have thought of myself if I were to fail to turn up at the predetermined hour. Perhaps they were already secretly amused by this young manager who had shown so much elan, persistence, and money too, in his attempt to secure an unproven player.

The 6,800 marks were gone. You might call it my apprenticeship fee. If so, it was a price worth paying (, which I later learned was secretly paid back by Benthien's successor, Wolfgang Klein). There might not be much to show for my first six months in the job but opinion about me had started to change. I was not to be found at the town's fashionable parties, firstly because I had no time, secondly since, contrary to the way I had been portrayed, I was hardly a socialite. As for the Ferraris and all the women that, together with partying, were supposedly my consuming passions, the Ferrari remained in the garage; the car which went with my new post being a dignified Daimler, while, thanks to the thick cloud cover at München-Riem, followed by the forced landing at Stuttgart-Echterdingen, I was now in a steady relationship. Elvira Lang was no longer nagging me about my driving. She had begun divorce proceedings.

12

Managerial Obstacle Course

Early in 1978 I called Hermann Neuberger. If I was to stand a chance as an absolute beginner in management, I would need the cooperation of that most powerful figure, the Bundesliga's chairman. The kind of team I had in mind was beginning to take shape. I still needed a new coach. The first few months had been enough to show me that Özcan was not the man with whom HSV were going to achieve success. More than offloading a couple of players was required in order to change the mentality of a side in which sloppy habits had taken hold. I was well aware of the danger that, with a weak coach, these would continue and soon rub off on their replacements. A trainer who commanded respect was needed. I knew just the man. He had coached FC Bruges and Feyenoord as well as the Dutch national side. Zonal marking and pressing, both concepts which were barely known about at that time in the West German game, were at the heart of his football philosophy. The man I had in mind for HSV was called Ernst Happel.

Ernst Happel, mind you, was not cheap. Nor, as a football obsessive, did he have, or appear to want to have, the first idea about anything else in life. The first time I contacted him, in order to find out if he would be interested, in principle, in coming to the Bundesliga, he set out his salary demands. He would be happy to come – for 300,000 marks a year. This was beyond anything being paid in the Bundesliga then. 200,000 was as far as Chairman Benthien was prepared to go. Happel's demand, in fact, would involve him paying more than 300,000, since this was the sum he expected to receive after tax. HSV's bill would therefore come to over 600,000 marks a year. I knew there was no point in talking to Benthien about it. At the same time, I was fairly confident that, if I first succeeded in dealing with the other problem involved in hiring Happel, then he might be ready to find a way to take on the former Dutch national manager.

This concerned the DFB's requirements which would-be Bundesliga trainers had to satisfy. A licence could only be granted following attendance at the sports academy in Cologne. Just as with Benthien, I knew there was no point in talking to Happel about this. He could be relied on to laugh at the suggestion that he first had to return to the classroom.

At the other end of the line, Hermann Neuberger was far from dismissive. He knew what Happel was capable of; his presence in the Bundesliga would benefit West German football. "The difficulty," he said, "is that any concession is going to undermine our training education model." He was already trying, nevertheless, to convince the relevant DFB committee that Happel should be allowed in without the licence.

A fortnight passed without hearing anything from him. The training staff issue remained unresolved. I considered the possibility of taking on Max Merkel, whom I spoke to on several occasions. The Merkel of that time was not simply a talker. He had a justified reputation, particularly for being a strong leader. My plan, if it was not possible to appoint my first choice yet, was to have Merkel instil discipline into the team, so that there was a foundation upon which, hopefully, Happel could later begin his tactical work. Merkel, however, shrank from the challenge. An alternative was Branko Zebec, whom I had also been talking to. My proposal immediately enthused the Eintracht Braunschweig trainer. I then had to downplay the probability that it would materialise – without letting on about Happel.

Neuberger rang. The news was not good. In spite of all my cajoling, the DFB would not budge, which meant Happel stayed put in Holland.

To describe Zebec as a stopgap appointment would be unjust. In 1969 he had led FC Bayern to its first title in thirty-seven years. As my Bayern teammates in the national side often told me, he was very popular. His training methods may have been tough, but they were efficient. His routines were full of variety. With Zebec, there was a good chance of success; so we took him on. At the same time, Happel continued to occupy my thoughts.

I was already aware that Zebec had a drink problem. It was something known about in the game, even if it was not, at this point, public knowledge. That is the way it was intended to remain. Liking to drink in large quantities, as he did, was not yet, I believe, considered an illness. The truth is, most treated the subject rather superficially. I naively hoped that Zebec would be able to wean himself away from the bottle by his own efforts. My job, as I saw it, was to play down the issue with him. It was something I had learned at Real Madrid: a good manager does all he can to relieve the trainer and players from the pressure of off the field concerns, so that they are free to concentrate on their key, footballing, duties. Only later did it become evident to me that addiction cannot be dealt with on your own.

Whenever I think back to these first six months at HSV I am still astonished at the way I threw myself into the job. What had become of the Günter Netzer for whom football may have been the priority, but who had time for other things as well? Now I was occupied morning, afternoon, evening and nighttime with the sport. I barely had a private life. Amazingly enough, this is when my relationship with Elvira began to develop. She stuck with me, although I barely had any time to spare for her.

A snapshot of that period makes it look as if all the decisions I took, and then set in motion, were part of a carefully prepared plan. A reasonable number may have been the consequence of deliberate thought, for example the observation that HSV needed a new trainer, or my basic analysis regarding the (unhealthy) state in which I found the team. Many, however, were really convictions, that came from the gut. These were choices which my instinct told me to make: to have a good, but not chummy, relationship with the Press; to steer clear of the big Hamburg social events; to be evidently working for HSV around the clock. These were not, whatever might be suspected, carefully calculated means by which to improve my image. I simply understood that I must avoid either leaving myself open to manipulation or becoming too expansive. Fortunately, I knew how to do it. Once again, I had tapped into a vein that, until then, I hardly knew I had. This was my ability to work exceptionally hard when required, leaving everything else to the side. The first months as a manager were stressful, but in a creative way. It was a fulfilling and therefore enjoyable time.

That Branko Zebec was above all an outstanding football trainer, I could tell from day one at the training ground. His spontaneous response to seeing Horst Hrubesch in action for the first time was one of shock. Or, at least, that is the impression he gave. "What can I do with him, this great big attacker, this colossus you have provided me with? He has no movement, he's like a monument," he said. Well, I thought, now the time has come to pay for being overzealous. Hadn't I known all along that my first was also going to be my last signing? I made an attempt to justify myself. "Look, Branko, we've also got Manni Kaltz. Can't you take advantage of his crossing? It's what he's best at. And put the colossus in the middle, ready to receive?"

Zebec looked at me pityingly, as if to say, "You've noticed that too, have you?" He then gestured towards one of the pitches, where Kaltz and Hrubesch were already following his instructions. It was not so much training as the narrowly focused rehearsal of an unvarying scenario. Kaltz crosses; Hrubesch heads. Kaltz crosses; Hrubesch heads. Kaltz crosses; Hrubesch heads. Nine times out of ten the ball ended up in the back of the net. If you had seen it, you could appreciate the Bayern goalkeeper Sepp Maier's later remark that Horst Hrubesch is the one footballer who would choose to take a penalty with his head. Cross, header … Goal! These two poor guys practiced until Kaltz's foot was almost falling off and Hrubesch developed a bump on his head. Neither was about to complain, though.

Instead, they were rewarded. Their routine soon became the talk of the Bundesliga. Its repetitiveness might be criticised – without anyone having a better alternative to suggest. Hrubesch's tally of thirteen goals, which compared to following years appears insignificant, is listed in the records for that season. What is not, but which I can remember very clearly all the same, is that he had already established himself as the life and soul of the side. Without making a great fuss about it, he concerned himself with each of his teammates, as well as the team and its mood as a whole. On the pitch he was intimidating; once the final whistle blew, he was affability itself. After Franz Beckenbauer had joined us several years later, there was a brutal collision between the two. It happened during the course of a midweek match. As we were about to take a corner against the visitors, VfB Stuttgart, Beckenbauer glided into the penalty box. I have no idea what he thought he was doing there. And even less as to what came over him when he decided he was going to jump for the ball. Hrubesch stormed in from behind him. Naturally climbing higher, he headed the ball into the back of the net, which is where Franz ended up too. He was taken to hospital with kidney bruising. For a short while there was concern that he might lose a kidney. Horst Hrubesch, although blameless, was inconsolable. Not until Beckenbauer, having convalesced, made his return, was he happy once again.

For having detected his gift as a footballer so quickly I probably have my instinct to thank, but the man's character was a gift in itself. Horst was a boon for us. Who would have guessed that this newcomer, who prompted ridicule, or pity at best, when he arrived in the wake of the troublemakers' purge, would turn out to be the catalyst for the team's new solidarity?

There was no doubt about its sporting class. Felix Magath was just beginning to break through as an intelligent playmaker; the defence, built around Ivan Buljan and Peter Nogly, two big guys and strong headers of the ball, was solid; running down the right wing, Manfred Kaltz was a sensation, while Jimmy Hartwig was the find of the season. By the time we gave 1. FC Köln a 6-0 kicking, people had only good things to say about HSV. And nobody was referring to me as a lazy playboy any more.

Occasionally, I had the time during this first season as a manager to stand back and feel proud. Such moments were rare. In this business there is always something to do. The team had been put together and a new trainer found. Things were running smoothly. That was not enough. The way I saw my job, wherever I could I had to shield the players and the coach from any problems. So, Elvira and I took Branko house hunting, in the mistaken belief that having a settled base would help him control his drinking. I also had to settle down Kevin Keegan. As Zebec put his training programme into place, he became a frequent visitor to my office. "Now, I really am leaving," he would begin. That was something about Kevin: he didn't like training at all. "Gaffer," he explained, "the coach is completely nuts." Having to train harder than ever before in his career was one problem. Another was the Kaltz – Hrubresch duo. "It's like at Liverpool," he moaned, "with Toshack up at the front, totally unaware of me." There was no need, on the other hand, for him to complain any longer about being alienated by the other players. The new harmony was the context in which, as an outstanding player, he was flourishing more than ever. Performance was what mattered. Kevin stayed on, remaining a frequent visitor to the office, with a steady stream of grumbles, demands and transfer requests.

He was, how shall I say, a little capricious. Life with him was never easy. From time to time he would play the diva. Whenever he phoned, I would tighten up automatically. Knowing his worth, he was able to make clever use of the high volume of interest shown in him. The following year we played in a tournament in Madrid. Once more he was outstanding. Barcelona subsequently offered him the then unimaginable salary of two million marks net. Kevin understood that we were unable to pay anything like that. The fact that he did not pack his bags on the spot says something about him. Instead, he reacted as I had at Borussia Mönchengladbach. "At least try and find some way of closing the gap," was his suggestion.

He wasn't thinking about taking over the matchday programme. He had other plans, following an offer he had received from The Washington Diplomats that he should go and play for them during the Bundesliga off-season. Although unprecedented, I did not think the idea a crazy one. He could spend his free time wherever he wanted, if that was the way of keeping him at Hamburg. The game had not yet become so commercialised then that one had to immediately worry that, if a player returned injured and could not be selected, the club might lose a million marks. If a single defeat could be pinned on his absence, however annoying and disappointing, it would not have the same consequences as today for, say, Borussia Dortmund or Bayern Munich to miss out on the Champions League by a single point, with the significant loss in revenue that implies. So long as Zebec and, above all, the chairman agreed with me that Keegan could go and supplement his income with three months kickabout on the Washington astroturf, then he was free to do so. Neither objected; Keegan was chuffed.

A few days later I was speaking with a journalist about this bold plan, since it now had to be made public. Keegan was scheduled to return from the States on 15 August, which meant he would miss the opening match of the season, against VfL Bochum. That did not seem particularly important to me. "What about if," the correspondent wanted to know, "HSV are champions ...?" As the league table stood, the question was not just hypothetical. "Then he will miss the first round of the European Cup as well." As I may have already mentioned, I am not very good on this kind of detail. No doubt I was in a muddle too about the rules concerning the number of foreign players allowed then. Was it yet three? Or still only one and a half (, from within the EEC)? ... Or something like that? I have difficulty taking notice of these things. So long as no complications arise, the probably ingrained inadequacy of those of us who tend to act on instinct can go unnoticed. Now I had a problem, which, taking him to one side during a tournament in Bordeaux, I shared with Keegan.

He may have been someone very preoccupied with money but, even more, Keegan was a competitive sportsman. I told him that his plan to spend the summer with The Washington Diplomats would only work if he was willing to miss the first round of the European Cup. The club, however strange it may sound, was prepared to begin the campaign without its most important player. Kevin, though, was not. He knew that the team was still in the process of developing and that the rough spots which continued to require ironing out could get exposed in the first round. Most of all, the possibility of playing against Liverpool trumped that of playing for The Washington Diplomats. "What if we get drawn against Liverpool and you have to play without me? It's out of the question." His verdict was clear.

Rather than relying on Keegan's sporting ambition to outstrip the lure of bettering himself financially, I preferred to find sponsorship deals. These would largely compensate for the gap between what we were able to pay him and the amount he might expect to earn elsewhere. With a few endorsements, his money concerns would soon disappear. Given the buzzing, extrovert personality of the 'Mighty Mouse', as Kevin was known, finding sponsors need not be a problem. Once we had done this, and with The Washington Diplomats project behind him, Keegan was finally content. For the next two seasons he was European Footballer of the Year.

At the same time, we were on course for the league title, as I clocked up my first twelve months in the job. No one had predicted it. There were concerns though. In the spring, Felix Magath came down with jaundice. We found ourselves wondering who we could find at short notice to fill the role of provider for Keegan. I had heard from Uli Hoeneß that he was not very happy at Bayern. Following four operations, he was struggling to recover his true form. We had got to know one another's very different personalities in the national team. Compared to him, I was an introvert. I pondered bringing him to HSV. In the event, his visit to Hamburg was brief. He arrived for a morning training session in good spirits. It was clear though, from the other players, that he was not fully fit. The team doctor, Ulrich Mann wanted to examine Uli at the Paracelsus Clinic in Ulzburg. Here he carried out an arthroscope under general anaesthetic. Afterwards, Hoeneß phoned a doctor he trusted for his opinion about this procedure. He apparently described it as criminal. A second call was made, to Paul Breitner. The two of them were still close at the time. Paul's advice was that he should head straight back to Munich.

I still do not know what all the fuss was about. I was unwilling to contradict our doctor, as Hoeneß offered his own, non-expert opinion on the state of his health. The following Saturday he appeared on the ZDF sports programme brandishing a six-inch long metal syringe. But it was not, as Mann confirmed to me, used at the Ulzburg clinic; Hoeneß had obtained it from his teammate, Jupp Kapellmann, a onetime medical student. That was taking showmanship a little too far, I think.

Even without Uli Hoeneß, and in spite of losing the last game, played at home at the Volksparkstadion against his Bayern, 1-2, we won the league. It was HSV's first title since 1960. Predictably, the place went wild. But the scene was not just one of joy; it was a shambles – the most alarming title celebration I have ever experienced.

Some idiot had cut through the pitch side fencing with a pair of bolt cutters. The spectators at the top of the stand surged downwards. Those below them were unable to get out because the exit gangways were too narrow. I didn't see it straightaway. Then I noticed something not right in the corner. There were five hundred stadium marshals and a deployment of three hundred police. The situation grew steadily worse. People were laid out on the pitch; overhead, helicopters hovered. It was an eery spectacle. In a relay, the helicopters lifted wounded out of the chaos below. Spectators shoved their way in all directions.

Somehow or other, the players, staff, Zebec and I made it to the dressing room. The team sat in a circle, stunned. Rumours began to circulate that there were fatalities.

It was hard to understand how come, in such circumstances, and knowing what turn the catastrophe was taking, the civic authorities did not cancel the celebrations which were planned to take place in front of the city hall. Seven thousand had gathered there in order to see us. They still did not know what had happened at the stadium, in spite of which we were conducted in an open-top bus to the town square. It was an absurd situation. We were meant to be in a buoyant party mood, at the same time that fans who wanted to join us might be dying. As he handed a sixteenth century map of Hamburg to Chairman Benthien, the mayor made a little joke about the yellow patch representing Rothenbaum, where the old stadium stood outside the city walls. Nobody was laughing though.

The mood was already tense when *Bild am Sonntag*'s early edition appeared with the headline: 'Five dead – Netzer to blame?' With an effort, I had let similar reporting of my mother's death wash over me. This was just as bad. The suggestion that I was responsible for stadium security was far-fetched. The paper's match correspondent was as outraged as I was by the headline. He kicked up such a fuss that it was dropped from the evening edition.

The next day I received news of the shocking toll. Five city hospitals had admitted a total of seventy-one people. The injured had lung contusions, broken bones, severe bruising, cuts and lesions, puncture wounds. Four remained in intensive care on Sunday night. The damage to the stadium was going to cost in excess of 100,000 marks, easily. Twenty thousand fans, for whom there was not enough space in front of the town hall, gathered at the Rothenbaum stadium in the evening instead. Rather than a peaceful gathering, brawls broke out once it became clear that the team was not going to appear there. The injured list grew longer. It was a poor decision on our part. On the Monday came better news: speculation concerning fatalities could now be officially denied. By midweek all those who had been in intensive care were continuing their recuperation in hospital. They were able to return home the following weekend.

13

Soaring and Wallowing

The eminent old gentlemen who ran HSV were very confident they knew what they were talking about. "Listen, young man," they said – I was already thirty-four – "you are new to business. Our old friend, Krohn also liked to dabble in the market you are suggesting. Did you know? He ended up 80,000 marks worse off. If he was not able to gain anything from it, then there is nothing to be hoped from it now."

They were referring to my predecessor's investment in pitch side advertising rights, and the subsequent hit he had taken. My ideas were in fact a little different. I had first discussed them with Caesar W. Lüthi and, with his approval, I was now canvassing his participation to the board, too. It was during my time in Zurich that I had got to know and respect Lüthi. An advertising man to his fingertips, he was something of a guru when it came to sport's, as yet untapped, marketing potential. Another of his outstanding characteristics was his persuasiveness, which I had evidently been won over by. Back in Zurich, he had mentioned to me that if ever I grew tired of football, I should come and work for his company. But I retained my enthusiasm for the game. I also had from him the price he was willing to pay for exclusive touchline advertising rights at HSV: 350,000 marks per annum.

The directors indulged me with their smiles. "Really, Herr Netzer. We know the Swiss to be serious businessmen. Highly serious. But it seems that you may have unearthed the exception. 350,000 for the advertising rights! He must be joking." With those words, my entry into the business side of the club appeared to be on hold.

A few days passed before I had another meeting with the board. I hoped that, with a crossed cheque of Lüthi's for more than 350,000 marks in my pocket, the affair might now progress. Benthien and his colleagues did not respond immediately. They took a while mulling sceptically over the cheque. In the end, they indicated that they would at least make enquiries as to whether it was bankable. Two days later, once they had received satisfactory confirmation, the deal was concluded. Lüthi then busied himself refinancing the sum he had paid HSV. It was not a grand act of patronage on his part; rather, a very good piece of business. How good, he demonstrated using an indicator board he brought with him several years later, when the partnership was extended. This showed the wickedly expensive rates he charged advertisers.

I had entered the world of licensing. Or, at least, I was taking a good look at it. This gave me an idea of just how much scope there was for sports advertising to grow. Although Lüthi was already involved with the DFB and the national side, it was not an area I, or the HSV directors, had previously given any thought to. Thanks to Lüthi's involvement and some generous sponsorship deals, over the next few years the club began to reduce its debt, which had now reached ten million marks. I was able to buy several new players: Holger Hieronymous from St. Pauli, Jürgen Milewski from Hertha BSC, and Duisburg's Dietmar Jakobs. For this, and other reasons, I was mocked by various journalists. They included Max Merkel, who, of all people, was working as a columnist at the time. He scoffed at me doodling and playing matchstick men at my desk. Football fans do not need to be told though that all three signings worked out well for HSV. So much for commentators' perceptiveness.

A lot of the things I undertook seemed to turn out well, even when I more or less stumbled into them. That was the case in early 1979 when a charity match on behalf of UNICEF took place in Dortmund. I can no longer remember who was playing whom. I think one of the teams, which included Franz Beckenbauer, was a World XI. Franz was still playing professionally, for The New York Cosmos. And, if the performance in Dortmund was anything to go by, still at the highest level. Branko Zebec was deployed as the World XI's coach. In the evening the three of us sat down and chatted. Zebec remarked to Beckenbauer in passing that he appeared to be in good form – something I already knew. "You would have no problem playing for us," he told him. Beckenbauer looked doubtful but said nothing. We bantered around the subject, without taking it any further. It was getting late when we said good night to one another.

I could not get Zebec's off-the-cuff remark out of my head. If HSV were to bring Franz Beckenbauer back to the Bundesliga, it would be a minor sensation, I thought. Was this fantasy, like Robert Schwan's idea to prise me away from Madrid? There was a difference: Beckenbauer's contract with The Cosmos was coming to an end, whereas, five years earlier, the ink was barely dry on mine. Thanks to the earlier experience, though, I understood the kind of positive publicity that could be expected to accompany his signing. Apart from which, it was obvious our team would benefit from having Beckenbauer in it. His reaction to Zebec's proposal may have been one of bafflement, but I took that to mean he was interested. Like me, he had yet to have his fill of football. When he quit the Bundesliga it was not because he was disenchanted with it. His enthusiasm for the game, and particularly for playing in this league, remained. Just before falling asleep, I made a mental note to find out from Zebec in the morning if he had been serious.

As it happened, he had not been joking. He could picture Beckenbauer fitting into the team. Before talking to Franz, I first had to check that the club possessed the necessary finances. Could it spare some of its limited resources to buy a thirty-seven-year-old veteran?

There were other issues to contend with. The point had been reached where Zebec's weakness for drink could no longer remain hidden. The fact that, until now, it had was fairly astonishing. For a long while the players had grown used to him arriving at training sessions drunk, incapable of giving a team talk. But they still had a lot of affection for the trainer, whom they considered to be quite a guy. With the likes of Horst Hrubesch, it was a solid group. If need be, they supervised their own training sessions, dispensing with Zebec's advanced tactics. It was natural at HSV then to assume responsibility. Regrettably, the game has changed since.

Journalists had to be considered too. Every day there would be some at the training session. They travelled with us to away games and abroad for European Cup matches. Not a word escaped regarding Zebec's alcohol intake. I can only speculate how come. Common decency perhaps; the ethical conviction that one should not drag someone's illness out into the public sphere. Besides, alcoholism was considered to be relatively harmless; not a great deal was known about it. What these journalists did know was that, leaving his drinking to one side, with Branko, HSV was going somewhere, and that could only benefit them. The Hamburg *Bild*, for example, had a readership of 600,000. HSV's success played its part in this. No one wanted to disturb the status quo with revelations of the trainer's problem. After all, there was no disputing that he was an exceptional trainer, who had shaken HSV out of its lethargy.

An away match in Dortmund changed everything. Because of a meeting in Hamburg, I travelled after the team. Arriving at Düsseldorf Airport, I was met by an HSV official in a worked-up state. Before mobile phones, news needed to be delivered personally to a manager on the move. What he had to tell me was not good. The trainer was in the district attorney's office in Dortmund, having been pulled over on the autobahn as he approached the city. He was travelling alone, heavily fuelled: the breathalyser test recorded that he had driven the three hundred and fifty kilometres almost three times over the limit. Later, I received further details from the attorney's office. Zebec had been driving erratically. Since no other car dared overtake him, a traffic jam had developed in his wake, before someone contacted the police and pointed Zebec out.

After I arrived at the attorney's, where I gathered the full extent of his disastrous day from him, Zebec was allowed to go. He was driven to the team hotel. The players later told me that his pre-match talk was one of the best he ever gave. Everything he said, as he outlined the tactics to be adopted in the manner of a chess grandmaster, was to the point. He was completely focused. Who could have guessed that something was not right with him?

I am talking about the hotel here, not later ... As normal, I had arranged that each room's minibar was empty. And, as usual, this didn't help at all. Branko, thanks to whoever his supplier was, began drinking again. As normal, he and the players arrived at the stadium half an hour before kick-off. If I could have got there at the same time, I might have been able to prevent what followed: not his illness becoming publicly known – that was bound to occur sooner or later – rather the manner in which it did, so that he might preserve his dignity. As it was, that was stolen from him too.

During the long minutes before the match, Branko could be seen hunched on the trainer's bench. He was in a deplorable state, and it was not hard to tell why. The photographers caught him in the moment he almost fell asleep, his head lolling forward; then again, as his glasses slid off, when he appeared to topple off his seat. If I had asked for professional advice earlier, I would no doubt have been told that he needed to go into rehab or seek help and that, to do either, he must want to take the step himself. The chances of that happening were nil. So it goes. In triggering the crisis, Branko's drive to Dortmund may have been his way of issuing a cry for help.

His illness made the headlines. Talk of it was no longer limited to confidential dressing room discussions. It was everywhere. Something special, such as our spirited display against Real Madrid in the European Cup a few days later, was required to push it into the background. Trailing 2-0 after the first leg, HSV gave the best performance I had ever seen from them. The excitement came close to matching that of our 7-1 thrashing of Inter Milan. There was a moment when it looked as though HSV was also going to have the problem we had with the televising of the tie in 1971. Broadcasters always try to drive a hard bargain. If the clubs hold out for more than the television executives are prepared to pay, they repeat their mantra, "OK, consider the situation calmly, and then consider it some more: we are not transmitting". Nevertheless, in contrast to the Mönchengladbach match, this time, for 200,000 marks, they did broadcast. This was a lot of money, but still short of what such a big game was worth. Millions were therefore able to watch HSV outplay Madrid, Uli Stielike included, in the first half. The score at that juncture was 4-1; after ninety minutes, 5-1.

I was the one who had brokered Stielike's move from Mönchengladbach. Chairman Bernabéu had asked my opinion about possible midfielders. Initially he was sceptical about taking on Stielike, his concern being that no one in Spain would be able to get their tongues around the difficult German pronunciation. He was to become known as Uli. S. Tielike. Ultimately, what mattered was that he was a very good footballer. As a sign of his gratitude, Bernabéu gave me an engraved Rolex watch.

The day after our semi-final victory the level of excitement remained high among the sports following part of the Republic. It was probably seen as some compensation for a Bundestag debate, being held in the wake of the Soviet invasion of Afghanistan, which resulted in a vote in favour of boycotting the Olympic games in Moscow that summer.

Meanwhile, the Zebec saga simmered on. Following defeat in the final to Nottingham Forest it boiled over. Frustrated by the English side sitting on its 1-0 advantage, the team had also turned to drink. The next morning, Zebec cancelled the scheduled team meeting, on the somewhat awkward ground that, "I am not training with drunkards". Already, in the week leading up to the final, he had strained its commitment to him by griping at the team. Now he was denouncing it. The downward spiral continued with their open defiance of him being caught on camera.

As for myself, I no longer had the strength to deal with the situation. Maybe I just wanted it to end. My involvement in the year long struggle with his alcoholism, our frequent nighttime talks, had worn me down. Again and again, it was me he chose to scapegoat when complaining, as he increasingly did, to journalists. I felt as if I had been left to deal with the problem alone. I remember the post-match conference he gave after we played VfL Bochum. Once more he was drunk. No HSV officials were to be seen. It was me who led him away from the podium. It made me sad. In December HSV fired the coach.

The separation was ugly. There was even a court case, in which the players testified, so that the redundancy settlement could be decreased. Not a glorious chapter. Branko Zebec finished his managerial career in West Germany with Eintracht Frankfurt. That did not end well either. Then he returned to his native Zagreb, where a few years later he died at the age of fifty-nine. He was a top trainer who had a problem, which he was unable to get on top of.

His dismissal lay behind Beckenbauer and myself almost having a falling out. Roughly six months after Zebec, at the time of the Dortmund charity match, had made his offhand proposal that he should come back to West Germany, I phoned Franz Beckenbauer. At the other end of the line, in New York, he clowned around and made a few jokes; he was not taking me seriously. Yet, for some strange reason, I had the feeling that this was only because he was unsure if my question, as to whether he retained some – just a little – desire to play in the Bundesliga again, was meant in earnest or not. Rather like I had in Dortmund, I got the impression that Franz's Bundesliga ambitions were not yet drained. Working with Branko Zebec was an additional incentive. We arranged to meet in New York. It seemed as good a place as any.

In the meantime, HSV had elected a new chairman, Dr Wolfgang Klein. He was equally enthusiastic about the possibility of bringing Beckenbauer to Hamburg. The two of us flew by Concorde. On arrival, it was soon obvious that Franz was not playing about. With him was his manager and adviser. Once again, I found myself in a hotel sitting down to negotiate with Robert Schwan. Thank God, the dress code in New York was more relaxed than it had been at the Madrid Ritz.

These were just the preliminaries. Franz had booked a table for later at 'Regine's', New York's hottest nightspot. As we ate and chatted there, I could tell that he was already decided on the move. For our part, the financing was worked out in advance by Dr Klein and myself. A British oil company had already assisted in bringing Kevin Keegan to the club. Without its help once more we would not have been able to meet the 1.2 million mark salary that Beckenbauer had in mind.

It was a contented scene which photographers, presumably American, burst in on. Usually there were plenty of celebrities at 'Regine's'. Tonight was an exception. Maybe the paparazzi were asking themselves whom they could snap in the absence of well-known New Yorkers? Who in Manhattan though knew of Franz Beckenbauer and Günter Netzer? There were obviously my friends in Harlem. But besides them? No doubt Franz, with Pele, had given football, or soccer, a higher profile. Nevertheless, he could still walk around the city like anybody else. Now the photographers' lenses were all pointing at him. I have since thought about it from time to time, without being able to say for sure who it was who set the West German Press on his trail. Someone must have leaked the news that we were in negotiations with him. My suspicion is that it was probably the very clever Robert Schwan.

We were all agreed: Franz would join HSV in November, once he was match fit. Dr Klein and I were happy as we flew home, knowing that we were in the process of achieving an especially spectacular coup. The report soon appeared in the Press. A few days later came the unsubstantiated news that Beckenbauer was renewing his contract with The Cosmos. I immediately picked up the phone. "What's going on?" I asked. Beckenbauer assured me, "There is no need to worry". The story must have been a fabrication.

He arrived on schedule in November 1980. About five hundred waited for him to touch down at Fuhlsbüttel, where he made his temporary home at the Intercontinental Hotel. The idea was that he should start playing as soon as possible. Because the next home game was only a cup tie against RW Frankfurt, his debut was postponed. I was at least enough of a businessman to realise that, even if Beckenbauer was playing, not many were expected to come to this fixture. Nor would the takings be what they might otherwise be, given the rule for cup games which divided advertising revenue equally between the home and away sides. Following his three-and-a-half-year absence, Beckenbauer's first appearance back in the Bundesliga would therefore be in Stuttgart, playing against VfB. Events were so fast moving that there was not enough time to inform their chairman, Gerhard Mayer-Vorfelder. He got worked up about this, complaining that the crowd was going to be much smaller than if he had known earlier. 'M-V', as he was known, and whose principal role at the time was as Baden-Württemberg's culture minister, had real concerns about VfB Stuttgart's finances. Years later, in fact even as I write, these have become critical, as everybody knows.

Beckenbauer's comeback had been low key. The move was working out well, however: he was back in West Germany, he liked it in Hamburg and he was collaborating with Zebec. Then, after he had been with HSV barely a month, came Branko Zebec's dismissal. Furious, he stormed into my office. "What is the matter with you?" he wanted to know. "Are you out of your mind? It was because of Branko that I joined you. Then you might as well get rid of me, too."

Expecting something like this, I had my answer prepared. "Franz, calm down," I said, "we are getting an even better trainer."

"There is none better," shouted Franz, as he stormed back out of the room.

"Franz," I called after him, "I have a feeling there is. Ernst Happel."

In spite of my plan for Happel coming to work in the Bundesliga being blocked by the DFB chairman's decision, he had continued to haunt my thoughts. Without being conscious of it at the time, I am surprised today at the relentlessness with which I pursued my goal. Regarding this resolution: it was not as if, when playing, I had given up every time I found an obstacle standing in my way. Instead, if possible, I preferred to sidestep each one. Dealing first with the Horst Hrubesch situation, I now overcame them. For a long time, I then confronted that of Zebec's drinking directly until, finally, it became too much. When the DFB said "No" to Happel I had accepted the blow, since there was no choice. It was me who then resubmitted his application. The time with Real Madrid, I have mentioned before, was the most important in my development, so far as I am concerned. Just getting through that difficult first year, not capitulating in spite of the pressure, was an experience which I was able to draw strength from. That is what I did now.

It was the DFB and its academy which, in the face of change, appeared to have given way. In spring 1980 1. FC Köln were allowed to take on the Dutchman, Rinus Michels, another coach of international renown but without a West German trainer's licence. I do not know what had altered for this permission to be given; whether it may have had anything to do with the national academy, in Cologne, being right on the club's doorstep. The most straightforward explanation was a growing awareness of the trend for football to become a more open sport, in which national boundaries no longer counted so much. There was little logic anyhow in players being free to go where they chose, while trainers were prevented from doing so. With Rinus Michels at Cologne, I now had a good chance of bringing Ernst Happel over from Standard Liège.

There was not a great deal that needed to be discussed. We

wanted Happel to come; Happel wanted to come. I arranged a meeting in a Cologne hotel when Liège played a European Cup tie against 1. FC Köln. Our brief conversation was mostly to do with the gross / net aspect of how he was going to be paid. Wolfgang Klein had already made clear that he did not want to get bogged down in the fine detail of tax law: that could be sorted out later, with the help of our sponsors. Beckenbauer was still moaning a bit about Zebec's departure, brought about by his drinking. Now that it looked as if Happel was set to take over from the caretaker, Aleksandar Ristić, two reporters from the Hamburg based news weekly, *Der Spiegel*, travelled to Bruges, where Happel lived. The interview turned into something of a binge, in which Happel drank the delicate pair under the table. When news of this got back to Chairman Klein he remarked, "Out of the frying pan and into the fire". Convinced that everything was going to be OK, I managed to calm his fears.

How can one describe Ernst Happel? In a word: a grouch. He was not forthcoming with others, or, rather, he had built a wall around himself, which it was hard to penetrate. Those who succeeded discovered a man whose conversation was not without a certain surly charm, and who, above all, liked to talk football, the subject which obsessed him and about which he knew everything; literally, everything. My old acquaintance, Ulfert Schröder once asked me for an interview with Happel. He reckoned he would get ten minutes with him, at the outside. Personally, I doubted whether their interview would last that long. I left them to get on with it, and returned to my desk. Three or so hours later, when I went back into the room, they were still there, Schröder listening alertly to Happel's flow of conversation, that was accompanied by a great deal of gesticulating and punctuated by laughter. Yes, laughter. It was a rare occurrence. Schröder had broken through the barrier. He later reflected that he had never spoken so little in three hours' conversation. Another time – I am not sure why – Hansi Müller, the Stuttgart midfielder, asked if he could have a talk with Happel. This time the chemistry was not so good. Happel brought the audience to an end with the words, "If you want to chatter, become a travelling rep".

He was the greatest trainer I ever worked with. Because of his special gift for tactics, in a different league even to Hennes Weisweiler. He barely discussed these with the players, giving them their instructions instead. It was not hard for them to see that these were effective and that following them was the key to success. This authoritative manner of Happel's did not come with the scornful attitude which Zebec's training methods occasionally revealed. A favourite drill of Branko's, who tended to look down on the players, had been to get them doing circuits until they could take it no more. Happel was interested neither in drills, nor in the players' views. He would listen to these, without them having any bearing on the decisions he then took by himself.

Horst Hrubesch, for whom Happel had a lot of respect, told an anecdote which illustrated the way in which the trainer totally ignored what he and his teammates might have to say. It was just before the European Cup Final in Athens against Juventus. Together with Manfred Kaltz, Felix Magath and Dietmar Jakobs, Hrubesch was invited by Happel to join him in a walk around a golf course. He said he wanted to get their views on whom it would be best to have marking Michel

Platini. They talked it over, almost in the Hennes Weisweiler manner, Happel using the informal, friendly "*du*", the players responding with "*Sie*". In the end, all four agreed that Jürgen Groh should be the man. Happel nodded. They parted with the players' self-esteem having received a boost before the big match. Happel then chose Wolfgang Rolff for the special task of shadowing Platini. He never, as Hrubesch related many years later, had any intention of taking their opinion into account in making his decision. The golf course stroll was simply intended to help strengthen their self-belief.

Being with Happel could be tiring. As with Zebec, there were times when I felt I needed to lighten the mood with my trainer. Like my Aunt Triene, he enjoyed having a gamble at the casino. That, and the good weather, explained why I always organised our training camps on the French Riviera, close to either Monte Carlo or Cannes. It is a myth though that he spent every night in a casino; he was, in fact, one of the hardest-working coaches I have known. Never ill; never late; always the last to leave.

On the other hand, he liked to be the first to leave a press conference. For Happel these were a real nightmare, which seemed to physically affect him. The best was the one in which he delivered two prepared sentences, got up and left. The last journalist to arrive had not yet sat down.

What counted, of course, was success on the pitch. There was no shortage of it with Happel. It did not take long before Franz Beckenbauer stopped his grumbling, to become the new coach's biggest fan. When he went into management himself, he would travel to Austria, where Happel had finally returned, to talk at length with him and profit from his advice.

Unfortunately, Franz did not have much luck as a player during the Happel era. He made only twenty-eight appearances, a record which was largely explained by injuries, including when he ran up to take a penalty in a tournament in Brussels and pulled an abductor muscle. In May 1982 he made his final appearance, against Karlsruher SC. He was substituted after forty-one minutes. It was an unspectacular end to a glorious career.

Another ending, during my time in Hamburg, came with the death of my father. He had got to know Elvira. The two of them had an excellent relationship. By this stage though he was very ill. The cancer he had was spreading. Increasingly, his leg arteries took the toll of his smoking habit. By the end he was limited to his Mönchengladbach flat; he no longer went outside. There is no doubt that his death was a release for him. At least he had lived long enough to see his son settle down with a woman, as he had hoped I would.

Elvira and I were now living together in a small flat by the Alster river, one of Hamburg's most pleasant neighbourhoods. Not that I was particularly aware of it. Years after, I belatedly realised that this was a city where I felt particularly at home. Its style, reserve and nonchalant calm chimed with my own approach to life, even if my manager's life could hardly be described as nonchalant. It was limited to the office, stadium and various restaurants I would take the bachelor Happel to, just to keep an eye on him. We had won the league another time. Better still, we were in the European Cup Final again. Everything was going well.

I remember then having a long conversation with Elvira. I told her how tiring I was beginning to find the job. The feeling that the existence I was leading threatened any chance of a good life was growing.

14

The Final Curtain

Leave early, was the advice in the hotel. If we wanted to get to the stadium punctually, that is what we needed to do. Allow at least three hours, they said, which I was immediately willing to believe. Driving in Athens can be hell in summer, and in the autumn too. Winter does not offer much respite. It was now spring; late May 1983. We were in Athens for the European Cup Final. It could be expected to be hell.

The friendly young man at reception tried explaining the best route to the stadium to our coach driver. I stood by, thinking that three hours of crawling along in heavy traffic was probably not the ideal way to maintain concentration in the build-up to a cup final. If we were to stand any chance in this match, we would need all our concentration. Our opponents were Juventus, the best team in European football at this time, without question. It included Platini, Gentile, Rossi, Boniek, Tardelli, and Dino Zoff in goal. Giovanni Trapattoni was still coach. He did not encourage elegant play. It was success which interested him, and which he achieved. On their good days though, that were frequent enough, Platini and Boniek added gloss to Trapattoni's functional game. Italian football had arrived at another of its high points.

By contrast, the West German game was still coming to terms with the controversies surrounding the national side during the world cup in Spain the previous year. Its reputation was in tatters following the awful foul committed by the goalkeeper, Schumacher on Patrick Battiston, which left the Frenchman without several of his teeth and in a, fortunately brief, coma. It could have been worse.

Earlier, in the group stage, the team, together with Austria, was suspected of colluding in a so-called 'non-aggression pact' which ensured that both sides, by playing unworthy tippy-tappy football between themselves, went through to the knock-out stages. All this may have had nothing directly to do with Hamburg SV but we could count on a less than friendly welcome playing at a neutral venue. The Turin side were clear favourites, as they knew. Back in Italy, the question was not whether they were going to win, but by how much. According to what I heard, Juventus had already hired a hall for the victory celebration. Posters with the words 'European Cup Winners 1983' were printed en masse and pennants manufactured in preparation for the great victory. These were the circumstances in which I thought it would be a good idea to leave well in advance.

The roads were clear. We arrived three hours early. The stadium gates had barely opened. This left us looking like an overeager school team unable to wait for the big occasion to begin. At least that is the way we – or I – pictured it, given that our chances were so extremely slim. Now there were these three hours of tedious waiting to be got through. I was worried that the players' nervous energy would gradually evaporate. Instead, they all remained cheerful. The mood was good, almost carefree. Why shouldn't it have been? The team might have nothing, realistically, to win, but nor did it have anything to lose.

This relaxed, almost detached pre-match attitude carried over into the game itself. Wolfgang Rolff dealt with Platini, just as Ernst Happel had intended during the walk around the golf course with his players. When Felix Magath scored in the eighth minute it gave us something to hold on to. He had an outstanding game, as did Rolff, and Lars Bastrup too. The way Happel deployed our inside-left was very clever. We knew that Gentile would follow him wherever he went on the pitch. When Bastrup kept heading to the right wing that is exactly what happened, leaving us free to roam on the left. Gentile grew so irate that he ended up slamming his elbow into our man's face. In spite of the pain – real pain – Bastrup carried on until the end, when it was discovered he had a broken jaw.

How could you avoid joining in the dressing room celebrations – unless, of course, you were Bastrup, slumped on the wooden bench, barely able to talk? All he managed to get out was, "I am going to kill him, I am going to sue him; I am going to sue him, I am going to kill him ..." This from the cultivated Lars, who in his spare time read Grass and Böll; not in his native Danish, mind you, but in the original. That was enough for many to regard him with suspicion. The team doctor for instance, who came up to me after he had carried out the medical which preceded Bastrup's transfer in 1981. "You know," he said, "I am pretty sure he's a communist." Above all, Lars was astute. I remember when I finally got round to asking about his political position, he told me that he sympathised strongly with Marxism. Without wishing to get drawn into a long debate, I was interested to know how this tallied with the immense amount of money he earned playing for us. Lars' response to this was a very dry one about taking the "long march through the institutions," as Rudi Dutschke had said back in 1967. "Every opportunity to undermine the capitalist system, I will take," he informed me. Following his football career, he studied literature and began a new one as a secondary school teacher.

Right now, what he had in mind was extreme direct action. As luck would have it, the two players picked for a doping test were him and Gentile. And, as neither was able to pass water, they ended up sitting together in the separate changing room where this was taking place, snapping at one another for the next two hours. As a precaution, I went along too and placed myself between them. When they were finally able to do what was required, our tense little group broke up. I took Bastrup straight to the clinic, where he received medical attention. At last, we were able to celebrate. What could be sweeter than one of the biggest European Cup upsets there has been? It was also one of the most satisfying achievements of my career. If ever there was a day to be jubilant, this was it.

There is a photo of me taken just after the Athens triumph. The look I get back from it, frozen in time, is that of a completely vacant, blank-eyed Netzer. Burnt out, with no fire remaining. It is an accurate representation of the way I felt. I no longer possessed any joie de vivre. It had been ground out of me. I should have announced my retirement straightaway. But how? Can you just walk away from something you helped to create, but which still needs to be consolidated? I gave myself one more year. In 1984 I would finally quit.

Not long after the cup victory, at the beginning of the summer break, HSV travelled to the USA for a friendly against The New York Cosmos. Even in America we were a big attraction at this moment, having also retained the Bundesliga title the previous month. After the match, Elvira and I were finally able to have a week's holiday, in Hawaii. At least it gave me a few days with no football, no sick nor exacting trainer, no diva-like players. Easy living.

On our return, we climbed into a taxi at Frankfurt Airport which would take us to the city, where Elvira's family lived, to spend a few days with them before heading back to Hamburg. The driver turned around to speak to me. "Herr Netzer, my sincere condolences. I feel sorry for you. You must be feeling very unhappy right now." I had no idea what he was talking about. Then he said to me, "Hennes Weisweiler has died".

The news hit me like a thunderclap. I headed straight back into the terminal building and phoned a Zurich journalist I knew well. After an unsuccessful spell with Barcelona and having subsequently managed 1. FC Köln and The New York Cosmos, Weisweiler's final post was with Grasshoppers. We changed our booking and flew to Zurich to be with Gisela, the second Frau Weisweiler. There I would learn more about his passing.

It had been a swift and relatively peaceful death. As Gisela Weisweiler recounted, the previous evening he had gone to bed in their villa overlooking Lake Zurich in a good mood. Shortly before 6.30 am he writhed for a short while, let out a groan and was dead. He was sixty-three, still strong and lively and full of enthusiasm. At sixty he had married Gisela. Their son, Johnny was born a year later. A fortnight before he passed away, Gisela and he had consecrated their marriage in a church ceremony.

Nothing appeared unusual, she recalled, on the day of his death. In the morning he had their son in bed with him, romping around. Later, he gave an interview to a youth magazine, before leading a brief Grasshoppers training session without incident. In the afternoon the family looked at a few houses. They were planning to move into somewhere smaller than their current, two hundred square metre home. During the previous weeks he had been working on his autobiography. It was to be called 'Hennes'. With his ghost writer, he had made a trip a fortnight before to retrace his roots. This journey into the past took him to the places that mattered most to him. They visited his parents' grave in Lechenich and, naturally, Mönchengladbach. The meal he shared with Helmut Grashoff, Borussia's old manager, the chairman, Beyer and treasurer, Gerhards continued until dawn. I am sure they talked about me and had a laugh over some of the old stories. I would have liked to have been there.

The final spot on the itinerary was Cologne Cathedral. The building meant a lot to him. That is why Gisela wished for him to be buried there. We called Karlheinz Thielen, the ex-international and current 1. FC Köln manager. He sounded irritated. "You are asking for the high and mighty and holy *Köln Dom*? Is that all?" Although Thielen thought this was unlikely, he promised to make some enquiries. Subsequently, a licence was granted for the funeral service to be held in the cathedral. Gisela asked me if I would make the address; but that was not something I could do. I was unable to speak in public about Hennes Weisweiler, my coach and patron, adversary and, yes, my friend.

Twenty thousand came to the funeral to say goodbye to this 'peasant', as he was affectionately known in Cologne. This peasant with the big heart. Amongst the congregation were all those who had shared his life and who had so much to thank him for: Berti Vogts, Wolfgang Overath, Jupp Heynckes, Wolfgang Weber, Rainer Bonhof, Franz Beckenbauer, Hennes Löhr, Helmut Schön, Jupp Derwall, Udo Lattek. We all came to pay our respects and display our affection.

In Hamburg, work continued. With each day it seemed to become harder for me. 1984 was the date I had set myself for packing it in. Happel reacted cussedly, cursing me for having got him to extend his contract only to leave him in the lurch now. So I stayed for another two years. Why did I not take care of my own interests, when I was feeling so exhausted? It was not that I lacked options, with Lüthi pressing me to finally come and join him. The answer, even if it is a rather precious thing to say about oneself, is that I probably had too strong a sense of duty. I couldn't simply depart. If I had done, I would have felt shabby, as though I were slinking away.

Staying on was a mistake. I was no longer fully committed. My enthusiasm had dwindled, partly because my instinct was no longer as lively and therefore reliable as it had previously been. Aiming to build on our success, we signed Dieter Schatzschneider and Wolfram Wuttke, one of the most outstanding players Germany has ever seen. Unfortunately, Wuttke was not one of the most outstanding human beings Germany has ever seen. I knew a little about this in advance but calculated that characters in the team like Kaltz, Magath and Jakobs would have a positive influence on him and that Happel in particular, with his pedagogic persuasiveness, could improve him. What happened instead was that Wuttke and Schatzschneider undermined the old man. Both of them were undisciplined and did the bare minimum in training. So they were unfit. Ultimately, they could not be relied upon. Happel began to leave them out. With these two playing, HSV were no longer a team, even if Schatzschneider was a much better footballer than Hrubesch. He scored fifteen goals in his debut season. But never the first, which is often the crucial goal.

If I had listened to my instinct, I would have signed the Korean player, Cha Bum from Bayer Leverkusen. My gut told me, "Do it," but I probably thought that he was too old, with the result that he would have limited re-sale potential. It was another mistake at a time when Hamburg, although not in decline, was no longer amongst the trophies.

During my time as manager, HSV were three times West German champions and twice runners-up. The club appeared in three European Cup Finals, winning once. Now I was tired; continually tired. I spoke with Lüthi. We agreed that I would come and work for him. I made the announcement: 30 June 1986 was to be my last day with Hamburg SV.

Twenty-four hours earlier I had travelled to Fürth in order to watch a promising centre-forward, Manfred Kastl. He did not contribute much on the day, but that was almost beside the point: he was only going to cost 50,000 marks. Another player, Dietmar Beiersdorfer, caught my eye too. That night I talked with both. Within half an hour an agreement had been reached with Beiersdorfer. Kastl, however, imagined himself (falsely) to be in a different league. He already had an agent. At around 2 am he phoned him. Contract negotiations with Maradona could not have been much more complicated. Here

I was in some anonymous hotel in Fürth in what was turning into an all-nighter, with a player who had not particularly convinced me that afternoon. Someone with potential, but no real successes he could yet point to. Three hours had already elapsed when this agent of his, a lawyer I think, whom he had dragged out of bed, arrived. This meant we were able to start all over again discussing all the banal details – moving costs, etc. On balance, both players turned out to be sound purchases for HSV. They each did pretty well at the club and, when the time came to move them on, their sale fees helped ease its financial difficulties. The important thing for me though about the exasperating negotiation with Manfred Kastl was that it confirmed the correctness of my decision: the next day I would celebrate my freedom from the responsibilities of football management.

That evening, after leaving work, I drove with Elvira down Rothenbaum Avenue towards the Dammtor district. We talked about Switzerland and my new job with Lüthi. We were in a good mood. Suddenly tears appeared in Elvira's eyes; the waterworks began. It was difficult for her, having lived here for eighteen years. I had been in Hamburg for eight years and felt sad too.

Something new lay ahead, that was certain. But what?

15

New Beginnings

Gottlieben is a beautiful little village overlooking a tributary of the Rhine, populated by three hundred and twenty-one people, as well as cows, rabbits, geese and ducks. It is a quiet, idyllic refuge to withdraw to. Ideal for a stressed-out football manager. Seclusion is what I was looking for. Here I could find it. Just like on every other occasion I made a new beginning, we lived in a hotel when I first went to work for Lüthi. The Drachenburg is a delightful place to stay, with unspoilt views onto a wonderful landscape, which Elvira and I were able to enjoy from our thirty square metre room. Peace at last.

Did I say peace? When right next to the hotel was a pier that attracted day trippers, bowling club and wedding parties, singing nuns, and midges in their millions.

Evenings, however, were quiet in our confined, even intimate space. Here I would like, in this account of my lifetime of outstanding achievement, to hint to the reader that there was a good reason why neither of us was tempted to throw ourselves into the Rhine: we were perfectly happy together in our love nest.

Why, though, did we hold back from finding a house, or at least an apartment, to live in? We weren't so hard up that we could not afford a sensible little place. Without ever talking about it, we both knew that Gottlieben, in spite of its typical Swiss tranquility, and being conveniently situated for my work in Kreuzlingen, was unlikely to be a long-term solution. Everything was too fluid to have any real idea as to what awaited us. For example, while I might have a job, what it entailed was not yet clear.

I have never been the sort of person who has a step-by-step career plan mapped out. Throughout my professional life, I had remained fairly insouciant concerning the direction it took. Was I now worried about the future? I suppose I must have been. The training I had received as a businessman was hardly something I could fall back on. That left football. The careers open to former players were either to coach, which I had always personally discounted, or to become a manager, something I no longer wanted to be. It was my accumulated experience which accounted for why, ultimately, I felt optimistic that I would never have a problem finding a situation and that I had a fair chance of developing a successful business career. I looked at the restaurant bankruptcy as a one-off.

An advantage I have always had is a good appreciation of what I am capable of and, equally important, what I am not fitted for, up to and including the things I am a complete loss at. Heading a football, for instance. Sports marketing and stadium advertising ought both to be within my area of competence. I had dealt with the second, which in those days earned more money than television advertising, at HSV. Other aspects of the industry I had yet to learn. I knew though that there was a lot of potential in sports publicity. That was clear from the ease with which Lüthi had been able to refinance the sum he paid HSV. Fortunate timing had played a part, too. The club, on the cusp of its national and international success, was soon regarded as a highflyer. To recognise an opportunity required a good nose, a well-developed instinct. Lüthi had it. It was also something he anticipated I would bring to his business. At least I assumed so. He had never actually described what he was expecting from me. His plans were rather vague. When I finally began working for him, it was evident that at this point he had no specific use for me. He seemed unable to spell out what he hoped I should do. Only later did his instinctive decision to hire me prove to have been, on the whole, a good one.

He appreciated that, as a prominent sportsman, I could provide his company with a widely recognised public face. But what is a poster boy meant to do all day? Obviously, I had nothing to do with Lüthi directly. As a good company man, I arrived promptly each morning at eight, smartly dressed, in accordance with his dress code, in a suit and rather too snug fitting tie. I left the office in the evening in the same regular fashion to head back home, and also at midday precisely, like everyone else, for the one-hour lunch break and a predictable traffic jam in the town centre. I was meticulous and correct, as I adapted to this new, for me, world of 'Twelve o'clock sharp'. No offence intended, but I was turning into an office drone. There were conference meetings to be attended, during which I had nothing to say nor decide. Afterwards I would return to my office and stare at the walls. After a year, I handed in my notice. Lüthi rejected it. He had plans for me.

In 1981 he had concluded the first agreement with the DFB for publicity rights to international games. He was quick to realise that these could be capitalised on not only for perimeter advertising but also for use on players' shirts and stadium announcement screens, as well as in the traditional matchday programme. Nor did Lüthi limit himself to football. At that time he also held the television advertising rights for ice hockey. To start with these operated at a loss. Having paid 800,000 marks to acquire them from the Swiss Association, we were only able to recoup 600,000 by broadcasts. They were limited to showing the rink side adverts.

My difficult first year was just over when I was invited to be part of RTL, the private network's pioneering football show, *Kick-Off*. The presenter was Uli Potofski and the director, Volker Kösters. I am not sure why he thought he needed me for the guest role. In the end, it was a classic case of miscasting. There was no doubting though that Kösters was a real TV expert. I managed to bring him on board at our company. His competence, Lüthi's vision and my status were to combine very well. I was back at work.

Our first destination was East Europe. I was the calling card and Kösters the pro. The first deal we made was with ZSKA Sofia. Everything was wrapped up in a matter of hours. We flew straight to the European Cup draw with our new partners in the LearJet we had somewhat untactfully arrived in. As luck would have it, Sofia were drawn against Bayern Munich. The sponsors rubbed their hands at the prospect they were going to share in. The deal worked out well for us too. We made 500,000 marks from it.

Lüthi's original idea was as simple as it was novel. The club hosting a match owned the TV and advertising rights to it. If the visitors were a foreign side, we purchased these rights from them. Most clubs were unaware at the time of what they were sitting on. When we first approached them, they were delighted to be receiving anything. The games which we looked forward to were those against any club with both a strong tradition and current XI, generating a high level of interest and viewing figures. These were the Italian, French, Spanish and English sides. When any were involved, we knew that the advertising industry would be likely to pay the full price. A famous club from one of the leading economies meant rich pickings for us.

There was an element of luck. We didn't always come out on top, but our calculations in those early days mostly worked out. Clubs took a while to appreciate their marketable value. The broadcasting circus had barely got going. Nowadays, getting the clubs to do business involves putting down a deposit, something only the biggest companies are able to afford. Back then, a significant, though unavoidable risk we took was that our expectations for the selling power of either a club or a match were not met.

Don't imagine that sports marketing in its infancy was a smooth, neat and tidy branch of the business. There were times it became a very rugged sector, in which one had to improvise wildly. It could, and did occur that those we were dealing with preferred to be paid in kind rather than money. I already had some experience of this while negotiating transfers at HSV. When we signed Miroslav Okonski, the Lech Poznań playmaker whom Paul Breitner once described as the Bundesliga's best, the Poles were part paid with refrigerators, TVs and sporting equipment. This was the kind of thing we got used to in our young business, LKW-Ladung, founded in Kreuzlinglen in Lüthi's head office, but which spent most of its time on the road in Eastern Europe.

Each week Kösters and I travelled east, where, to give an example, we would trawl through the DDR from head to toe and from side to side, signing up all the clubs and associations we could. We ended up with a good catch. At times we had as many as fifty of one and fifteen of the second on our books. They were not pleasure trips. I am fond, I don't mind admitting, of creature comforts, plush hotels. I like to eat well. When I drink wine I am looking for a smooth, noble vintage. However, all these weaknesses had to be left at home when we went on our travels. There were plenty of times I had the feeling we had wound up in the meanest dive, or spent the night in the filthiest hotel that Europe had to offer. These were the kind of hotels in which one hesitated to take one's clothes off, since the building appeared to harbour the majority of the world's bug population. Whereas this would have deterred the young Netzer, I was not particularly bothered. I liked this job. It was enjoyable work and I was grateful to be occupied. If foul food was part of the deal, I could adapt. It is important to be able to adjust to different situations. My willingness to do so is perhaps one of the most important clues to my success. Everything, I believe, depends on being able to adapt. If I have decided to do something, then I will carry it out, without whining about its grim aspects.

What mattered was that the people I met in this period were anything but dirty, mean or foul. Nearly all were hospitable, and the friendliest of all were in Georgia. With them, you could invariably count on being offered hospitality in a particular sense of the word. Weren't these drinking sessions in fact attempted murder? Although well intended, they could be gruesome affairs.

I had never enjoyed alcohol that much but, in these new surroundings, the time had come to stand up and be counted. I pulled through. Once, I even got paid the dubious compliment that I drank like a horse. It was lucky I knew how to because this did not just help in doing business, it was a basic requirement. Previously, I had mistreated my knees; in Eastern Europe it was the turn of my stomach and liver.

Various HSV banquets had provided me with the right training. There was the experience, following a UEFA Cup match against Bordeaux in spring 1981, when we were driven to an estate outside the city. It was already past midnight. The meal, accompanied by a selection of clarets, began at about two and continued until the final whistle blew shortly before 8.30. Fortunately, no one asked me to give my opinion on the game, which we had lost 1-2. I would not have been able to.

Here, on the other side of Europe, even tougher questions were asked of one's body. I learned from those we dealt with that the first day of any negotiation was one on which business was left to the side. Instead, you got to know each other a bit over a few drinks. The business of the day was to drink your potential partner under the table.

One of our trips took us to Moscow for a few days. By this stage we had learned a few tricks to lessen the effects of the demon vodka. For example, to drink something sweet in between, such as lemonade, to balance it. I can no longer remember which club it was we were dealing with there. Whoever it was, this turned into another all-night drinking session. Around four o'clock, the chairman asked us back to his house to carry on there. His wife may have been a ballerina with the Bolshoi Ballet but she received no special treatment as a result: he roused her and instructed her to fulfil her role as hostess. The poor woman rustled up some food and brought out glasses and a fresh bottle of vodka. By the time we got away, to finally drive back to our hotel, it must have been six am.

As arranged, at ten we arrived for the meeting, shattered and still under the influence. Our host though was still in bed. The return flight was scheduled for 1 pm. With one eye on the clock, we stayed for as long as we could. At the final moment before we had to go, he eventually appeared. We handed him the contract. He signed it. I was astonished. "Do you not want to read it first?" The Russians laughed. Raising his hand affably, the chairman replied: "Nah, what could be wrong with it? After last night we know you are sound people. The same must go for the contract." It held good for the twelve months until its expiry. An extraordinary, one-off – and drunken – display of trust.

Not much was known about my working life with Lüthi. Who could say at this point what Netzer was doing with himself? The public saw me sitting next to Potofski in the RTL studio, without knowing that I was otherwise either putting my body on the line working in the Soviet Union or enjoying Switzerland's peace and quiet.

The move there was turning out well. I finally had a private life, with which came responsibilities. On 1 February 1987 Elvira and I were married in a small mountain church in Lauenen, close to Gstaad. There was no need for a wedding in order to have a contented and stable relationship with Elvira. We chose to marry because we wanted children. All the wedding preparations were carried out by the Sachss, who took it upon themselves to deliver an almost unimaginably beautiful, stylish and perfect ceremony. Elvira had first met Günter Sachs when he was the photographer for a calendar she appeared in. For a number of years now, she had been friends with him and his wife, Mirja.

With the arrival of our daughter on 28 July 1987, hotel room living became even more *gemütlich*. We had been there for over a year, and would stay another twelve months with Alana.

Whoever still likes to think of me as a jet-setting playboy should know that in all the time since she was born, in spite of my hectic business life, there has only been one occasion when I have been away from the family for more than three nights. And the reason for that was that, coming back home from accompanying the national side on a short tour of Moldavia and Turkey, I thought the airline I was using might be a bit dodgy. After the Moldavian game, I had to return to Zurich and then, the next day, take a flight back to Turkey. Rather than fly to Zurich a second time on a suspect Moldavian Airlines plane, so that we could then all travel together to the USA for a six weeks trip at the time of the world cup, I met up with them in the States instead. I remember at some point, when Franz Beckenbauer and I were talking about our children, mentioning to him that in our profession it is unusual to see much of them growing up. Franz said, "How could I have noticed my kids growing up? I was still a child myself."

This family holiday we were now going on was the reward for having clocked up a million air kilometres. It was a hard-earned prize. The family is us and Alana. I think she is happy. She grew up alone, without any brothers and sisters. We wanted to have more. We would like to have had a second child. And, when Alana was two years old, we almost did. Elvira was expecting again. It was a day when I drove to the office as normal. Elvira said she was going to the clinic later on for a routine check. She was four months along. It was a nice day; I enjoyed the short drive from Gottlieben to Kreuzlingen, thinking about our baby. At midday Elvira phoned the office. "Please come to the clinic straightaway."

"What's the matter? Has something happened?"

"Please, just come. Quickly," she pleaded.

The child being carried in the mother's womb was dead. At such moments there is no comfort to be found. I could not console Elvira and she could not console me. Because of the danger of blood poisoning, she remained in the clinic. I drove back to where we lived, alone. I had to take care of Alana.

The grieving was more poignant than I can write here. It took a long time before we overcame our loss. Her doctor advised Elvira against further pregnancies, as the chance of endangering her own life was too great. So, Alana grew up alone, which she enjoyed a lot. I think – no, I know – that she is happy.

As I have already mentioned, I am a man who, after he has received a blow, quickly turns to the future. I was feeling bad. It felt like time to move out of the hotel. Thirty square metres is not enough space for three people and their grief.

Moving out was not as easy as that. First, we had to get through a fire. Elvira had recovered. We were coping reasonably well. The first we knew about it was when a fireman knocked on our door one night. I was still asleep. He told Elvira that we needed to get out of the burning building without delay. She eventually succeeded in waking me. Outside in the courtyard we stood holding Alana, and a few essentials we had grabbed. These included what my wife, in the heat of the moment, considered I could not do without the following day: a tie. There were one or two other items. Not much. If the fire had got out of control and burnt everything we had left inside, the story of me going into work in pyjamas and tie is one I would have had to keep from getting out. But the damage was not that bad.

What had happened was that a deep fryer on the upper floor had exploded. By chance, a room maid, who did not usually sleep up there, heard the noise from the attic. Apart from her, we were the only people in the hotel, which was shut for business in the winter. This exceptional maid reported to the fire brigade fast enough that, although they had to come from Konstanz, since there was no station in Gottlieben itself, the firemen arrived in time to douse the fire at its source, before it got out of hand. We could return to our room. My suit was intact. But we needed to get out of there. That was enough of hotel living.

There was a small furnished house available only a street away. The question was, did we want to settle down here? A nagging feeling told us to carry on looking. Something that needed to be taken into account was the Swiss tax law which lays down that you must live in the same canton as you work – or pay the premium. We were thinking about Zurich. In the meantime, we took the small house for three months, with the idea of seeing what happened next. It was an interim measure which lasted for two years. Still, we had our plan now to put down roots. It had become clear to us that we wanted to stay in Switzerland for good. I had my work, which I enjoyed. I was watching Alana grow up. Life was peaceful here. We felt right.

Every now and again I receive phone calls from Germany, asking if I would be willing to give an interview about the football back home. On other, rarer occasions journalists travel to interview me in Switzerland. Sometime at the end of the nineties, I drove from Kreuzlingen to Gottlieben with a pair from *Der Spiegel* who had come to ask me about the current crisis in German football. We sat in a restaurant down by the jetty, eating and drinking some wine and chatting. I told a few of the old stories. Afterwards, I showed them the hotel room where we had lived. As for the state of the national game, that was not something I was able to set right. When the two departed, I was left with the silence of the Swiss mountains. There are worse lives.

By this point in ours, we had made the move to Zurich. Finding an apartment to buy there had soon developed into a major headache. What we were looking for was a place along the lines of our old Hamburg home, with its high, stuccoed ceilings and parquet floor. The problem was not that such properties were lacking in Zurich but that they were already occupied, less well constructed and three times as expensive as in Hamburg. We decided that, even if we had had the money, we were no longer interested in buying.

Today we are still renting a single storey apartment. I am not complaining. Two hundred and fifty square metres is not so small. Because the family feels completely at home in Zurich, nor do I mind making the one hundred and fifty kilometre round trip, driving to and from work in Kreuzlingen.

The previous tenant had been an old lady living on her own. A certain amount of renovation was needed when we moved in. Since the flat is in a listed building, we received some help with this via a grant from the Swiss government. Once the work was completed, we were finally able to take our possessions out of storage, where they had been kept for the last six years back in Hamburg. We had almost forgotten what they looked like.

Renting in central Zurich obviously makes no sense financially. The cost of living is even higher for its citizens because we are expected to subsidise the lakeside districts, which pay fifteen to twenty percent less in tax. Perhaps I have already mentioned that good sense is not one of my strongest points? Do I really need to drive a Ferrari these days? Soon I will be paying more tax than if I was back in Germany.

16

Black Ferrari

It is no longer such a peaceful life. Fridays had been kept aside for the family, whenever possible. That is now increasingly seldom. The easy life that I prefer is almost a thing of the past. Every now and again, I receive signals from my body. My knee, whose state I managed to conceal from the Real Madrid doctor when I had the medical, aches a lot of the time. It is not going to get any better and will have to be operated on. I no longer practice sports. I find jogging too boring. Do I really want to trot through the woods on my own? As I only used to run under duress, with a pistol, so to speak, in my back, I am hardly going to start again now of my own free will. I used to enjoy tennis. Unfortunately, it's bad for the knee. As for golf, I am not sure that checked trousers are really my style. Or whether I would have the necessary composure to choose between a wood and an iron. Maybe sometime later.

From time to time Elvira grows worried, in what I think is a rather exaggerated manner. I doubt if I would have tolerated her concern when I was playing. Not without appearing a wimp, anyway. Once we were at my friend, the former editor of *Die*

Welt newspaper, Claus Jacobi's, where he offered us very good, very clean vodka. I probably enjoyed myself a bit too much; the following morning I felt slightly strange. My circulation did not seem right. It wasn't the first time. I planned to spend the first half of the day lying down, reasonably confident that in the afternoon I would be feeling better again. Elvira, though, instinctively feared there was a serious issue and decided to call a doctor. He came and examined me without delay. His opinion was that there was nothing obviously the matter with me. I gave him a very good and very expensive bottle of wine to thank him for this welcome news. Not long after he left, he must have started to have second thoughts about his diagnosis, which he had made a little too hastily, perhaps. He came out again and recommended that, to be certain, I should go and be tested at the clinic. Elvira fully agreed with this. The results of the ECG I then had suggested to the senior consultant that there was an irregularity. "You cannot seriously think I am going to let you leave," he said. "You will have to stay in intensive care for forty-eight hours where we can keep an eye on you." This was Christmas Day. While my girls, Elvira and Alana, celebrated at home, I remained under observation, sound as a bell but sour as hell.

Four days a week, no work on Fridays: that was the plan. For a while after making the move to Zurich I stuck to it. We had been eager to live there and enjoy the city's cosmopolitan way of life. I was willing to pay the price of the daily one hundred and fifty kilometre return commute to Kreuzlingen. In the meantime, the relationship between Volker Kösters, my companion on East European trips, and Caesar W. Lüthi deteriorated. Eventually he was fired. CWL TeleSport found itself without a managing director. "You know what I am thinking," Lüthi said to me, indicating his trust in an innocent, but very determined manner, "you can take over. You really can." Representing the firm is one thing; running it is another. But it worked out well. We were four men and three women who functioned as an effective unit.

At the end of the nineties, Leo Kirch came to Lüthi with a proposition: he wanted to buy the company. He knew, being perhaps an even greater visionary than Lüthi himself, how, with CWL TeleSport, he could exploit the world cup rights to the full. The price he was willing to pay was appropriately high. Without revealing it here, it was enough for Lüthi and his wife Eva, who had controlled the company's finances, to retire on comfortably. The problem was they did not take into account how much he depended on his working life. With nothing to do, his health declined rapidly and in 2002 this man, to whom I owe so much, died.

TeleSport turned into KirchSport, now a fully owned subsidiary of the Kirch media empire. My new boss fascinated me, both on account of his thinking and his deep, deep humanity. It is a simple example maybe but this was made apparent on the night of a dinner he gave for 2,500 guests, many of them well-known faces from the television. Those at Kirch's table included his bookkeeper, porter and chauffeur; he wanted to be amongst his workforce. Not only was he mentally alert; little escaped his impressive sixth sense. We got on from the outset. "You're getting fat, old boy," he greeted me to one of his supper parties, and it was true, I had put on a pound or two.

The firm was in a very good position. We had the advertising rights not only for Bundesliga match broadcasts but also for the world cup. When Germany was chosen to host the 2006 edition these became pure gold. Then Kirch went into liquidation. What were we to do? We did not want the opportunity to slip through our hands. All of those involved in running the company were determined to keep it going but we lacked the means for a management buyout. Investors were needed. Those we found were Robert Louis-Dreyfus, who had already brought success back to Adidas, his friend and partner, Dr Martin Steinmeyer, as well as Dr Christian Jacobs from Bremen, and Sheikh Kamel too. Just to be clear, I was not amongst the new owners benefitting from these lucrative rights, to the tune of roughly 300 million euros. My percentage was a very small one.

It was a lot of hard, but enjoyable, work. So was my other job. The one with Gerhard Delling. Even when, as was frequently the case, he tried to wind or send me up. For instance, by introducing me, as the cameras began to roll, as a player who used to like running about, "many years ago". A particularly nasty trick he pulled was when we were in Malta for an international. Berti Vogts, who had infamously dropped Stefan Effenberg during the 1994 World Cup, was still coach. He had now recalled him. It was not the best decision he ever took, as I personally told him – but that is another story. The point here is that Delling left me blowing in the wind.

Before transmission, there was a technical run-through, in which the lighting and sound engineers made sure their equipment was set up correctly. That something was different during this rehearsal could not have escaped my notice. Normally, Delling stood to my right. This time he positioned himself on the other side. For some technical reason, he explained. I knew nothing about such things; if it was necessary for me to stand to his left or right, I was happy either way. The broadcast began. Delling stood in the lee of the wind, his hair perfectly in place. Upwind, I was unable to provide any analysis because I was too busy sweeping mine away from my face. Delling continues to deny it, but I know this was the aim. Insult was added to injury when he and the crew, having a good laugh at my expense, began calling me "L'Oréal Hairspray".

This is just to illustrate that my working relationship with Gerhard Delling is ... first class. We have become friends. Real friends, not just colleagues who get along, an acquaintance that frequently goes by the name of friendship in this business. For me, the word implies something deeper. I think Boris Becker also falls into this category. In Zurich he has often come and had kitchen table suppers with us. We have got beyond the small talk stage. I now consider him a friend. Since the word is an important one for me, I do not use it lightly to describe people I would actually rather not get too close to.

Delling and I are on yelling at one another terms. During the 2002 Japan / South Korea World Cup – which we commentated on from a Hamburg studio – we had one of our loudest disagreements. Neither he nor I know what it was about any longer. It was probably the result of being tense, nervous and on edge. By the time the two of us, together with his wife, arrived at the studio we were shouting at each other. When he let me out, I slammed his car door so violently that, as he later told me, he briefly wondered whether he might have to go to the garage for a repair. I was pretty amazed myself that the hinges did not come off. It didn't improve his mood. I thought that might be it. A couple of minutes later the disagreement was forgotten.

He had found a parking space. We took up our positions at the studio table, where we began laughing and kidding about. No detailed post-mortem was required since we both knew we were partly to blame.

He and I have similar mentalities. There is no need for us to sit down before an international and work out the kind of things we are going to say. There are no prepared gags; the mickey-taking is all spontaneous. Perhaps the best example of our intuitive understanding came after the European Championship qualifier against Iceland in 2003. It had been an abysmal performance. 0-0 versus Iceland. Delling and I were simply doing our job, which was to describe what we and all the other viewers had just witnessed. He remarked, not unoriginally I thought, that the crisis of Saturday night viewing had reached a new low. Afterwards the coach, Rüdi Voller exploded in his interview with Waldemar Hartmann, "I am not listening to any more of young Günter's and Herr Delling's bullshit ..." We were all astonished by the inappropriate tone he had adopted. Even without his outburst, the two of us felt the need to talk – and drink. As soon as we were off air, we disappeared to a bar where we thought we might not be found. But naturally, all the German football journalists gathered in Iceland tracked the two of us down. They clamoured for a statement. Since we were not going to retract any of our criticism, it got blown up instead, a development which neither of us was looking for. The following days saw our little dispute exaggerated in parts of the Press, until it reached the same proportions as the one which was then taking place between Chancellor Schröder and President Bush. Unlike them though, there was no need for Rudi Völler and me to get up on a podium to clear the air. Even without the long talk we had together, that was obvious to us. Our quarrel was never really that important.

I have known Gerhard Delling apparently since 1982, when I was managing HSV. I don't, but he does have a clear memory of the date. He was working for North Germany Radio, in their Kiel studio, when I was invited to participate in a sports discussion there. Having accepted, I left Hamburg on a winter's day in good time. I had barely got out of the city when the rain started to come down onto the icy road in sheets. In spite of the conditions, which made driving almost impossible, I felt I ought to continue, having said I would be there. I finally got to the studio with a quarter of an hour of the broadcast remaining. A long while after, Delling told me how the fact that I still made the effort to come had made an impression on him. When he interviewed me for forty-five minutes in 1992, I could sense what seemed to be a good understanding between us.

As the French World Cup approached, I was still under contract with Swiss television. My time working for them had begun a few years earlier, with me less than happy about the commentary position I had been given for internationals, somewhere high above the corner flag. A match against Italy was no exception. I was wandering back to my seat for the second half when a chance encounter took place. Another TV reporter asked me for my thoughts on the upcoming forty-five minutes. It had already occurred to me, as I now told him, that, "a crucial change has taken place: the Italians have lost their most important player". Tardelli may have been unspectacular but, once he was pulled off injured, the visitors would no longer have the man who drove their game along. Very few probably noticed this. "Without him," I continued, "it will be different. If the Swiss are alert and adapt their tactics too, they have a good chance of winning." Which is what happened.

Subsequently, I received a job offer from Berni Thurnher, a sort of Swiss Thomas Gottschalk. Two days after the game, he called me to ask if the idea of providing occasional match analysis for Swiss television appealed at all. "Yes," I replied, "so long as I get a better seat than the one above the corner flag." It was arranged that I should have a view from the halfway line. For that I was prepared to take a slight drop in pay.

I have occasionally been asked in Germany whether the Swiss do not mind one of us commenting, sometimes critically, on their national side. That has not been a problem. Perhaps because of a difference here between our two countries, which I noticed early on. It was soon clear to me that Switzerland is not a footballing nation in the way that we are. So, its performances need to be assessed differently. I made sure that I adopted the right tone. Not only was there no problem, it was a great success. Thurnher is someone else I need to thank for having spotted a dormant talent of mine.

It was an enjoyable time. I sat with other reporters, amongst whom it was easy to discern, from the conversation, what the game's points of interest were. Making a fluent assessment at half-time was harder.

During the 1996 European Championship held in England, I had a further encounter with Delling. Before Switzerland's confrontation with the hosts, he questioned me about the Swiss game. A colleague of his who worked in the Southwest regularly watched the Swiss emissions. This was Volker Kottkamp. It was he and WDR's Klaus Schwarze, someone I had in a way grown up with, who a little while later came up with the idea that I might be part of the ARD team covering the 1998 World Cup. Even if it was clear by now that Switzerland were not going to qualify, many of the games would still be shown there. My employers were therefore quite happy that I should commentate for ARD.

The only contractual condition I laid down was that I wished to work with a single, named co-presenter. ARD, on the other hand, wanted the agreement to include a term stipulating that I was to be partnered by a variety of different hosts. Without being able to explain exactly why, I continued to press for just the one, authoritative commentator, namely Delling. ARD's directors may not have intended that, in taking someone like me on, I should have a hand in staff issues, but I held firm, confident that I was going to prevail. In the event, I did. It was not that I had anything against any of the others. Working with Waldemar Hartmann, for example, would have been a pleasure. Once more, it was just my instinct guiding me. With Delling, this would work.

I think that was more foresight than fancifulness on my part, based on at least some understanding of the medium. I had already had one bad experience, due to a programme being put together carelessly. This dated back to 1988, when Uli Potofski and Burckhardt Weber launched *Kick-Off*, with my involvement, for RTL. Potofski and Weber's pioneering show was a way of celebrating the Bundesliga. All that SAT. 1, the public channel, later did was to refine it. The project was a sound one to begin with; I had a subject to talk about, which I knew my way around. I was there to share my knowledge of the game, nothing more. It was Helmut Thoma, the leading director at RTL, who did us no favours by turning *Kick-Off* into a three-and-a-half-hour extravaganza. That is just too long for a broadcast devoted exclusively to football. Ask me a question about the game itself and I will provide an answer. I can be counted on to serve up all there is to know about it and to illuminate many interesting aspects. But, please, a show ...

The real show, out on the pitch, is another matter. My ritual when preparing to take a free kick triggered anticipation around the stadium. The solitary hero in the arena, doing what a man has to do. Whatever it may have looked like, there was nothing studied about this 'ritual'. It was simply the process by which I 'entered the zone'. The way I moved my body and used my feet on the pitch was particularly my own. Like a fingerprint, or the way one speaks. It was a form of expression I mastered from a young age, in which I felt confident. Perhaps football players are performers – but not entertainers, even if they are enjoying themselves. Which is the aim: to amuse ourselves. If a million strong public is spectating and enjoying itself too that is an added bonus. But, at heart, this is not showbusiness. Certainly not where I am concerned.

I still do not commentate as naturally as I played the game. I feel awkward holding a microphone. That has made me the despair of the sound technicians because the alternative, of wearing a small microphone fixed to a lapel, is much harder for them to modulate. It is not the only aspect of working in contemporary television which I find difficult, in spite of my otherwise well-developed business skills. At the time of the French World Cup I was offered a lucrative sponsoring deal. All I had to do was to have the company's logo stamped on my shirt collars. Just the idea of walking around like an advertising pillar repelled me. I thanked them and turned the offer down. It is not something I can see myself changing my mind about in the future. A friend was prompted to make the witty suggestion that I should have the word 'Expert' written on my shirt collars.

Delling and I are not thinking of making any major changes to the way we cover matches. Why should we, having won television's top award, The Grimme? I have never made a big fuss about the titles, West German Championships and two Player of the Year awards I collected. Winning The Grimme Prize was different, because it marked an achievement in a field that is not really mine. For the jury, who know much more about it than I do, to make this choice shows we must be doing something right. When I remember the way in which, back in 1998, I naively thought I would cover the world cup and then return to the peace of the Swiss mountains, I cannot help feeling we have come a long way.

Some might ask themselves whether Delling and I sometimes use the singular '*du*' between ourselves now. In fact, it is not only for the cameras that we address one another formally; we simply forgot to progress to '*du*'. Calling the other '*Sie*' has become one of our jokes. Otherwise, we are happy when the football gives us reason to be and, by contrast, sullen when it does not. We receive less criticism than we used to for our own criticism of others: that oversensitive fashion seems to be on the wane. We just carry on, sticking to the facts, rather than stirring things up unnecessarily. The thing we like most, whenever it is possible, is to enjoy and compliment the spectacle being presented.

After all, it is just a game. But the support Rudi Völler received after our disagreement, particularly from politicians wanting to strike a populist chord, makes me wonder. A couple of weeks later came the next broadside. This time it was for something I had written about the Bayern Munich player, Michael Ballack. Or, to be precise, what the journalist I spoke to about him had written. My argument was that Ballack was neither an orchestrator nor a strategist, and that this was probably because he was a product of the East German football system, which favoured the group at the expense of individual initiative. This was a fairly banal observation, intended to explain why Ballack was failing to develop his undoubted potential at Bayern. What was expected of him there was the one thing he was unable to deliver.

When the article appeared, a minor storm erupted. The indignant tone those criticising me took was that I was insulting East Germans. This was a wild interpretation but one which the populist politicians happily seized upon. The kind of hypocrisy and disregard for the truth which still make me livid. My instinctive dislike of them explains why I am able to avoid a conflict of interest between my work as a commentator and my job in advertising. I know how to keep the two separate. I have to, as the so-called most powerful man in world football. The man who owns the lucrative marketing rights to the 2006 World Cup and the Bundesliga. The man without whom no football can any longer roll – at least not on the telly. And finally, according to the critics, the man who decides whether it rolls favourably or not. Good, good ... this sort of stuff gets written ...

Most of the time nowadays I am dressed in a suit and tie. That goes with the job. It does not bother me. Once in a while I will take a week off. Then we drive to Sylt, one of the nicest spots in Germany. On arrival I will head to 'Zanzibar', where mine host and good friend, Herbert Seckler takes good care of me. It's my canteen when I'm there – the best canteen in the world. Time flies by on the peninsula.

Most of the time, I am flying somewhere. A typical week might find me in London on the Monday, talking to British TV executives. In the evening I take the return flight to my wife and daughter. On Tuesday I am in Hamburg for the ceremony in which Uwe Seeler is given the freedom of the city. Wednesday, it is Frankfurt am Main for the world football congress meeting to begin the work of the committee handling the 2006 World Cup. Then I travel to Munich on Thursday to meet Dr Günter Struwe, ARD's programme director, who wants to discuss a quiz show to be recorded in Hamburg, which I promise I will take part in with him. Friday, I am back in Zurich, commuting to the office in my car.

At some point, Elvira told me I was getting too old to be driving a red Ferrari. I now drive a black one instead. Am I complaining? Heavens, no! It is the life I wanted. A very good life. There's nothing I would change about it. I am a lucky devil.

Acknowledgements

Thanks are due to Gertje Berger-Maaß at Rowohlt Publishers for her friendly and patient cooperation, which has made this English version of *Aus der Tiefe des Raumes* possible. Thanks too to David Exley at Beamreach Printing for all the know-how he has brought to its production.

Picture Acknowledgements

Although every effort has been made to trace copyright holders and clear permission for the photographs in this book, locating the provenance of them all has not been possible. The publisher would welcome the opportunity to correct any omissions.

Cover photograph and plates 3, 5 and 6: ©Getty Images
Plates 1 and 4: ©Alamy